Second Edition

ASSISTIVE TECHNOLOGY

ACCESS FOR ALL STUDENTS

Lawrence A. Beard
Jacksonville State University

Laura Bowden Carpenter
Auburn University at Montgomery

Linda B. Johnston
The University of Tennessee at Chattanooga

PEARSON

Boston   Columbus   Indianapolis   New York   San Francisco   Upper Saddle River
Amsterdam   Cape Town   Dubai   London   Madrid   Milan   Munich   Paris   Montreal   Toronto
Delhi   Mexico City   Sao Paulo   Sydney   Hong Kong   Seoul   Singapore   Taipei   Tokyo

Vice President and Editor in Chief: Jeffery W. Johnston
Executive Editor: Ann Castel Davis
Editorial Assistant: Penny Burleson
Vice President, Director of Marketing: Quinn Perkson
Marketing Manager: Erica DeLuca
Senior Managing Editor: Pamela D. Bennett
Production Manager: Meghan DeMaio
Creative Director: Jayne Conte
Cover Designer: Bruce Kenselaar
Cover Image: Fotosearch.Com, LLC/Royalty Free
Full-Service Project Management/Composition: Joseph Barnabas Malcolm/GGS Higher
   Education Resources, PMG
Printer/Binder/Cover Printer: R.R. Donnelley & Sons
Text Font: Palatino

Library of Congress Cataloging-in-Publication Data
Beard, Lawrence A.
  Assistive technology : access for all students / Lawrence A. Beard, Laura Bowden Carpenter, Linda Johnston.—2nd ed.
      p. cm.
  Prev. ed. cataloged under Johnston, Linda.
  Includes index.
  ISBN-13: 978-0-13-705641-5
  ISBN-10: 0-13-705641-9
  1. Children with disabilities—Education—United States.   2. Self-help devices for people with disabilities—United States.   3. Special education—Technological innovations—United States.
  I. Carpenter, Laura Bowden.   II. Johnston, Linda.   III. Johnston, Linda., Assistive technology.
  IV. Title.
  LC4019.J576 2007
  371.9'0433—dc22

                                                                                    2010005165

10 9 8 7 6 5 4 3

www.pearsonhighered.com

ISBN 10:   0-13-705641-9
ISBN 13: 978-0-13-705641-5

PREFACE

NEW TO THIS EDITION

The second edition of *Assistive Technology: Access for All Students* continues to provide both inservice and preservice educators with an introduction and overview of assistive technology (AT). It is a resource and guide for training preservice and inservice teachers to meet the diverse needs of students with disabilities. In addition, the revision is relevant for those educators who are preparing students with disabilities to meet the challenges of both postsecondary education and post- employment opportunities. This revision includes the following:

- The introductory chapter (Chapter 1) has been reorganized with updates of specific laws related to AT and expanded to include ethical standards of practice and professional development.
- Revisions include a new chapter (Chapter 2) on Universal Design for Learning (UDL) and Response to Intervention (RTI) and how AT plays an important role in each.
- Chapters 3–8 have been updated to show current, evidence-based practices in the use of AT devices and application of services.
- Chapter 9 highlights the role of AT in helping students be successful learners in community-based programs.
- Chapter 10 describes how AT allows persons with disabilities access to interpersonal and social networks.
- Every chapter has been updated with the latest AT resources.

The second edition will benefit the reader by introducing and expanding the following premises:

- Educators now teach a wide range of students from very diverse backgrounds. It is important that educators know and understand laws and legislation that mandate AT in both the classroom and the workplace. Educators must differentiate instruction and understand how to accomplish this endeavor. AT is an essential and powerful way to meet the mandates of RTI and UDL.
- Educators must have an understanding of ethics as it applies to AT. They must understand various codes of ethics and how ethics relate to the use of AT, and that they are bound by these codes of conduct. Professional development is part of the commitment of the professional.
- Inservice and preservice educators must have a knowledge base of various types of adaptations to meet the unique needs of each student. Educators need to understand how to make these adaptations in every aspect of the student's life. AT is a means by which adaptations can be made for students. The adaptations can begin at birth and continue through the adult years. This begins in the preschool setting and continues as students transition to postsecondary of the employment sector.

- Inservice and preservice educators must understand the various types of AT that are available to them and how to locate and find funding for the devices.
- Community-based services are essential for generalizing and applying classroom knowledge to the adult world. AT serves as an important tool in helping students with disabilities become successful adults.

ORGANIZATION OF THIS TEXT

This text is organized into 10 chapters. Chapter 1 provides an introduction and overview of the laws that govern the use of AT and provides the reader with a synopsis of ethics as it applies to AT. New to this text is a chapter (Chapter 2) on Response to Intervention and Universal Design for Learning. Chapter 2 show how these two compliment each other in making the general education curriculum accessible to all students.

Special Features

ORGANIZING FEATURES Each chapter begins with a Chapter View and a Chapter Focus. These two features provide an overview and introduction of what is covered in each chapter. A Chapter Review provides a summary at the conclusion of each chapter.

ASSISTIVE TECHNOLOGY SNAPSHOT Each chapter contains an in-depth snapshot of a real-life situation that relates to the use and understanding of AT. The AT Snapshot is referred to throughout each chapter as it relates to specific information.

ASSISTIVE TECHNOLOGY FOR STUDENT LEARNING The AT for Student Learning section connects AT directly to student learning. This section is specific and based on the information covered in the chapter.

ASSISTIVE TECHNOLOGY SPOTLIGHT This section of each chapter features AT that is applicable to the information covered in the chapter. This provides the reader with hands-on applications of AT.

MARGIN NOTES Each chapter contains notes in the margins that ask the reader to react to different types of situations. These notes provide the reader with an opportunity to apply what has been read.

DIVERSITY The topic of diversity is covered extensively throughout the text.

COMPANION WEBSITE The Companion Website features PowerPoint slides and AT application activities with real-life situations involving many different types of individuals. The AT resources featured in the chapters can be linked to directly from the Companion Website.

ACKNOWLEDGMENTS

Thank you to all of our reviewers, whose comments and suggestions made this a better book: Steffanie Bowles, Marygrove College; Sumita Chakraborti-Ghosh, Tennessee State University; Richard Evans, Jr., James Madison University; Mary Hilsenbeck, University of Louisville; and Ann Orr, Eastern Michigan University.

To Drs. Raymond Elliott, Tommy Russell. and Charlie Horne, who guided and mentored us through the doctoral program at the University of Alabama.

To all our teacher education candidates at our respective universities who instilled in us the importance of preparing all educators to work with a diverse student population.

To my mother Nita, my sister Cindy, and my brother Kris, who don't always know what I'm talking about, but still listen, thanks. To my daughter, Laurel, who keeps things in perspective by reminding me that autographed copies go for more on eBay, thanks. To my best friend and right hand, who never hesitates to either pull or kick me in the right direction, Patricia Hill, thank you for the encouragement. To the faculty and administration here at Jacksonville State University, thanks for allowing me to stay involved. To Linda and Laura, the best partners in crime an author could have, it's been an experience and the two of you are the best. And finally, to the best group of present and future teachers here at Jacksonville State University for keeping me on my toes and asking me the tough questions, keep asking.

—*Lawrence A. Beard*

I wish to thank my colleagues and co-authors, Larry and Linda. This project has been a true collaborative effort. Both of you have proven to be dedicated, creative, knowledgeable, and committed. You are the best! I am grateful for the friendship of my longtime friend, Randy Estes. Randy keeps me focused on the important things in life, including constant reminders of why special educators must be effective teachers. My husband Jim continues to be a source of encouragement and support for my life's work. Thanks for helping me make all my dreams come true.

—*Laura Bowden Carpenter*

To my husband Charlie, who is the light of my life and continues to encourage and support me in life's endeavors. To my daughter and son-in-law, Becky and Paul Crawford, both educators, who instill in me and remind me of practicality in the preparation of all teacher education candidates. To my grandchildren, Emma Campbell and Liam, who represent the future of everything I do in the preparation of teacher education candidates. To Nickolas and Kevin, who have inspired me. To Dr. Valerie Rutledge, my department chair, who encourages me and continues to provide me with many opportunities that have opened many doors. Finally to my co-authors, thanks; it was a joy to work with both of you on this second edition.

—*Linda B. Johnston*

BRIEF CONTENTS

CONTENTS

1

Assistive Technology
An Introduction and Overview

CHAPTER VIEW

- Assistive Technology Snapshot
- Introduction to Assistive Technology
- Assistive Technology Defined
- Laws and Assistive Technology
- The Assistive Technology Continuum
- Funding for Assistive Technology
- Assistive Technology and Ethical Standards of Practice
- Professional Development
- Assistive Technology for Student Learning
- Chapter Review

CHAPTER FOCUS

1. Who needs to know about AT?
2. Where did the definition of AT originate?
3. List the laws related to AT.
4. What are the characteristics of the AT Continuum?
5. How is assistive technology funded?
6. How can the AT Continuum guide professionals in selecting the type of technology needed by a student?
7. Why do professionals need a code of ethics for practice?
8. How might AT enable students with disabilities to meet general education curriculum standards?
9. How do students with disabilities who need AT services benefit from effective professional development for educators?

Assistive Technology Snapshot

MEET ANNA SLOVIC, PAUL RAMIREZ, MARY O'DONALD, YUN LEE, AND CATHERINE WYATT

Anna Slovic is a student at a local state-supported university. She is currently pursuing her degree in special education. As part of her teacher preparation program, Ms. Slovic must take a course in assistive technology (AT). She has just been admitted into the professional education program and has taken the introductory special education course. She knows a little about assistive technology, but she knows that there is much more to learn about how assistive technology services and devices support learning in the general education curriculum for students with disabilities.

This is Paul Ramirez's first year as the principal of Garcia Elementary School. He has attended many professional development events to prepare him for this position. Mr. Ramirez understands educational technology for enhancing teaching. However, one area that he feels he must learn more about is the assistive technology that five of his students use to be successful learners. More experienced principals have warned him that assistive technology is expensive and, many times, unnecessary.

Mary O'Donald has been a special educator for 23 years. For the past 3 years, she has taught in a resource room, where she teaches learning strategies to students with mild disabilities. The district special education supervisor came by to visit and discussed the possibility of Ms. O'Donald becoming a consulting teacher for three students who are included in general education classes. Each of these students relies on assistive technology for access and support in class. Ms. O'Donald has tried to keep up with current technology, but she is not confident that she has the knowledge and skills to support the students' use of assistive technology.

Yun Lee teaches world history at SeaView High School. He loves his job and cares deeply about the well-being and education of all his students. He was invited to attend the Individualized Education Program (IEP) meeting for a student who will be in his class next fall. During the meeting, he was asked to explain the types of teaching and learning activities that he requires for his course. Then the IEP team determined what kinds of assistive technology the student might need to be a successful learner in world history. Mr. Lee wishes to remain optimistic about how he can meet the academic needs of the student, but he knows he has limited experience and very little knowledge about assistive technology.

Catherine Wyatt is a vocational rehabilitation counselor. Her job includes assisting students with disabilities in making the transition from school to the adult world. She has been working recently with a student who wishes to go to college. The student uses a wheelchair and requires technology for communication. Ms. Wyatt needs to know what kinds of expectations the student will meet in the postsecondary environment and what types of support the student will need to be a successful student. She wants the student to be prepared to make a successful transition.

These professionals all have something in common: They need to know more about assistive technology. They should begin by learning how to define assistive technology and by understanding the laws that provide for it as well as the ethical standards of practice that support professionals. This and subsequent chapters describe what professionals must know about assistive technology to provide services and successful learning opportunities for students with disabilities.

INTRODUCTION TO ASSISTIVE TECHNOLOGY

Today the challenges of teaching a diverse student population are at the forefront of all education initiatives. At no other time have all students had such an opportunity to be educated by a team of professionals in an inclusive setting. Students with disabilities, English Language Learners (ELL), students at risk for school failure, and students who are gifted now have the opportunity to learn from one another in inclusive educational settings. Many students have benefited from inclusive settings that boast of well-prepared and caring teachers, effective strategies, and appropriate resources to meet their needs. For some, however, the road has been a journey of trials, discrimination, and even some errors.

Educators now have the opportunity to individualize instruction with many technological devices never before available in education. Many teachers have these devices available to them in their own classrooms. Not only educational or instructional technology but also assistive technology (AT) can be customized to meet the needs of students with disabilities. Although AT is widely used to ensure that students with disabilities may participate in the general education curriculum, AT can also be used with ELL, students at risk, and students considered to be gifted. AT can open a new world for students in inclusive settings, as well as for adults throughout the life span. AT makes it possible for students with disabilities to access the general education curriculum and be successful learners. Many professionals seek a merging of educational technology with AT to make learning accessible and reach a diverse student population (Cavanaugh, 2007).

Assistive Technology Defined

To understand AT, we must first define the term and understand how it evolved for students with disabilities. *Assistive technology,* as we know it today, evolved from the definition in the Technology-Related Assistance for Individuals with Disabilities Act (Tech Act) of 1988 (Public Law 100-407). **Assistive technology** is defined as an item or piece of equipment or product system acquired commercially, off the shelf, modified, or customized, and used to increase, maintain, or improve functional capability for an individual with disabilities.

What are the components of the AT definition?

LAWS AND ASSISTIVE TECHNOLOGY

The Technology-Related Assistance for Individuals with Disabilities Act of 1988

Better known as the Tech Act of 1988, the Technology-Related Assistance for Individuals with Disabilities Act (P.L. 100-407) was signed into law by President Ronald Reagan. The original 1988 law provided funding for states to develop consumer information and training programs that were designed to meet the needs related to assistive technology of individuals with disabilities. The act defined two different areas related to AT and delineated *assistive technology services* and *assistive technology devices*. An **assistive technology service** is any service that directly assists an individual with a disability in the selection, acquisition, or use of an AT device. An **assistive technology device** is any piece of equipment or

> 1. Evaluating the needs of individuals with disabilities for AT devices.
> 2. Purchasing, leasing, or providing for the use of AT devices by individuals with disabilities.
> 3. Selecting, designing, customizing, applying, and maintaining AT devices.
> 4. Coordinating and using other therapies and services with AT devices.
> 5. Training and technical assistance for individuals with disabilities.
> 6. Training or technical assistance for professionals.

FIGURE 1-1   Assistive Technology Services   *Source:* Adapted from U.S. Congress (1988).

product system, whether acquired commercially, off the shelf, modified, or customized, that is used to increase, maintain, or improve functional capabilities of individuals with disabilities (U.S. Congress, 1988). The latter still is used frequently for educational purposes. In understanding the term *AT services*, the Tech Act outlined AT services within the law (see Figure 1-1).

REVIEW FIGURE 1-1. How might a student's IEP team find this information useful in planning for AT?

Under this law, grants were provided to states to support systems change and advocacy activities related to statewide programs of technology-related assistance for individuals with disabilities. The Tech Act of 1988 was a monumental mandate because it was the first law that actually provided a venue for the use of AT devices. In 1994, the Tech Act was amended (P.L. 103-218) to revise and extend programs of the Technology-Related Assistance for Individuals with Disabilities Act of 1988 and for other purposes.

Telecommunications Act of 1996

President Bill Clinton signed a major reform of telecommunications legislation on February 8, 1996. The Telecommunications Act of 1996 (P.L. 104-104) provided benefits to all citizens as it related to the information superhighway that carried the United States into the 21st century. The act contained provisions that opened the doors to connect all classrooms to the information superhighway by 2000. It also provided provisions for libraries to be connected. Accessibility guidelines related to this act were published in the *Federal Register* in 1998. In part, the accessibility guidelines provided for accessibility, usability, and compatibility of telecommunications equipment covered by the Telecommunications Act. The guidelines specifically provided the requirements for accessibility, usability, and compatibility of new products and those products in existence that need changes or upgrades to improve functionality. This legislation and the ensuing guidelines provided a foundation for ensuring that the information superhighway became accessible to all individuals.

Carl D. Perkins Vocational and Technical Education Act of 1998

The Carl D. Perkins Vocational and Technical Education Act (P.L. 101-392), better known as the Perkins Act, was first authorized in 1984. In 1998, the act was reauthorized and provided individuals with academic and technical skills for success in a knowledge and skills economy. Some of the activities supported by the Perkins Act include access to career and technical education for students with disabilities and the purchase of equipment to ensure access to the latest technology.

Funds provided by the Perkins Act are allocated to both secondary and postsecondary schools (Association for Career and Technical Education, 2005).

Assistive Technology Act of 1998

The Tech Act officially ended in 1998 with the passage of the Assistive Technology Act (P.L. 105-394) signed into law by President Bill Clinton. The purpose of the act was to support programs and grants to states to help them address the technology needs of individuals with disabilities. The Assistive Technology Act consisted of four sections:

Title I	State Grant Programs;
Title II	National Activities;
Title III	Alternative Financing Mechanism;
Title IV	Repeal and Conforming Amendments.

Title I	Designed the awarding of grants to states to support capacity-building and advocacy activities. These grants were designed to provide assistance to states in the maintenance of comprehensive statewide programs of technology-related assistance.
Title II	Provided for the coordinated effort in research related to AT that incorporates principles of Universal Design for Learning (UDL).
Title III	Provided grants to states to help pay for the federal share of costs related to the establishment, administration, or expansion related to alternative financing for AT systems for individuals with disabilities.
Title IV	Repealed the Tech Act of 1988 (1998 Amendment to Section 508 of the Rehabilitation Act).

Federal mandates have specifically addressed AT during the past two decades. However, it is important to remember that support for students to gain access to general education was mandated as early as 1973 in federal legislation.

Assistive Technology Act of 2004

The Assistive Technology Act of 2004 (P.L. 108-364) redirected funding to individuals by providing direct aid to individuals with disabilities. The reauthorization of the Assistive Technology Act of 2004 redefined the purpose of the Assistive Technology Act of 1988, which helped states develop the infrastructure to get assistive technology to individuals. Due to the reauthorization, the focus of the law became delivering AT to persons with disabilities rather than on developing the delivery structures. Under this act, states can use 60% of AT state grants on direct-aid programs, including AT reutilization programs, AT demonstration programs, alternative financing programs, and device loan programs. States may also choose to use 70% of the state AT grants on direct-aid programs and may have full discretion when allocating funds for at least two and up to all four of the programs cited. The Assistive Technology Act of 2004 also created greater accountability for how states use AT grants and requires that states continually evaluate the effectiveness of programs. Millions of Americans with disabilities depend on

AT to function in their daily lives. The federal government has established funding, through the Assistive Technology Act, to help individuals with disabilities gain access to technology.

Education for All Handicapped Children Act of 1975

Public Law 94-142, the Education for All Handicapped Children Act (EHA), was signed into law on November 29, 1975. This landmark legislation changed education for school-age children with disabilities. The act ensured that all students with disabilities had access to a **Free Appropriate Public Education (FAPE)**, which ensures that all children with disabilities have available special education and related services to meet their unique needs. The law further stated that the Individualized Education Program (IEP) would contain a statement of specific education services provided to the student and the extent to which the student would be involved in the general education program. The services and participation in the general education program have evolved much since passage of this law. In 1975, educators were creating their own devices to help students be successful in the general education setting. These supports would later be known as AT.

In 1986, the EHA was reauthorized (P.L. 99-457) and added services for infants, toddlers, and their families. The Individualized Family Services Plan (IFSP) was included in this reauthorization and opened the door for infants and preschool children to begin receiving services and utilizing AT devices. These early devices were primarily the light-tech type, as described by Vanderheiden (1984), which will be defined and discussed throughout this text. These devices enhanced students' opportunities to be educated with their peers in the general education classroom and to learn valuable skills.

Individuals with Disabilities Education Act of 1990

The legislation continued in 1990 when the EHA was again reauthorized, with its name changed to the Individuals with Disabilities Education Act (IDEA) (P.L. 101-476). In this revision the Individual Transition Plan was added and became part of the student's IEP. As part of the IEP update, a transition plan is designed for each student with a disability. AT devices must be a consideration for the transition plan and must be provided if the IEP team considers it necessary and appropriate for the student's success as a learner. Transition and AT are discussed further in Chapter 8.

The 1990 IDEA amendments added autism and traumatic brain injury as disability categories. As more students were determined eligible in these categories, supports and related services became important components of the IEP.

Individuals with Disabilities Education Act of 1997

The IDEA was reauthorized in 1997 (P.L. 105-17). IDEA (1997) stressed **Positive Behavioral Intervention Supports (PBIS)** as a means for addressing issues related to the behavior of a student and how behavior is related to learning. The IDEA also addressed the participation of students with disabilities in district and state testing and the general education curriculum. These three major additions to the law could provide impetus for the use of appropriate AT devices.

The changes that occurred with the 1997 amendments made it very clear for educators that students with disabilities were to be educated with their peers. These changes resulted in colleges and universities preparing preservice educators to work with a more diverse group of students. General educators were taught strategies to support students with disabilities in the general education classroom. The use of AT services and devices became widespread. Educators wanted and continue to seek professional development related to AT. As illustrated in the Assistive Technology Snapshot at the beginning of this chapter, educators find themselves in the role of planning and delivering services for all students. Thus, the need for knowledge regarding AT continues to grow, and it is critical that educators have the opportunity to participate in professional development opportunities that support that need. More about professional responsibilities can be found in later in this chapter.

Individuals with Disabilities Education Improvement Act of 2004

In 2004, IDEA was reauthorized. The Individuals with Disabilities Education Improvement Act of 2004 (P.L. 108-446) added to the definition of AT. The original definition of AT, as defined in the Tech Act of 1988, remained basically unchanged except for the clarification that the term does not include surgically implanted medical devices or replacement of such devices. According to Mandlawitz (2005), this addition resulted over the concern that school districts may be held accountable for the provision of cochlear implants for children with hearing impairments. Cochlear implants are discussed in detail in Chapter 8.

In addition, the term *Universal Design for Learning* was introduced. Although addressed in other legislation, this was the first time it appeared in the amendments of special education law. The definition was derived from the meaning found in Section 3 of the Assistive Technology Act of 1998. **Universal Design for Learning (UDL)** is a concept or philosophy for designing and delivering products and services that are usable by people with the widest range of functional capabilities and that include products and services that are directly usable (without requiring assistive technology) and products and services that are made usable with assistive technology (Sec. 602[35]). The law requires that states and school districts develop and administer assessments, to the maximum extent possible, using UDL principles (Mandlawitz, 2005). Both the use of AT and the concept of UDL must be considerations addressed by the student's IEP team. More about UDL and its relationship with AT is found in Chapter 2. The details of the collaborative team processes are found in Chapter 3.

Section 504 of the Rehabilitation Act of 1973

Two significant pieces of legislation that are critical in understanding AT are both civil rights legislation for individuals with disabilities. These were passed almost two decades apart—however, both made significant contributions in support of the success of individuals with disabilities. The first, Section 504 of the Rehabilitation Act of 1973 (PL 93-112), required that reasonable access be provided for all individuals with disabilities. This law affected both the public schools and the general society outside school buildings: it guaranteed public access to all public buildings. Access had to be made for individuals with disabilities both in schools and in the broader public sector. Prior to this, most legislation addressed only school-age children. Section 504 extended to the entire workforce. Today many individuals believe that this law set the tone and foundation for both IDEA and the Americans with Disabilities Act.

Americans with Disabilities Act of 1990

On July 26, 1990, President George H. W. Bush signed into law the Americans with Disabilities Act (ADA; PL 101-336). This act prohibited discrimination in employment and in transportation, and it provided access for public accommodations and telecommunications. The ADA Amendments Act of 2008 (PL 110-325) became effective on January 1, 2009. These amendments make minor changes in the language and definitions; however, the major intent and provisions of the original law remained intact.

The ADA also implemented the concept of normalization. ADA guaranteed access in the employment sector for individuals with disabilities and also prohibited discrimination in the workplace against individuals with disabilities. The ADA required that telephone companies provide relay services for individuals who are deaf and those with speech impairments so that they may use telecommunication services. These are described in Chapter 8.

No Child Left Behind Act of 2001

The No Child Left Behind Act (NCLB, PL 107-110) was passed into law on January 8, 2002. It is the reauthorization of the Elementary and Secondary Education Act of 1965 (PL 89-10), which is the primary federal law affecting education from kindergarten through high school. Although not a law that focuses primarily on AT, the four principles of the NCLB do affect students with disabilities. These four principles—(a) accountability for results, (b) more options for parents, (c) greater local control of and flexibility in the use of federal funds, and (d) an emphasis on using best practices based on scientific research—have thrust students with disabilities into the mainstream of general education in greater numbers. The Individuals with Disabilities Education Improvement Act of 2004 is aligned with NCLB to provide increased support and improved outcomes for students with disabilities. Because students with disabilities are expected to become proficient in subject matter, AT will provide access for them to be successful learners in the general education classroom.

Federal legislation has served to protect and provide equal access for individuals with disabilities. Through the passage of many laws, all individuals are now on an equal basis. Through the use of AT devices, individuals with disabilities can now lead productive, independent lives, which was impossible in the past. The Elementary and Secondary Act is scheduled to be reauthorized by the 111th Congress. The Council for Exceptional Children (2009) recommends that the reauthorization carefully balance the major components with the Individuals with Disabilities Education Improvement Act so that the rights of persons with disabilities are protected.

TABLE 1-1 Web Resources for Assistive Technology Laws	
1998 Amendment to Section 508 of the Rehabilitation Act http://www.section508.gov	Provides Section 508 information and guidance. Multiple links including a summary of the law.
Individuals with Disabilities Education Improvement Act of 2004 http://idea.ed.gov	Resources and information about this act.
Americans with Disabilities Act http://www.ada.gov	Information and technical assistance regarding the Americans with Disabilities Act as well as the ADA Amendments Act of 2008.
Section 504 of the Rehabilitation Act of 1973 http://www.section508.gov/index.cfm?FuseAction=Content&ID=15	Summary of Section 504.
No Child Left Behind Act of 2002 http://www.ed.gov/nclb/landing.jhtml	Summary of the law with informative links.
Assistive Technology Act of 2004 http://www.ataporg.org	The Association of Assistive Technology Act Programs (ATAP) is a national, member-based organization, comprised of state Assistive Technology Act programs funded under the Assistive Technology Act (AT Act). Highlights Tech Act Projects.

Technology can support students as they strive to become successful learners. Education is a lifelong process that begins at birth and continues through a lifetime. AT can empower individuals with disabilities to access, acquire, and accept new opportunities. Understanding the legislation that has shaped the field of AT allows professionals to form a solid knowledge base that can be applied in practice. Table 1-1 provides additional resources related to legislation and AT.

THE ASSISTIVE TECHNOLOGY CONTINUUM

Technology does not have to be sophisticated and expensive to be effective. The Individuals with Disabilities Education Improvement Act of 2004 defines technology in a broad sense to include the range of very sophisticated high-tech innovations to the simplest, everyday, light-tech devices. The selection of devices must be a careful and well-thought-out process. Just as it may be harmful to the student to select an inappropriate device, it may be harmful to select a device when one is not needed. Assessing the needs of the individual student improves the chances that the correct device will be used to improve student outcomes. AT assessment should determine what combination of specific technology and services would best meet the needs of the individual student. Chapter 3 describes more about AT assessment.

One effective method of visualizing and understanding the range of the various types of AT is to think of AT on a continuum. This continuum provides a range of consideration for AT devices varying from no tech to light tech, to high tech. These terms were first described by Vanderheiden (1984). Assistive Technology Spotlight 1-1 in this chapter features the AT Continuum.

No Tech

Professionals must be careful not to fall into the trap of the so-called technological imperative. Just because something exists does not mean it must be used. The focus of AT is on the student and the student's current individual needs, not on the device or the student's needs in the near or distant future. If the student is not ready to use a device or cannot at the present time use a device, frustration can develop that may lead to AT abandonment. The team must take the time to consider carefully how the student may benefit from an AT device and whether the task can be accomplished successfully without the use of technology. Valid and reliable assessment is critical in determining whether a device is needed. Chapter 3 provides more information on assessment.

Light Tech

You are most familiar with this type of technology because you have used it yourself. All those gadgets, gizmos, thingamajigs, doohickeys, and other items with colorful names are considered light tech. Regardless of what we call them, they are simple tools that make life's daily activities easier, or in some cases, possible.

Light-tech AT devices are nonelectronic and relatively inexpensive. They may be as simple as pencil grips to help students with fine-motor problems grip pencils properly, magnifying glasses to enlarge print or special paper with raised lines for the visually impaired, or eating utensils adapted to help a student self-feed. Light-tech devices are simple to use and should be considered after the no-tech devices in the continuum.

High Tech

High-tech devices are generally electronic, usually tied to a power supply, and typically require careful planning so that they are not too intrusive. A cost factor usually must be considered. Some good examples of high-tech devices are a wheelchair that climbs stairs and a laser cane for people who are blind. A great deal of computer hardware and software also provides screen magnification, synthesized speech, tactile display, or combinations of these. Other devices also can be used, such as talking scales, talking glucometers, talking clocks, color identifiers, talking compasses, and other devices that allow for speech output. Some students with disabilities must have high-tech devices to be successful learners.

Give an example of a no-tech, light-tech, and high-tech device related to a content area. See the Companion Website for the latest AT devices.

Cost cannot be a consideration in providing the type of AT a student with a disability needs for access to the general education curriculum. Thus, identifying resources for possible funding for AT is a critical professional skill.

FUNDING FOR ASSISTIVE TECHNOLOGY

Funding for AT is often fraught with contention because families find themselves at odds with the school in the provision of needed AT. While this may happen, more can be achieved by a spirit of collaboration. A proactive strategy that promotes collaboration is one in which the team develops a funding strategy. Devices vary in cost from inexpensive for light-tech devices (such as pencil grips or special paper) to very expensive for high-tech devices. After first determining that a student would benefit from AT and then identifying the type of devices a student may need, funding may become an issue. It is then crucial for the team to confirm that the student will need the AT to access the general education curriculum and to be a successful learner. Again, this emphasizes the importance of accurate AT assessment and knowledge of the AT Continuum.

For students who are eligible for special education services under one of the 13 disability categories defined by the Individuals with Disabilities Education Improvement Act, it is the responsibility of the local school district to pay for any AT device or service included in the student's IEP. For AT that may serve more of a medical need than an educational one, Medicare, Medicaid, and private insurance may help finance technologies prescribed by a physician or a related service professional, such as a speech-language pathologist or an occupational therapist. AT for vocational success is all about helping the student enter and maintain a job in the workforce. Using the correct terminology enables the team to determine the correct funding source.

CW Other than the school district, where might an IEP team find funding sources for AT devices? See the Companion Website for access to funding sources.

Although resources (other than the local education agency) for affordable AT may be limited, families and schools should consider other sources, such as special needs libraries, lending libraries, disability organizations, voluntary organizations such as church groups and service clubs, local businesses and vendors, and families and friends. Table 1-2 lists sources for AT funding.

Professionals and families working with students with disabilities making the transition to a postsecondary setting should be aware of sources for AT and how to access the resources. This is important once the student has moved to a postsecondary school. Section 504 of the Rehabilitation Act of 1973 requires that the postsecondary school provide AT devices as a reasonable accommodation so that the student has full access to the institution of higher learning. In addition, some state departments of vocational rehabilitation may provide AT funding for their clients.

AT can be costly. However, the bottom line is that the local education agency has a legal obligation to provide the AT devices and services stated in a student's IEP. It is important for the school and family to work together to make sure the AT device is what the student needs to be a successful learner. Professionals must understand their roles and responsibilities in ensuring that students with disabilities receive the AT devices and services they need. Conflicts can arise between stakeholders. It is critical for every professional to adhere to the ethical standards of practice for educators when making decisions regarding AT for students with disabilities.

ASSISTIVE TECHNOLOGY AND ETHICAL STANDARDS OF PRACTICE

Classrooms are becoming more diverse as students with disabilities are included for access to the general education curriculum. Educators who find themselves teaching students with disabilities are faced with complex conflicts, challenges and

TABLE 1-2   Funding Assistive Technology

ATSTAR http://www.atstar.org/atinfo/funding.htm	Assistive Technology Strategies Tools Accommodations and Resources question-and-answer format addresses funding issues.
The Alliance for Technology Access http://www.ataccess.org http://www.ataccess.org/resources/low costnocost/LowCostNoCostATAguide.pdf	The alliance is a national network of AT resource centers, individual and organizational associates, and technology vendors and developers. Includes a *Guide to Low-Cost / No-Cost Online Tools for People with Disabilities*.
United Cerebral Palsy http://www.ucp.org/ucp_channeldoc. cfm/1/14/86/86-86/2938	Assistive Technology Funding Search Tips.
Other Sources of Funding http://trace.wisc.edu/archive/fintech/ fintech.html	An excellent handbook on funding assistive technology through Medicaid, private insurance, and Social Security.
A Listing of Alliance for Technology Access (ATA) Centers and Community Technology Centers (CTCs) Network http://www.ataccess.org http://www.ctcnet.org	Some ATA centers accept donations of used computers, then refurbish and distribute them to adults with disabilities and to families of children with disabilities. Some community technology centers also recycle equipment for people in their communities.
Volunteer and Charitable Organizations http://www.elks.org/lodges/default.cfm http://www.easterseals.com http://www.lionsclubs.org	Lions Club, Elks Club, Easter Seals, church groups, and local charitable organizations may provide support to purchase technologies.
NECTAC http://www.nectac.org/topics/atech/ funding.asp	The National Early Childhood Technical Assistance Center supported by the U.S. Department of Education's Office of Special Education Programs.
Funding Source for Computers http://www.givetech.org/	Funds from Give Tech may be available for persons with severe disabilities.

issues. The solutions for these may be found within professional organizations that support teachers. Such organizations define and expand on a code of ethics and professional standards of practice that serve as guides for ethical practice.

Ethics

The area of AT has grown immensely within the last decade. Professionals involved in the assessment and planning process for AT services and devices for students with disabilities generally adhere to the standard code of ethics for their profession. **Ethics** is defined broadly as standards of conduct related to a specific profession. For special educators, the Council for Exceptional Children (1993) Code of Ethics applies; for speech-language pathologists, the American Speech and Hearing Association Code of Ethics applies. Most states have now adopted professional ethics and standards of practice for all educators. Readers are directed to each state department of education for more information for particular states. All professionals should be members of their professional organization.

None of us would like to use the services of any professional who does not subscribe to and adhere to the professional code of ethics and standards of practice created by and for members of the profession and based on extensive research and dialogue among professionals in the field, and are often evolving as the field advances. Professional standards take into consideration the legal and ethical aspects of practice. When a person enters a profession, he or she is expected to follow the ethical standards of practice developed by his or her professional organization. As more and more general education teachers find themselves teaching students with disabilities, it becomes a necessity for them to understand and adhere to the ethical standards developed for teachers who work with students with exceptionalities.

Rehabilitation Engineering and Assistive Technology Society of North America

The use of AT by students with disabilities in the general education classroom has grown. Due to the increasing number of students who use AT devices, the Rehabilitation Engineering and Assistive Technology Society of North America (RESNA, 2005) has adopted a mission statement and code of ethics for AT.

RESNA is an interdisciplinary association for the advancement of rehabilitation and AT. Table 1-3 describes RESNA and other professional organizations. The RESNA mission statement and code of ethics are specific to AT. While many professions are represented by their own codes of ethics, the RESNA mission statement and code of ethics guide the optimal standards for AT providers.

The Council for Exceptional Children

Students with disabilities are, by their very nature, vulnerable. They have been historically discriminated against and have received below-standard educational services. To prevent further discrimination and to support high standards of educational services, the Council for Exceptional Children (CEC) has a code of ethics for educators of persons with exceptionalities.

The CEC was organized in 1922 by a group of professionals interested in the education of persons with disabilities. Since that time, the CEC has grown to be the largest international professional organization dedicated to improving educational outcomes for individuals with exceptionalities. The organization advocates for appropriate governmental policies, sets professional standards, and provides opportunities for professional development. In addition, CEC advocates for newly and historically underserved individuals with exceptionalities and helps professionals obtain conditions and resources necessary for effective professional practice (Council for Exceptional Children, 2008). The CEC code of ethics and standards of practice may be accessed through the CEC website (see Table 1-3). Parts of the CEC code of ethics and standards of practice will be integrated and explained in other parts of this chapter.

Professional Ethics and Special Education

Ethics can be defined simply as doing what is right. However, ethics must be considered from all aspects. As educators, we must look at doing what is right and we must have a solid understanding of what technology can and will do for the student.

Webquest
1.1

To see the CEC Code of Ethics, go to http://www.cec.sped.org/Content/NavigationMenu/ProfessionalDevelopment/ProfessionalStandards/EthicsPracticeStandards/default.htm

Why would general education teachers need to understand the ethical standards of professionals who work with students with disabilities?

TABLE 1-3 Professional Organizations Related to Assistive Technology

Council for Exceptional Children (CEC) http://www.cec.sped.org/	CEC is the largest international professional organization dedicated to improving educational outcomes for individuals with exceptionalities, students with disabilities, and the gifted. CEC sets professional standards, provides continual professional development, advocates for newly and historically underserved individuals with exceptionalities, and helps professionals obtain conditions and resources necessary for effective professional practice.
The Technology and Media (TAM) Division of the Council for Exceptional Children http://www.tamcec.org	TAM is the official division of CEC that works to promote the availability and effective use of technology and media for individuals with disabilities and/or who are gifted.
International Society for Technology in Education (ISTE) http://www.iste.org	ISTE provides leadership and service to improve teaching and learning by advancing the effective use of technology in education.
The International Technology Education Association (ITEA) http://www.iteaconnect.org	ITEA is the largest professional educational association, principal voice, and information clearinghouse devoted to enhancing technology education through technology, innovation, design, and engineering experiences at the K–12 school levels. Its membership includes individuals and institutions throughout the world in more than 45 countries, with the primary membership in North America.
Rehabilitation and Engineering Assistive Technology Society of North America (RESNA) http://www.resna.org	RESNA is an interdisciplinary association of people with a common interest in technology and disability. Its purpose is to improve the potential of people with disabilities to achieve their goals through the use of technology. The organization serves that purpose by promoting research, development, education, advocacy, and provision of technology, and by supporting the people engaged in these activities.

Along with the concept of "Can we do this for the student?" educators must consider the question "Should we do this for the student?" We must examine the consequences of our actions on the student, the school, and the environment in which the student must function (Vertrees, Beard, & Parnell, 1997).

Assistive Technology Considerations and Ethics

The IEP team must consider who is going to train the personnel (not just the students) in the appropriate use of the AT. It is the responsibility of the IEP team to ensure that everyone involved follows ethical standards of practice when making AT decisions and implementing AT devices and services. All professionals involved in this process are expected to adhere to the code of ethics set by their professional organizations. The IEP team may suggest that teachers and service providers undergo professional development to be able to use AT effectively.

Webquest 1.2

To see the National Education Association (NEA) Code of Ethics, go to: http://www.knea.org/profession/codeofethics.html

PROFESSIONAL DEVELOPMENT

Technology is a rapidly growing, changing, and expanding field. It remains a significant challenge for professional educators to obtain the knowledge and skills related to the newest technology. The field of AT is no different from other areas of technology. Professional educators can stay current in technology by engaging in meaningful and purposeful professional development that allows the professional to pursue a program of continuing education. These opportunities advance knowledge and skills so the professional educator can maintain a high level of competence. This advancement allows the professional educator to respond to the changing needs of persons with exceptionalities (Council for Exceptional Children, 1993).

Professionals can advance their knowledge and skills in many ways. Most school districts provide inservice opportunities, which can be powerful opportunities for learning if they adequately address the professional needs of the educator. For those educators who need specialized training, professional conferences and topical workshops are provided by professional organizations. For example, RESNA provides a variety of online courses, programs, and electronic-based information, as well as an annual conference, to facilitate the skills of those who work with persons who use AT. Table 1-3 lists other professional organizations that provide similar resources for professionals who need to know more about AT services and devices.

Professional Publications

Another resource for educators wishing to advance their knowledge base and skills in the field of AT is the professional literature available on this subject. Professional journals are found in a variety of formats—including electronic, print, and CD-ROM. The electronic journals may be obtained through library databases and the Internet. Most professional organizations in the field of AT publish professional literature, and most of it is available electronically. One of the benefits of belonging to a professional organization is the opportunity to receive professional publications as part of membership. For example, RESNA publishes a journal for professionals involved in the application of AT and rehabilitation technologies and the delivery of related services. The Technology and Media (TAM) division of the CEC also publishes a journal and a newsletter providing professionals with information on new technologies, current research, best practices, relevant issues, and national political events.

Professional Organizations

Teachers are responsible for joining and participating in professional organizations that advocate for the profession of teaching, for improving student outcomes, and for advancing professional growth. Most organizations of teachers define ethical standards of exemplary professional practice. Teachers who find they are teaching students who learn differently and need AT to access the general education curriculum should identify those professional organizations that provide standards for practice and resources for teachers using AT. Table 1-3 lists professional organizations of interest.

Planning for Professional Development

Teachers need a systematic and effective method of planning professional development opportunities. One suggestion for structuring a professional development plan is to engage in a self-assessment activity. Using standards of best practice provided by professional organizations may provide a method of self-assessment. Assistive Technology Spotlight 1-2 (found later in this chapter) provides a method using the top 10 skills required for being proficient in assistive technology. The professional rates him- or herself as "novice" or "proficient" in each individual area. For those areas marked "novice," the professional can begin a search to find the appropriate professional development opportunities to move from "novice" to "proficient."

> Whose responsibility is it to make sure professionals have current training in specific areas of need?

ASSISTIVE TECHNOLOGY FOR STUDENT LEARNING

Accessing the General Education Curriculum

With few exceptions, students with disabilities are expected to meet the same high academic standards as their peers without disabilities. The Individuals with Disabilities Education Improvement Act (IDEIA) of 2004 and the No Child Left Behind (NCLB) Act of 2002 support the philosophy that all children, regardless of disability, should have access to the general education curriculum. Understanding the meaning of AT, the terminology associated with AT, and the laws and ethical standards that mandate AT are essential for learning how AT allows students with disabilities to access the general education curriculum and be successful learners.

ACCOMMODATIONS AND MODIFICATIONS   For the purposes of this text, the terms *accommodations* and *modifications* are used to describe how students with disabilities can access the general education curriculum and be successful learners. **Accommodations** allow students access to the general education curriculum. They may include changes in teaching strategies, adaptations to the physical environment for physical access and to facilitate learning, and assessment of needs such as how a student responds in learning situations to demonstrate acquired knowledge or skills. A student's IEP team should address major decisions about accommodations for students with disabilities.

Modifications relate more to curriculum issues. Modifications provide changes in content or level by altering standards or expectations. Any decision to change curriculum content or the level of expectation from the required standard should be made by the student's IEP team. When modifications are made to a student's curriculum, the IEP team should also address assessment and grading issues.

The IEP team has the responsibility, first, to identify how the student will access the general education curriculum and, second, what accommodations and modifications the student will need to do so. In making these decisions, the IEP team must first determine the learning goals for the student. Then the team must decide what related services and/or accommodations and/or modifications (such as AT) the student will need to reach such goals. Deliberations and considerations must include the delivery of instruction, the environment where the student will receive instruction, and assessment issues. AT devices can be considered for each of these components. For example, the student may need to use a closed circuit television (CCTV) to read print materials such as texts, handouts for learning, and assessment materials. Without AT, many students with disabilities have limited or no access to instruction and to assessment.

The IEP team also should take a very close look at materials that the student needs for access and then should determine how AT devices and services may support and allow for successful student learning. For example, a student with a visual impairment may benefit from better illumination of print materials. A student using a light box that provides the appropriate lighting for a handout such as a map may accomplish this. As the IEP team and the teacher address those issues related to instructional materials, the team might ask the question "How might we select and use materials that reach many students with diverse needs?"

STANDARDS-BASED INDIVIDUALIZED EDUCATION PROGRAMS The Individuals with Disabilities Education Improvement Act of 2004 mandated that all students with disabilities have access to the general education curriculum. Thus, educators should set goals for ensuring that students have that access (McGrath, Johns, & Mathur, 2004). To perform well on mandated high-stakes assessments, students must have appropriate access to the content of the curriculum. AT services and devices provide access. The IEP team may consider AT services and devices a related service. They may also consider AT services or devices for accommodations and/or modifications.

A **standard** is the expectation students must meet at the end of each academic year. Teachers must teach the curriculum standards that each state has determined all students will meet. This enhances the opportunity for all teachers to be familiar with state standards based on the general education curriculum. When teachers know and understand the state's curriculum standards, they can arrive at more informed decisions that will enhance the student's performance toward meeting the state standards as well as how AT might be used in this endeavor.

Students can access the general education curriculum in an inclusive setting. While teachers must determine how they will teach toward the standards and make the curriculum meaningful for each student, it is the IEP team that will ultimately decide how the student will meet these standards.

A standards-based IEP is one that determines how students with disabilities will work toward achieving the standards. A standards-based IEP is responsive to the student's individual needs, and it also defines how students will show that they meet state standards (Snell & Brown, 2006). The targets for all students are grade-level proficiency and achievement of long-range educational outcomes that support graduation, career preparation, and lifelong learning.

What standard is appropriate for the student?

Is the student able to perform the skill at his or her designated grade level?

If not, would appropriate light-tech AT enhance the performance? If so, what type of light-tech AT would work?

If not, would appropriate high-tech AT enhance the performance? If so, what type of high-tech AT would work?

How will the AT be assessed to determine if this enhanced the student's performance toward meeting the standard?

FIGURE 1-2   Determining Appropriate Assistive Technology for the Student for a Standards-Based Individualized Education Program

Students can participate in meaningful ways in the general education curriculum and meet standards in ways that are appropriate for them. The delivery of instruction can be modified to accommodate every student, based on the individual needs of each student. AT helps accomplish this.

Ranging from light tech to high tech, AT has been very useful in accomplishing educational goals. IEP teams must ask themselves if students can perform the standard skills without any modifications or accommodations. If they can, specially designed instruction is not necessary. When designing a standards-based IEP, Figure 1-2 can guide the team in determining the appropriateness of the performance outcomes for each student and how AT might affect student achievement. Utilizing the AT Continuum, Figure 1-3 illustrates how a goal is related to a state standard based on the eighth-grade science curriculum.

Confidentiality and Privacy Issues

As required by law and supported by CEC, professionals working with students with disabilities must adhere to strict policy regarding privacy issues. CEC standards remind professionals that they must maintain confidentiality of information

State Standard: To know the planets in relation to the universe.

IEP Goal: Sarah will demonstrate expressive language by responding to questions.

High-Tech AT

When given a multiple-choice assessment about the planets, Sarah will use the screen reader on her computer and her alternate keyboard to respond to the questions.

Light-Tech AT

When working in small groups in science class, Sarah will respond to yes and no questions about the planets by pointing to yes and no picture symbols affixed to her desktop.

No-Tech AT

The teacher will read the questions to Sarah, and Sarah will respond orally to each question with the correct answer.

FIGURE 1-3   Curriculum Standard and the Assistive Technology Continuum

about students with disabilities and their families. In addition, professionals should respect confidentiality when communicating with parents. This includes any issues related to the AT and the student with a disability.

Under federal law, students with disabilities and their parents are entitled to certain rights. Those include the right to procedural safeguards and due process. The Individuals with Disabilities Education Improvement Act of 2004 incorporates and expands on the tenets found in the Family Educational Rights and Privacy Act (FERPA). In general, FERPA gives parents certain rights with respect to their children's educational records maintained by the local education agency (FERPA, 2005). Schools must also have written permission from the parent or eligible student to release information from a student's record. It is good practice to remind the members of the IEP team about FERPA and other procedural safeguards for students with disabilities.

ASSISTIVE TECHNOLOGY SPOTLIGHT 1-1

The AT Continuum

Self-Assessment for Professional Development: Where Are My Areas of Need?

1. After taking the self-assessment, make a list of any areas that you marked "novice."
2. Begin a search for sources that provide professional development in these areas so that you can move from "novice" to "proficient." For example, you can search for workshops, professional literature, online courses, college courses, and so on.

ASSISTIVE TECHNOLOGY SPOTLIGHT 1-2

Self-Assessment for Professional Development:
How Do I Rate on the Top 10?

	Skills	Novice	Proficient
1.	Educational implications of characteristics of various disabilities.		
2.	Definitions and terminology related to students with disabilities and assistive technology.		
3.	Rights and responsibilities of students, families, teachers, and other professionals related to assistive technology.		
4.	Laws, policies, and ethical principles regarding assistive technology.		
5.	Role of the teacher in planning and implementing an individualized program for students with disabilities who use assistive technology.		
6.	Strategies of consultation and collaboration regarding students who use assistive technology.		
7.	Principles of universal design for learning.		
8.	Implementation of assistive technology in planning daily instruction.		
9.	Maintenance of assistive technologies.		
10.	Incorporation of the use of assistive technology to conduct assessments.		

Chapter Review

- As early as 1973, students with disabilities received accommodations to receive a Free Appropriate Public Education. Many of these accommodations have been in the form of AT: an item or piece of equipment or a product system acquired either commercially, off the shelf, modified, or customized and used to increase, maintain, or improve the functional capability of an individual with disabilities. AT was formally defined in 1988 with the passage of the Tech Act. From the subsequent Assistive Technology Act of 1998 to the Individuals with Disabilities Education Improvement Act of 2004, AT has continued to evolve.
- In 1975, students with disabilities were granted a Free Appropriate Public Education (FAPE), according to the Education for All Handicapped Children Act. This was the beginning of special education and related services designed to meet individual needs. During this era, educators were designing their adaptation devices for students to use to be successful in the general education curriculum. This law was further expanded in 1986 to include services for infants, toddlers, and their families.

- The name of the Tech Act was changed in 1990 to the Individuals with Disabilities Education Act, commonly referred to as the IDEA Amendments. This revision added the transition plan as part of the IEP update. AT was again mandated as part of the transition plan if the IEP team so determined.
- In 1997, the IDEA was again reauthorized. The amendments stressed three areas that have implications for AT use. The first was Positive Behavioral Intervention Supports (PBIS) to address behavior in a positive way. The second provided students with the opportunity to take part in both districtwide and statewide testing programs. The third granted students access to the general education curriculum. Congress made it very clear that students with disabilities were to be educated with their peers, thus changing much of the way colleges and universities trained preservice educators. The emphasis shifted to teacher preparation programs that provided expertise to work with more diverse student populations within both public and private school settings. In 2004, when the Individuals with Disabilities Education Improvement Act was passed, AT was defined for the first time within the law. The term *AT* did not then include surgically implanted medical devices or replacement of such devices.
- The legislation for AT continues to evolve as FAPE is made available for all students. The Americans with Disabilities Act (ADA), signed into law in 1990, further emphasized the need for AT within the employment, transportation, public accommodations, and telecommunications sectors. This law prohibits discrimination against individuals with disabilities. Federal legislation makes it possible for all individuals to have equal access and to be productive citizens.
- The general education teacher can use the technology continuum to provide FAPE to meet the needs of, and use appropriate devices for, all students with disabilities. The Assistive Technology Continuum provides educators with a wide range of devices from high tech and sophisticated to the simplest imaginable, all of which they can customize for their teaching strategies.
- The funding for AT devices must be provided by the school system if the IEP team decides it is appropriate for the student. Other possible funding sources are Medicare, Medicaid, and private insurance. AT also may be secured through lease options or lending agencies.
- Educators who find themselves teaching students with disabilities can find answers to questions from the professional organizations that support teachers. These organizations provide codes of ethics and professional standards of practice, which serve as guides for ethical practice.
- Ethics is defined broadly as standards of conduct related to a specific profession. Professionals involved in the assessment and planning process for AT services and devices for students with disabilities generally adhere to the standard code of ethics for their professions. For special educators, the CEC code of ethics applies.
- All students must meet the curriculum standards set forth by each state to be successful on mandated assessments. For this to occur, teachers must teach to state curriculum standards for all students. The IEP team must design a standards-based IEP with appropriate modifications and accommodations for each student. Consequently all students must have access to the general education curriculum. Delivery of instruction is a consideration, as is where the student will receive instruction. AT devices can be a consideration in each of these areas.

- Teachers need a systematic means by which they can plan for professional development opportunities. They can develop a plan and engage in self-assessment activities using the standards of best practice provided by professional organizations.
- Professionals working with students with disabilities must adhere to strict policies regarding privacy issues. The CEC standards remind professionals of the confidentiality issue. Students with disabilities and their parents are entitled to certain rights that include the right to procedural safeguards and due process. The Individuals with Disabilities Education Improvement Act of 2004 incorporates and expands on the tenets found in FERPA. FERPA gives parents certain rights with respect to their children's educational records maintained by the local education agency.

References

ADA Amendments Act of 2008 (P.L. 110-325). Retrieved April 29, 2009, from http://www.ada.gov/pubs/ada.htm

Amendment to Section 508 of the Rehabilitation Act of 1998 (1998). Retrieved March 10, 2005, from http://www.section508.gov/index.cfm?FuseAction=Content&ID=14

Assistive Technology Act. (2004). *ATAP Press Release: Congress passes the Assistive Technology Act of 2004.* Retrieved April 10, 2005, from http://www.ataporg.org/ATpressrelease.pdf

Association for Career and Technical Education. (2005). *Carl D. Perkins Act—Background.* Retrieved December 12, 2005, from http://www.acteonline.org/policy/legislative_issues/Perkins_background.cfm

Cavanaugh, T. (January, 2007). Assistive educational technology takes shape: An interview with Dr. Terry Cavanaugh. *FCTD News and Notes.* Retrieved on April 29, 2009, from http://www.fctd.info/resources/newsletters/displayNewsletter.php?newsletterID=10043

Council for Exceptional Children. (1993). *CEC Code of Ethics.* Retrieved on April 29, 2009, from http://www.cec.sped.org/Content/NavigationMenu/AboutCEC/CECsMissionandVision

Council for Exceptional Children. (2008). *CEC's Mission and Vision.* Retrieved on April 29, 2009, from Council for Exceptional Children. (2009). *Public policy agenda for the 111th United States Congress: January 2009-2011.* Retrieved on January 14, 2010 from http://www.cec.sped.org/AM/Template.cfm?Section=Home&TEMPLATE=/CM/ContentDisplay.cfm&CONTENTID=11301 http://www.cec.sped.org/Content/NavigationMenu/AboutCEC/CECsMissionandVision

Family Educational Rights and Privacy Act. (2005). *General information.* Retrieved March 16, 2005, from http://www.ed.gov/policy/gen/guid/fpco/ferpa/index.html

U.S. Congress. (1988). U.S. Congress, Pub. L. No. 100-407.

Individuals with Disabilities Education Improvement Act of 2004. Pub. L. No. 108-446. 118 STAT.2647.

Mandlawitz, M. (2005). *What every teacher should know about IDEA 2004.* Boston: Allyn & Bacon/Pearson Education.

McGrath, M. Z., Johns, B. H., & Mathur, S. R. (July/August/September 2004). Tips to help special educators deal with NCLB. *CEC Today, 10*(7), 1.

No Child Left Behind Act of 2001. Pub. L. No. 107-110. 115 STAT.1425.

Rehabilitation Engineering and Assistive Technology Society of North America. (2005). *About RESNA.* Retrieved March 12, 2005, from http://www.resna.org/AboutRESNA/AboutRESNA.php

Snell, M. E., & Brown, F. (2006). *Instruction of students with severe disabilities* (6th ed.). Upper Saddle River, NJ: Merrill/Pearson Education.

Telecommunications Act Accessibility Guidelines, Final Rule. Published in the *Federal Register*, February 3, 1998. 36 CFR Part 1193.

U.S. Office of Special Education. (2005). *Individuals with Disabilities Education Improvement Act Resources.* Washington, DC: Author.

Vanderheiden, G. (1984). High and light technology approaches in the development of communication systems for the severely physically handicapped persons. *Exceptional Education Quarterly, 4*(4), 40–56.

Vertrees, D., Beard, L., & Parnell, E. (1997). Special education technology: . . . and then what? *Florida Technology in Education Quarterly, 9*(2), 26–36.

2

Assistive Technology, Universal Design for Learning, and Response to Intervention

CHAPTER VIEW

- Assistive Technology Snapshot
- Universal Design for Learning: An Introduction
- Response to Intervention
- RTI and UDL
- AT: UDL and RTI
- Assistive Technology for Student Learning
- Chapter Review

CHAPTER FOCUS

1. What is Universal Design for Learning (UDL)?
2. What is Response To Intervention (RTI)?
3. How do UDL and RTI compliment each other?
4. How is Assistive Technology (AT) useful in both the RTI process and the UDL concept?

Assistive Technology Snapshot

MEET MRS. MCDOUGAL

Mrs. McDougal is the school administrator for Freedom Elementary School. Freedom Elementary School is a small elementary school (preK–5 grade) in a rural setting. The school has a diverse student body ranging from English Language Learners (ELL) to students from high socioeconomic families. The school is well known for its caring and effective teachers and for consistently meeting adequate yearly progress. All students with disabilities are thoughtfully and meaningfully included in the general education curriculum to the maximum extent possible. The school was the first in the district to use the response to intervention process for reviewing interventions for students who were low achieving. To maintain the high standards of the school and to meet the needs of all students, each teacher is encouraged to attend meaningful professional development events. Each teacher has been trained in identifying students who need interventions to be successful learners.

Mrs. McDougal is also a successful grant writer. Therefore the school is the frequent recipient of funds from a variety of grant sources. Recently, Mrs. McDougal received a grant application that provides funding for educational technology. She understands that she must write a proposal that not only shows a need for such technology but also how the technology will impact student learning. The funding from this source would be a significant boost to the already existing technology. Mrs. McDougal's plan is to begin with the upper grades and create classrooms that are flexible as well as ones that use a variety of strategies, resources, and assessments to meet the needs of each student. She wants an effective classroom that provides equal access to learning for all students.

UNIVERSAL DESIGN FOR LEARNING: AN INTRODUCTION

In the Assistive Technology Spotlight, you learned that Mrs. McDougal wants to structure the classrooms in her school to meet the diverse needs of the students. She understands that the students in her school are typical only because they represent a wide range of learning styles, abilities and backgrounds. In planning for this diversity, she knows, as do other instructional school leaders, that in order to positively impact student learning, her teachers must have flexible teaching styles and incorporate teaching strategies to meet the needs of all students. With careful planning and intentional design of instruction, all learners can be successful. Universal Design for Learning is one concept or philosophy that emphasizes instruction and services that can be used by students with the widest range of abilities (Taylor, Smiley, & Richards, 2009).

The term *Universal Design for Learning (UDL)* comes from the field of architecture. The term started in architectural design when federal mandates provided for universal access to buildings and structures for individuals with disabilities (Lieberman, Lytle, & Clarcq, 2008). The definition is derived from the meaning found in Section 3 of the Assistive Technology Act of 1998 (see Chapter 1 for more information on this act). It refers to UDL as a concept or philosophy for designing and delivering products and services that are usable by people with the widest range of functional capabilities and that include products and services that are directly usable (without requiring assistive technology) and products and services that are made usable with assistive technology (Sec. 602[35]). According to Connell, Mace, and Mueller (1997), universally designed products and environments are equitable and flexible, simple and intuitive, and tolerant of error; require low physical effort; provide perceptible information; and provide the size and space necessary for approach and use. See Table 2-1 for more information about the Center for Universal Design and principles of design.

Give an example of how a classroom teacher might incorporate the UDL framework into specific content areas.

These guiding principles enabled educators to begin designing a framework that enhances the ability for all students to access the general education curriculum as well as provide a framework for all learners to be successful. As UDL relates to education, it is a means to adapt—for all learners—all materials, methods, strategies, and delivery of instruction and evaluation instruments that are accessible and without barriers. In essence, educators can design appropriate educational programs so that all students have access to successful learning.

One way to achieve this is to respond to individual differences by using the concept of UDL, which provides a map for creating flexible goals, strategies, resources, and assessments that accommodate the needs of a diverse group of learners (Meyer & Rose, 2002). This allows all students to achieve by identifying and removing barriers from pedagogy and resources, thus employing a philosophy of flexibility. The framework for UDL, as it relates to education, can assist educators to know and understand that materials used within a curriculum are barrier-free, and options to access and use them to engage learners will lead to a

TABLE 2-1   UDL Resources

Center for Universal Design http://www.design.ncsu.edu/cud/	The Center for Universal Design is a national research, information, and technical assistance center that evaluates, develops, and promotes universal design in housing, public and commercial facilities, and related products.
Teaching Every Student www.cast.org/teachingeverystudent/	Teaching Every Student (TES) supports educators in learning about and practicing universal design for learning (UDL).
Tool Kits for Teaching Every Student www.cast.org/teachingeverystudent/toolkits/	The Center for Applied Special Technology (CAST) UDL Toolkits help educators to understand and apply UDL principles in classrooms and to train others in UDL. Using the UDL framework, the toolkits support varied learning styles, needs, and preferences for teachers and students. Interactive activities, tutorials and tools are provided online; similar versions can be downloaded or printed.
UDL Planning for All Learners www.cast.org/teachingeverystudent/templates/UDLSolutionsTemplate.pdf	The Deriving UDL Solutions Template helps teachers select, assemble, and create flexible learning materials and methods, including tools, digital content, and Web-based materials to minimize barriers for students. Teachers can download it in Microsoft Word or PDF format to use on screen or in print.
National Instructional Materials Accessibility Standard (NIMAS) http://nimas.cast.org/index.html	NIMAS guides the production and electronic distribution of digital versions of textbooks and other instructional materials so they can be converted more easily to accessible formats.

better learning environment for all students (Hitchcock, Meyer, Rose, & Jackson, 2002; Meyer & Rose, 2002). Within this framework, materials that are universally designed enhance the education of all students (Hitchcock, 2001).

As we look at UDL, it is important to remember that it is more than a technology: It is a philosophy that drives the creation of the UDL classroom. UDL provides equal access to learning for all students, and it is in place before any student enters a classroom. Technology will play a critical role in designing a classroom for all students. Within the context of the UDL classroom, AT provides access that meets the individual needs of each student with a disability. However, more and more educators are becoming increasingly aware of AT and are using it to meet the needs of all students within their classroom. For students with a diagnosed disability, AT is considered by the IEP team after evaluating the student and the UDL environment to determine specifically what AT will enable the student to be a successful learner and to access the general education curriculum.

Ideally UDL should already be in place in all classrooms. IDEIA 2004 (see Chapter 1 for more information about this law) provides funding for technologies that support the principles of UDL. The concept is found throughout the amendments of the law. Providing the instructional resources that apply the concept of UDL has great implications for all students but especially for those who learn differently—as do many students with disabilities. As the IEP team considers what accommodations and modifications a student may need to be a successful learner, much can be accomplished if many of the supports are already in place in a

AT	UDL	Examples
Specially considered for an individual student with a disability	Used by a wide range of students	Laptop computers and screen readers are provided for all students who are reading below grade level in Mrs. Fuller's biology course. John has an orthopedic impairment and needs a specially designed switch to access his computer.
Utilized by a student with a disability to meet the expectations for the curriculum determined by the IEP team	Make the curriculum accessible for students with diverse needs	All students in Mrs. Fuller's biology class may choose to take examinations on the computer or with paper and pencil. Beth has a cognitive impairment and takes her modified biology test on the computer.
Decisions about AT are made by special educators and the student's IEP team	Decisions are made and implemented by general educators	Mrs. Fuller utilized the state course of study, state adopted texts, and technology to design her UDL biology course. She provided multiple representations of course materials for students to be successful learners. Beth's and John's IEP teams determined the goals and AT they would each need to be successful learners in Mrs. Fuller's biology class.

FIGURE 2-1 The Differences Between AT and UDL

classroom. The IEP team's responsibility is then to match the existing resources to the individual needs of the student.

What happens when a student is not making progress in the general education curriculum? Best practices dictate that every school should have a process for considering what might be impeding the learning of a student. This process includes a team of professionals who comprise a preferral team. These teams design educational supports for students who are low achieving or who have behavioral issues that are interfering with academic achievement. Response to intervention (RTI) is one method of providing these supports. RTI presumes that the student has been exposed to high-quality, evidence-based instruction and behavior supports in the general education setting. The successful implementation of the UDL classroom depends on resources and materials that are chosen based on high quality and research. The use of UDL and the process of RTI are in place for all students—not just those identified as having a disability. Many students who have access to both UDL and RTI may never need more intense, individualized interventions. For other students, however, the process of RTI provides a problem-solving framework to diagnose a student's learning problems and provide intensive interventions that include the use of AT.

RESPONSE TO INTERVENTION

The Individuals with Disabilities Education Improvement Act (IDEIA, 2004) provides for each local education agency to use the practice of RTI as part of the evaluation process for determining if a student is identified with a specific learning disability (SLD). This process implements the practice of a comprehensive approach that emphasizes the use of scientifically based research interventions (Johnson & Smith, 2008). RTI has been described as an alternative to the IQ severe discrepancy model used for many years in the identification of students who might have an SLD. The severe discrepancy model was the wait-to-fail model. Students were falling behind, often as long as 3 to 5 years, prior to an initial referral for services. The traditional form of instruction for many students remained the same and no differentiation or specific interventions were implemented until the student received a diagnosis of an SLD. Fuchs & Fuchs (2006) indicated that RTI is a multilayered system that can prevent academic and social failure before a student is unnecessarily or prematurely identified as having a disability. The RTI model can serve as both a means to improve instruction, whether it is delivered in the general education classroom or in the spectrum of special education services, if the student is diagnosed with a disability. The resources for providing services to any child should be allocated appropriately in order to secure the child's success.

Jimmerson, Burns, and VanDerHeyden (2007) suggested that RTI might be a systematic utilization of the data in order to allocate appropriate resources to assist in student learning for every student. This would help the process to identify students who are actually in need of special education services. RTI can be a source of identification in the process of SLD, as well as a source to consult in the determination of whether and what interventions work so that a student is most successful.

Typically the RTI models use anywhere from two to four tiers of interventions. The tiers depend in part on the needs of the student and how well the instructor can deliver the instruction at each tier. The model used by educators to improve instruction and student learning involve more tiers so that the intensity of instruction is greater. The standard treatment is usually more individual or what one might term as the pull-out method of delivery of instruction for students (Strangeman, Hitchcock, Hall, & Grace, 2006). While both have been used by educators, the specific difference in the two is that the RTI model provides for intervention to occur within the general education classroom and targets the specific needs of the students. UDL and RTI can mesh with each other to provide a basis for meeting the needs of all students within a general education classroom. The UDL concept can provide an environment and accessible curriculum materials to accomplish the goal of RTI and a means to access the general education curriculum. Again, AT can be a vital support for students who need more intensive instruction.

Give an example of how the RTI process can be incorporated into the educational process to improve student learning.

For more on the UDL concept, see the Companion Website.

RTI AND UDL

RTI and UDL compliment each other because they both relate to the education of all students. RTI is more process-oriented and is used to make decisions about a student who is at risk for school failure. RTI helps to make decisions about what specific interventions best meet the needs of each child so that the child will be successful in accessing the general education curriculum. UDL assists a student in being as successful as possible in the general education curriculum. RTI and UDL are both aimed at improving student outcomes by providing educational supports (Strangeman, Hitchcock, Hall, & Meo, 2006). The UDL concept, along with the integration of AT, can assist collaborative teams in expanding the interventions for all children to be more successful in accessing the general education curriculum. The RTI process, when meshed with the UDL concept, gives much to teams when they are making decisions regarding specific interventions for each student. The significance of meshing the RTI process with the UDL concept could result in fewer referrals for special education services and provide a means to expand the interventions found to be useful to meet the diverse needs within each classroom (Strangeman, Hitchcock, Hall, & Meo). The use of technology as a possible intervention can be a means to differentiate instruction for a large number of students. The technology in most classrooms today provides teachers with a strong intervention that is useful for many students.

Would RTI be necessary if the principles of UDL were followed?

AT: UDL AND RTI

While technology is not a requirement for developing and implementing both RTI and UDL, it is common in the UDL classroom (Council for Exceptional Children, 2005). Technology enables the UDL designer to meet the challenges of the UDL framework. Using technology allows for faster creation and design of curricula. For students with diverse learning needs, technology enhances curriculum and instruction, provides access to curriculum and learning, and engages and motivates students in meaningful learning experiences (Council for Exceptional Children; Crowder, 1999). The utilization of technology, specifically AT, can be a very strong intervention for many students.

RTI and UDL provide for the creation and design of instructional materials and activities that enable students with differing abilities to attain learning goals. These goals are achieved with flexible curricular materials and activities that provide alternative learning opportunities for the various ways students learn. These options are built into the design of the materials (Crowder, 1999). Thus, UDL products present multiple approaches to meet the needs of diverse learners and allow educators to customize teaching for individual differences (Rose & Meyer, 2002). With this in mind, educators can use these approaches for designing specific interventions for each student in the RTI process and thus meet the specific needs of each student and make the classroom more universally accommodating for all students. For example, teachers may use software that accompanies a text, and the software offers reading supports, such as a speaking voice or visual highlights. Other computer programs that use technology to support the achievement of each student would also be a consideration for all students in an effort to better incorporate the UDL concept within each classroom.

How would teachers at all levels use UDL to improve instruction?

For more on AT software for use with RTI, see the Companion Website.

ASSISTIVE TECHNOLOGY FOR STUDENT LEARNING

UDL and RTI: An Impact on Learning for All Students

The UDL and RTI models have a critical implication for all students. Educators who address the UDL concept for classroom design and adaptations for the curriculum make the learning process optimal for all students. The RTI process is one that provides classroom teachers with input from other colleagues on the successful implementation of various interventions based on the individual needs of each student. As introduced in the Assistive Technology Snapshot at the beginning of the chapter, it is important that educators are open to redesigning their classrooms based on the UDL concept. With this in mind, the RTI process would then assist teachers in providing better accessibility, interventions, strategies, and evidence-based research interventions that adequately meet the needs of all students. The RTI process has been described as a science because it is constantly evolving in the decision process that relates to practice (Jimerson, Burns, & VanDerHeyden, 2007). The practice of integrating UDL and RTI will improve the delivery of instruction and reduce the

ASSISTIVE TECHNOLOGY SPOTLIGHT 2-1

UDL and RTI: Consideration for Thought

1. UDL provides an accessible classroom for all students to learn.
2. RTI provides a process for the consideration of interventions that can change the way instruction is delivered to better meet the needs of a specific student.
3. UDL provides for adaptability within the classroom.
4. RTI provides for the use of scientifically based research strategies for students within the intervention process.
5. UDL and RTI are constantly assessed to make sure each student receives the opportunity for optimal learning within each classroom.
6. Within the UDL concept, the materials, the strategies, and the means of assessment are designed to be flexible enough to meet the needs of all students (Hitchcock, Meyer, Rose, & Jackson, 2002).

number of referrals for special education. Students receiving better interventions in the classroom to accommodate each learning style perform better academically. When UDL and RTI are combined, the use of AT can be a powerful and critical support in enabling all students to progress in the general education curriculum.

Chapter Review

- The term *Universal Design for Learning (UDL)* came from the field of architecture.
- The UDL framework suggests that educators adhere to three key principles by providing (a) multiple representations of information, (b) multiple means for students to express their learning, and (c) multiple ways to motivate and engage students (Meyer & Rose, 2002).
- UDL provides equal access to learning for all students,
- The Individuals with Disabilities Education Improvement Act (IDEIA, 2004) provides for each local education agency to use the practice of RTI as part of the evaluation process for determining if a student is identified with a specific learning disability (SLD).
- The RTI models use anywhere from two to four tiers of interventions. The tiers depend in part on the needs of the student and how well the instructor can deliver the instruction at each tier.
- UDL and RTI can improve the outcomes of all students when used properly.
- The practice of meshing UDL and RTI not only improves the delivery of instruction but also reduces the number of referrals for SLD.

References

Connell, B. R., Jones, M., Mace, R., Mueller, J., Mullick, A., Ostroff, E., Sanford, J., Steinfeld, E., Story, M., & Vanderheiden, G. (1997). *Principles of Universal Design.* Center for Universal Design. Retrieved on April 29, 2009, from http://www.design.ncsu.edu/cud/about_ud/udprincipleshtmlformat.html#top

Crowder, E. (1999). Universal design: Ensuring access to the general education curriculum. *Research Connections in Special Education, 5,* 1–8.

Council for Exceptional Children (2005). *Universal Design for Learning: a guide for teachers and education professionals.* Upper Saddle River, NJ: Pearson.

Fuchs, L. S., & Fuchs, D. (2006). A framework for building capacity for responsiveness to intervention. *School Psychology Review, 35*(4), 621–626.

Hitchcock, C. (2001). Balanced instructional support and challenge in universally designed learning environments. *Journal of Special Education Technology, 16*(4), 23–30.

Hitchcock, C., Meyer, A., Rose, D., & Jackson, R. (2002). Providing new access to the general curriculum: Universal design for learning. *Teaching Exceptional Children, 3*(2), 8–17.

Jimerson, S. R., Burns, M. K., & VanDerHeyden, A. H. (2007). *Handbook of response to intervention: The science and practice of assessment and intervention.* New York: Springer.

Johnston, E. S., & Smith, L. (2008). Implementation of response to intervention at middle school: Challenges and potential benefits. *Teaching Exceptional Children, 40*(3), 46–52.

Lieberman, L. J., Lytle, R. K., & Clarcq, J. A. (2008). *Getting it right from the start: Employing the universal design for learning approach to your curriculum.* JOPERO, 79(2), 32–40.

Meyer, A., & Rose, D. H. Universal design for individual differences. *Educational Leadership,* 39–43.

Strangeman, N., Hitchcock, C., Hall, T., & Meo, G. (2006). *Response to instruction and universal design for learning: How might they intersect in the general education classroom?* Retrieved March 11, 2009, from http://ldonline.org/article/13002

Taylor, R. L., Smiley, L. R., & Richards, S. B. (2009). *Exceptional students: Preparing teachers for the 21st century.* Boston: McGraw-Hill.

3

Assistive Technology
Evaluation

CHAPTER VIEW

- Assistive Technology Snapshot
- Collaborative Teaming
- Referral and Assessment for Assistive Technology
- Assistive Technology for Student Learning
- Assistive Technology Spotlight
- Chapter Review

CHAPTER FOCUS

1. What kinds of teams might be formed to guide decision making for students with disabilities?
2. What is the role of the individual team member?
3. What is the role of the team in assessment for assistive technology?
4. What are the steps in referral and assessment for the assistive technology (AT) process?
5. How can the Ongoing Assessment AT Checklist be useful in making future assistive technology decisions?

Assistive Technology Snapshot
MEET ERNIE HILL

Ernie is a 3-year-old currently enrolled in the preschool program at Johnson City Elementary School. He lives at home with his mother, Patricia Hill, a social worker at the local hospital. Ernie's father died when Ernie was 2.

Ernie was diagnosed at birth with **spastic paraplegia (increased muscle tone within legs), microcephaly,** and a seizure disorder. His most recent evaluation indicated that he needed **pervasive level of supports (extensive supports).** Ms. Brooks, Ernie's preschool teacher, thinks that AT would help Ernie with the developmental delays caused by his diagnosed disabilities. She feels that even limited self-initiated movement would help Ernie with his skills in adaptive and social and emotional development.

Since birth, Ernie and Mrs. Hill have received services for his disabilities and delays from an early intervention program. Early intervention helped Mrs. Hill procure a pediatric wheelchair for Ernie when he outgrew his stroller. The occupational therapist (OT) and physical therapist (PT) determined the correct type of chair to meet Ernie's needs. (An **occupational therapist** designs programs and delivers instruction utilizing appropriate materials to assist individuals' participation in useful activities. A **physical therapist** works with individuals to develop and maintain muscular and orthopedic abilities through movement.) Even though the chair was designed for Ernie for independent sitting and participating in activities placed on his tray, his mother used it primarily as a stroller to transport Ernie from one location to another. She continued to hold him for feeding and placed him on the floor in a beanbag chair for other activities. Consequently, Ernie was not accustomed to sitting in his chair for extended periods of time.

One of Ms. Brooks's goals was for Ernie to have more independence in the classroom. However, he was unable to maneuver the wheelchair due to the location of the wheels. He was unable to access activities at the table because the chair and table were in different heights. He also faced other obstacles in the classroom environment, which resulted in his inability to participate in group activities. For example, when his peers joined the teacher for circle time, they sat on the floor. Ernie was unable to do this, so he appeared not to be part of the group. Also, Mrs. Hill frequently did not bring Ernie's tray to school, so he was unable to participate in many of the daily activities. Ernie did not like to sit in his chair and expressed his displeasure by crying loudly. Ms. Brooks was unsure how long Ernie should sit in the chair, so she spent a great deal of her time getting him in and out of the chair. Ms. Brooks also wanted Ernie to eat lunch in his wheelchair with his classmates in the lunchroom, but Ernie refused to eat while in the chair.

After a week, Ms. Brooks realized that she needed assistance to enable Ernie to meet his goal of independence and improvement in the developmental domains. In addition, Ernie began to exhibit behavioral problems that she had not previously witnessed or found in his records. After consulting with Ernie's preschool special education teacher, Ms. Brooks scheduled an Individualized Education Program (IEP) team meeting to address AT issues.

In addition to the regular members of Ernie's IEP team, Ms. Brooks invited the school system AT specialist. The team met and used a systematic problem-solving approach to help Ernie and Ms. Brooks. The team was in complete agreement that the current seating was inadequate and that perhaps it exacerbated his physical and emotional problems. The AT specialist was assigned the task of assessing Ernie for appropriate AT devices to increase positive student outcomes. Until this assessment is completed, the OT and PT will work closely with Ms. Brooks and Ernie's mother to position and seat Ernie in safe and appropriate ways for learning activities, for play, and for eating. The team asked the AT specialist to complete the functional assessment as soon as possible and convene another IEP meeting to determine AT outcomes for Ernie.

Webquest 3.1

You have just been assigned a student with cerebral palsy. Go to http://www.merckbooks.com/mmha/index.html and find the definition for cerebral palsy.

Webquest 3.2

Models of collaboration: You have just been told you will be teaching in a fully included classroom for the fall. Go to http://learningdisabilities.about.com/od/publicschoolprograms/p/collaboration.htm and discuss the models of collaboration discussed on this site.

In addition to the regular members of Ernie's IEP team, Ms. Brooks invited the OT, PT, and the school system AT specialist. The OT designs programs and delivers instruction utilizing appropriate materials to assist individuals' participation in useful activities. The team met and used a systematic problem-solving approach to help Ernie and Ms. Brooks.

COLLABORATIVE TEAMING

As you can see from Ernie's situation, the decisions regarding AT are made as a team. The concept of a team that comes together to devise an educational plan for the student originated with the Education for All Handicapped Children Act in 1975, which was discussed in Chapter 1. Collaborative teams offer different models that provide ways for educators to work together. Three different team models have evolved through the years and provide individuals the opportunity to come together to plan the student's educational program. These team models include the (a) multidisciplinary model, (b) interdisciplinary model, and (c) transdisciplinary model.

Multidisciplinary Model

The multidisciplinary model is the oldest and is based on discipline-specific expertise. The input and expertise of many individuals are drawn upon when planning the educational program for the student. The AT specialist fulfills an important role in the planning and input of a student's IEP. The role of the AT specialist is defined later in this chapter.

Interdisciplinary Model

When utilizing the interdisciplinary model, members of the team conduct their evaluations separately but come together to plan and develop the student's education program. Team members work together to share information and plan intervention strategies specific to each student. The family is an integral part of the interdisciplinary team. Team members are responsible for implementing the interventions that are discipline-specific. For example, the AT specialist provides significant input based on the results of the AT assessment.

Transdisciplinary Model

A major characteristic of the transdisciplinary model is that one professional serves as the coordinator and is responsible for the implementation of most of the services for the student. In many cases, this is the special education teacher.

In this model, the AT specialist provides results of the AT evaluation and one person would be the primary service provider for implementing the use of AT for the student. Ernie's IEP team followed this model.

The Individualized Education Program Team

Friend and Bursuck (2002) suggested that effective teams remember why they are a team, set aside personal differences, and design the best program for students with disabilities. Most often, this team is the student's IEP team. In Chapter 1, the composition of this team was introduced. The role of each member of the team is essential in the formal assessment process and in collaborative problem solving. When making decisions regarding AT, considerations for the team include (a) participation in and documentation of the AT assessment process; (b) determination of student and teacher support for AT use; (c) evaluation of a student's academic progress after utilizing AT; and (d) problem solving to eliminate barriers that the student, family, teachers, and other service providers may encounter in implementing AT.

Roles of Individualized Education Program Team Members

The collaborative teaming process involves the participation of many individuals in planning an IEP that is appropriate for the student and ensures delivery of a Free Appropriate Public Education (FAPE). The IEP team members have several tasks to complete as they design an IEP, including (a) determining which team members should serve as part of the student's IEP team, (b) discussion and review of assessment results, and (c) writing the various parts of the IEP based on those results. These tasks address present levels of educational performance, annual goals, benchmarks, least-restrictive environments, and how and when progress will be reported.

The members of the IEP team all contribute to each part of the IEP. The specialties of individual members vary and are determined according to the needs of the student. The AT specialist is an essential member of the team. Other members of the collaborative team may include the general education teacher, special education teacher, school administrator, Local Education Agency (LEA) representative, parents, school psychologist, school counselor, physical therapist, occupational therapist, social worker, school nurse, speech-language pathologist, representatives from community-based agencies, and (when appropriate) the student. Each IEP team member serves a specific function and provides input in many different ways to ensure that the student receives the best possible program that meets individual needs and provides access to the general education curriculum. Every team member is important to the student and the process.

ASSISTIVE TECHNOLOGY SPECIALIST   The AT specialist conducts a complete AT assessment on the student to determine the correct AT device(s) needed to access the general education curriculum. The AT specialist is a major player in determining, and often helping to build or make, the AT device. The purpose of the AT evaluation is to determine what AT devices will be as effective and unobtrusive as possible while reducing the barriers that prevent access to the general education curriculum. The AT specialist assists in defining goals and benchmarks as they relate to IEP development for the student.

GENERAL EDUCATION TEACHER   The Individuals with Disabilities Education Improvement Act of 2004 requires that a general education teacher be part of each IEP team if the child is or will be participating in the general education curriculum. General education teachers have much documentation related to the student's performance in the general education classroom and can contribute much to the development of the IEP. Their contribution includes knowledge and documentation of the grade-level course of study standards and curriculum. They know and understand how the student can access the general education curriculum and what types of supports may be provided to achieve this goal.

General education teachers can be very good sources of information about what AT, if any, the student might need. General education teachers also provide input into the assessment process through both informal and documented assessments conducted in the classroom. The general education teacher must have input into the best ways to adapt the curriculum to make it accessible to meet the needs of each student.

SPECIAL EDUCATION TEACHER   Special education teachers take on different roles, depending on the needs of the student. Functions can range from an itinerant, inclusive resource-room teacher to a consultant to a general education teacher. Special education teachers usually schedule, organize, and do much in the way of conducting the IEP meeting. Special educators can provide information related to assessments, as well as how best to access the general education curriculum based on the student's prior history. They also provide expertise in defining AT devices or services that will help the student succeed. It is often the special educator who makes the referral for an AT assessment. Special educators know and understand disability law, policy, and regulations as well as the various types of disabilities and often can relay this information as it relates to planning instructional programs.

SCHOOL ADMINISTRATOR   As the instructional leader, the school administrator is responsible for oversight of all curriculum programs within a school. He or she is a role model for teachers. Teachers often take their cue from the school administrator. If the school administrator conveys, through program development, that he or she believes all children can learn, other staff will follow that lead. The school administrator must make sure that all students receive a Free, Appropriate Public Education (FAPE). Therefore, it is important that the school administrator not only be present and be part of the IEP team, but he or she should also contribute to its actual development. Some school administrators are responsible for scheduling and conducting IEP meetings. Some designate administrative assistants, school counselors, or other teachers to represent them at IEP meetings. In addition, the school administrator may serve in a second role: the Local Education Agency (LEA) representative.

LOCAL EDUCATION AGENCY (LEA) REPRESENTATIVE   The IEP team often includes an LEA representative from the local school district. Although the roles of the LEA representative vary somewhat from district system to district system, it is important for each IEP team to have such a representative. The LEA representative could be the director of special education services, curriculum coordinator, assistant school superintendent, or (as mentioned above) the school administrator. The LEA representative speaks on behalf of the school system.

PARENTS   The parents of the student are an important part of the team. The language of the law is very strong regarding the participation of parents in the IEP process. Parents know the child better than anyone. A parent can be the most supportive person for an educator, and educators should value their input as such. Parents provide support for their children across all environments. They continue at home what is often introduced in the school environment. If AT is important to the success of the child in meeting his or her annual goals, it is vital that parents and representatives of the school system work collaboratively. Such collaboration also lessens the likelihood of AT abandonment if the child is working with the AT device across all environments.

SCHOOL PSYCHOLOGIST   The school psychologist usually administers formal and other assessments deemed appropriate by the referral team. The school psychologist works with the team to interpret the test results. The school psychologist analyzes assessment data to make accurate and practical recommendations that can help develop the IEP. Some states have persons certified by agencies such as a state department of education to perform these services. For example, in Alabama a psycometrist is certified to perform evaluation services.

SCHOOL COUNSELOR   Counselors serve many functions in the development of the student's IEP. They can assist in the interpretation of assessments and can report on issues related to information received from the student's teacher(s). School counselors also provide counseling services if the IEP team deems that appropriate for the student. If AT is needed, the counselor may counsel the student as he or she learns to use the AT device in the school setting.

PHYSICAL THERAPIST AND OCCUPATIONAL THERAPIST   These professionals work in a nonmedical manner with the student who has physical disabilities. The physical therapist (PT) provides input regarding physical functioning in appropriate activities as they relate to gross-motor skills, positioning, and movement. The occupational therapist (OT) provides input regarding activities related to fine-motor and visual-motor skills of the student. PTs and OTs often participate in the IEP process when assessments reveal that these services are needed. These services are called related services in the development of an IEP. PTs and OTs also help the AT specialists to decide what type of AT devices and services are needed.

SOCIAL WORKER   Social workers spend much time bringing together community agencies to assist the student. They can gather information on the child outside the school setting. This helps the IEP team to make decisions regarding implementation across all environments. If AT is needed, the social worker can also contribute to deciding how it might work across all environments.

SCHOOL NURSE   These professionals help during the screening process. They screen students for vision and hearing loss. For a medically fragile student, they may help explain the student's medical history. This provides the IEP team with a basis for the selection of AT devices or services.

SPEECH-LANGUAGE PATHOLOGIST   The speech-language pathologist (SLP) provides services related to speech and language both in isolation and in the general education classroom. The SLP is an important part of the IEP process as it relates to augmentative alternative communication (AAC) devices. The selection of the appropriate AAC device is important for communication, and the SLP has major input into this decision as a member of the student's IEP team.

OTHER MEMBERS   Other professionals represent vocational rehabilitation (VR), human services, preschool service providers, and other medical professionals. All are potentially part of a student's IEP team. These professionals can provide specialized input in the development of the IEP to best meet the needs of the student.

STUDENT   The student for whom the IEP is being written should be present, whenever appropriate. Students must understand and feel that they are part of the development of their IEP early in their school careers. Students can add valuable input when present by leading their own IEPs, presenting information about themselves, and talking with members of the IEP team. If AT is needed, students should help determine the type of AT they would feel most comfortable using. If students are involved in the decision-making process, they are more likely to use their AT devices across all environments.

Team Participation and the Assessment Process

As stated above, each member of the team has specific roles. Friend and Bursuck (2002) suggested that those roles include professional, personal, and team roles. In the professional role, each contributes from his or her expertise. For example, Ms. Brooks would contribute for Ernie her understanding of what typically developing preschool students are expected to accomplish. In addition, she would provide information about how Ernie is presently performing in her preschool class. This allows the team to make decisions about how AT can support Ernie in the preschool class. Other members of the team may include the same members who were on the student's evaluation team, but new members may be added to meet a variety of student needs (Best, Heller, & Bigge, 2005). For example, the AT specialist was added for Ernie.

Each member also has a personal role on the team. Personal characteristics can make positive contributions to the process. For example, the team member who is an encourager will encourage the members when the process is challenging.

The third role suggested by Friend and Bursuck (2002) is the team role. For example, a team member may be adept at clarifying the intent of the team and expressing it in ways that all team members understand. According to Friend and Bursuck, common roles are necessary for the effective functioning of the team. These roles may include team facilitator, timekeeper, recorder, and reader. These roles may rotate so that all persons can participate in the teaming process. The active participation and contributions of each member of the team are vital to ensure successful student outcomes.

It is imperative to recognize the important role of the family in the teaming process. Again, the mandate of the Individuals with Disabilities Education Improvement Act of 2004 includes family members as an integral part of the collaborative team. It is incumbent on other team members to encourage and value effective and active family participation, as well as to assign team roles to the family members. Table 3-1 provides resources to support collaborative efforts of the team.

What personal characteristics do you have that will be assets to a collaborative team?

Student and Teacher Support

To meet the unique needs of the student with a disability, it is often necessary to supplement individualized instruction with additional services. These services are known as **related services**. These services, identified by the IEP team, assist the student in benefiting from special education. After the team completes the

TABLE 3-1   Collaboration and Teaming for Assistive Technology

Educational Change http://newhorizons.org	Site focuses on fostering educational change and includes a section on special education and collaboration.
Special Education Resources for Teachers and School Administrators http://seriweb.com http://www.techlearning.com/article/2818	Contains a collection of Internet-accessible information resources of interest to those involved in the fields related to special education.
International Council for Exceptional Children http://www.cec.sped.org	Official website for the International Council for Exceptional Children.
Technology Use for Students with Disabilities http://www.closingthegap.com	Website that advances the use of technology for students with disabilities. Includes examples of special education and collaboration.
Comprehensive Site for Teachers http://teacher.net http://www.readingrockets.org/article/211	Includes several chat rooms on current topics that are related to collaboration.
National Board for Professional Teaching Standards http://www.nbpts.org	This site for the National Board for Professional Teaching Standards includes standards for the voluntary certification of accomplished teachers. Many of the assessments for National Board certification include demonstrated knowledge and skill in collaboration.

multifactored evaluation, it is vital that needed supports be identified. These supports may include instruction in AT use and maintenance for the student, family, and teacher; peripheral support for AT use in the classroom; and/or environmental changes in the classroom and home setting to accommodate the AT.

Problem Solving

Almost all the activities and tasks confronting the IEP team can be conceptualized as some type of challenge or problem to be solved (Friend & Cook, 2003). Often the term *appropriate* in "Free Appropriate Public Education (FAPE)" creates tension and argument about what AT is appropriate. Due to the complex issues involved in the use and provision of AT, problem solving is an essential part of the IEP process. Problem-solving issues vary in intensity and may be confronted and resolved based on a reactive approach or a proactive approach.

PROACTIVE VERSUS REACTIVE   In the case of Ernie, the preschool teacher engaged the team in proactive problem solving in planning Ernie's preschool program. She used the appropriate AT to determine a level of independence for Ernie. Although it is inevitable that crises and dilemmas will occur even using a proactive approach to planning, this style of problem solving is the most desirable. Reactive approaches usually require more time and effort to correct an existing problem than to prevent the problem from occurring.

Engaging in a proactive problem-solving approach helps predict or anticipate what problems and barriers the student, family, teachers, and other service providers may face in implementing the AT. Taking the time at this stage to eliminate possible barriers and problems before they occur creates solutions that can be implemented to ensure student progress. This also allows the team to form a culture of collaboration before frustration and negativity become part of the problem-solving process.

The process of evaluating all student academic outcomes is an ongoing role of the collaborative team. This enables the team to closely monitor the student's progress and to problem-solve. Failure to conduct effective and efficient evaluation of AT may lead to a decrease in desired student outcomes and to AT misuse, nonuse, and eventual abandonment.

One of the greatest challenges for teachers of students with disabilities is to help make reasonable accommodations and modifications in the educational environment so students gain access to the general education curriculum and receive the FAPE that is guaranteed by law. (Accommodations and modifications are defined in Chapter 1.) Many accommodations consist of simply rearranging the environment for safety and access. A simple accommodation could consist of moving a student with a visual impairment closer to the front of the room to better see projected materials. Some students may require a more extensive equipment accommodation. For example, a computer system with an alternate or modified keyboard or specialized software could be the AT that would enhance a student's participation in the general education program. Chapter 1 describes the AT Continuum and the range of related options.

AT, like education, should not be approached with a "one size fits all" mentality. AT should be specific to the needs of the individual student. As in the case of Ernie, the decision should be the result of using a functional assessment process such as the Referral and Assessment for Assistive Technology (RAAT) process. This process is discussed in detail later in this chapter.

Assistive Technology Considerations

The Individuals with Disabilities Education Improvement Act of 2004 mandates that school districts use a team approach to develop the student's individual education program. These team members are knowledgeable about the student, and one of them should have significant knowledge regarding AT devices and services, as defined in Chapter 1. Collectively, they should have appropriate knowledge about AT to make an informed decision regarding the devices and services for the student. This does not mean that each member should be an expert in AT, but each should know AT well enough to help the team reach consensus regarding the appropriate AT for the student.

IEPs are developed based on intensive, focused, multifactored evaluations. Student goals are written based on the individual needs of the student. These needs are determined by the data collected during the assessment process. AT is a tool to help the student meet the individual IEP goals determined by the IEP team. Therefore, outcomes for the student must be written first in order as a process to determine what type of AT device would be appropriate. Best practice indicates that the type of AT device(s) should be one of the final decisions made by the student's IEP team. The interrelatedness of assessment, IEP goals, and AT is presented more fully in the last section of this chapter, Assistive Technology for Student Learning.

CONSIDERING INDIVIDUAL NEEDS   First and foremost, AT is a tool and one must not lose sight of that. AT is used to help the student meet individual needs and, as such, serves the student by helping him or her meet IEP goals and other curriculum standards. It is helpful to remember that the student is the primary focus, not AT. Scherer (2008) emphasizes the importance of keeping the focus of AT on the unique needs and preferences of the student. She also found that there are distinct differences in how AT users and AT nonusers approach the selection of AT devices. Having knowledge of these differences enables the team to continuously review the needs in every environment where the AT will be used.

Second, AT is specialized and is designed to help the student meet individual educational goals. Using one particular AT device across goals is a plus. Conversely, an individual piece of AT should not be overlooked because it can help a student meet only one goal in one area. If the device helps the student meet that goal, it should be a consideration. If one high-tech device may help to meet several goals for a student at minimal levels, this should be a factor when consideration is given to AT by the student's IEP team. The team must not lose sight of the needs of the student when determining AT.

Third, AT, ranges on a continuum from no tech to high tech. (The technology continuum is discussed fully in Chapter 1.) Generally speaking, the more high tech the device, the higher the costs and the longer the time involved in acquisition, training, and use of the device. Legally, cost cannot be a factor in the determination of AT, but realistically, the cost to the individual school district is a consideration. The team must help determine whether a particular device would simply be a "nice thing to have" or if it would help the student meet the individual goals for the educational program. Serious disagreements often develop between school districts and families related to the definition of *appropriate*. For example, a student with poor handwriting skills might benefit from a word processor with an enlarged keyboard; however, a pencil grip and paper with raised lines could also stabilize the pencil and improve handwriting, thus providing the same result. Funding conflicts are real issues and must be addressed as soon as they occur. (Chapter 1 has more information on AT funding.)

REFERRAL AND ASSESSMENT FOR ASSISTIVE TECHNOLOGY

Evaluation and assessment for AT are closely related and integrated within the overall assessment of a student suspected of having a disability or already diagnosed with a disability. As long as a thorough and functional assessment is adopted and followed, the AT assessment should provide the necessary data for the IEP team to make decisions regarding specific AT devices and services. It is important that all team members and additional stakeholders understand the selection process. The assessment process should also be global enough to include information from a variety of sources.

The process described in this chapter is Referral and Assessment for Assistive Technology (RAAT). It is a four-step process for determining the individual needs of the student and for providing the appropriate AT, ongoing support, and continuous assessment to meet those needs.

Step One: Referral for Assistive Technology Assessment

The specific procedures for referring a student for an AT assessment vary according to the official policies and procedures of the school district. This chapter considers the process from the point at which the school receives the referral. This may be an initial referral, a referral of a transferring student, or a request for a student already receiving special education services. A family member, a referring agency, a physician, a teacher, or another school professional may make the referral. Assistive Technology Spotlight 3-1 is an example of a referral letter written by a parent.

After the referral is made, the team meets to consider the request. All prior and current assessment data should be considered in the referral. The more information provided in the referral, the better idea the team has about whether the assessment should take place. The school district will have a form containing the information the team must consider. The team will want to organize and consider the following information:

- Student data or personal information
- Medical data for vital concerns
- Vision and hearing reports
- Information about any technology or equipment currently in use
- Background information regarding any related services provided previously for the student

Once the team has all the assessment data and hears the concerns of the family and other team members, the decision to assess may be made.

Step Two: Conducting an Assistive Technology Assessment

As mentioned, the student's instructional program must be tailored specifically to that student's abilities and needs. A multifaceted procedure addresses the unique needs and abilities of the student with a disability. An AT assessment is based on information gathered from a variety of sources, including the student's records, additional informal observations and information gathering, and formal assessment of the student's existing skills. It is the job of the AT specialist to conduct the assessment, but team members have a significant role in assisting the specialist. When the AT specialist has not been in the original referral meeting, the specialist will want to gather some general background information in addition to that found in the student's records. This may be obtained through direct observation of the student in several environments and through formal and informal interviews with family members, teachers, and the student.

DIRECT OBSERVATION   During direct observation, the AT specialist spends time focused on observing the student's abilities and skills, including the following:

> Cognitive skills
>
> Current use of any AT devices
>
> Sensory skills
>
> Motor skills
>
> Communication skills
>
> Social skills

For the older student with a disability receiving transition services, the specialist may wish to observe independent living skills and vocational performance. (More about transition may be found in Chapter 9.)

When very young children with disabilities are assessed, it is helpful to include a family assessment. (A discussion of the specific assessment needs related to young children may be found in Chapter 4.) The specialist should record this information for reference as decisions are made about particular types of AT devices. The student observation form found in Table 3-2 can be an effective data-collecting device.

The first column provides an opportunity to note the time, date, and environment. The time and environment may have significant relevance to the student's abilities and the expectations for that student in that learning environment. The second column provides a reminder of the abilities that are being observed. To get a total picture of the student, all these areas should be considered during observation. The third column provides space for remarks, memos, and pertinent quotes from other people regarding the student.

These observations should take place across times and environments. For the older student who changes classes multiple times per day, the observations should be made, if at all possible, in all of the environments. For example, the

TABLE 3-2   Student Observation Form

Name of Student:
Observer:

Date/Time/Environment	Observations	Comments
	Cognitive factors	
	Current use of AT	
	Sensory skills	
	Motor skills	
	Communication skills	
	Social skills	

expectations for a student in physical education are different from the expectations for the same student when he or she is in a history class. For the younger student, it would be helpful to observe during active learning events as well as playtime. Depending on the student, it may be helpful to observe the student in nonacademic settings, such as during extracurricular activities and within the home and community.

Observations provide feedback to the IEP team on behaviors that may be interfering with the student's ability to be a successful learner. They also allow comparisons to be made between behaviors of the student with a disability and typically developing peers. If it is not possible to observe in multiple environments, the assessment may rely on interviews with parents, teachers, and the student when appropriate.

INTERVIEWS   Interviews allow the specialist to gather information about specific areas of interest and give parents, teachers, and the student opportunities to express their experiences, interests, and concerns. Some formal assessments contain interview components, relying to some degree on reports from parents or other individuals who are familiar with the student. AT specialists may develop their own interview questions. These interviews can yield a wealth of useful information, including the following:

- Family concerns and expectations
- Perceived needs and abilities of the student
- Academic expectations
- Diagnostic information
- Medical information

In addition, for older students with disabilities making the transition from school to the adult world, the interview should include independent living skills and vocational performance.

As a service provider, teacher, or family member, you may be asked to address these matters. You should do so accurately and honestly. Participating in an interview for assessment helps to identify concerns and goals reflecting the student's needs at school and at home.

FORMAL ASSESSMENT   A formal AT assessment generally involves selected activities in predetermined environments. One area of need in AT is the development and publication of formal AT instruments. Because these instruments are scarce, the AT specialist may use instruments that were not designed specifically for assessing AT but that allow inferences to be made about how the student's skills are interrelated with the need for AT. The specialist may need to match assessments and parts of assessments to the student with regard to age, experiences, cognitive level, behavioral issues, and social skills. A summary of all the information collected during the AT assessment will be the foundation on which to make decisions about whether AT is needed for successful student outcomes.

PUTTING IT ALL TOGETHER   When the referral, information gathering, and assessment procedures are completed, the AT specialist will be able to construct a comprehensive picture of the student's strengths and needs. A formal, written report should be compiled by the specialist and presented to the student's IEP team. The format of this report may vary depending on the school district.

Step Three: The Individualized Education Program Team

The selection and implementation of AT are not individuals' decisions and should be approached with the team concept in mind, as already discussed. The IEP team, which is multidisciplinary in nature, will make its decisions based on the report given by the AT specialist and in light of other information found in the student's IEP. The team should carefully consider the student's learning goals and see how the AT allows the student to access the curriculum.

Recall that Ernie's teacher wanted Ernie to be more independent and to initiate learning activities. So the IEP team decided, based on assessment, that Ernie needed more stable seating in the form of a customized pediatric wheelchair with a tray that would allow him to complete tasks independently. In addition, the team decided that Ernie should use adapted eating utensils with built-up handles so he could initiate self-feeding at school and at home. The team also decided to have Ernie begin working with switches so that in the future he could manipulate a powered wheelchair. Although not noted in the background information, the AT specialist realized after observing Ernie in multiple settings that Ernie's speech was delayed and that he did not make transitions easily. The IEP team decided that Ernie could begin using a picture schedule to help him with the transitions. The AT specialist, with the assistance of the teacher and the SLP, designed a stable communication board with a picture schedule on it. The AT specialist also included other pictures that helped Ernie express his needs in more appropriate ways. The SLP will work with the teacher to help Ernie pair words with the pictures he uses for communication.

Other decisions made by an IEP team include training needs for the student and for those working with the student. This includes the family. Training issues should be discussed and decisions made at the time the IEP is developed. The team may consider device trials before making a full investment in the AT device.

DEVICE TRIALS   After the team decides that the student needs AT for access and support and determines the device or devices the student may need, it is time for the team to procure the device. Because many devices are high tech and expensive, the team should research the devices they consider. Failure to do so may result in overspending or underspending. The team should try to use the device on a trial basis. This may involve borrowing it for a while. Loaner programs, perhaps in your area, are available. (Chapter 1 includes resources for AT device loans and for funding.) If a loaner program is not an option, perhaps the device can be leased for a short term. If another student has outgrown or abandoned a similar device, it might be borrowed for the trial period. During the trial period, the student and others who will be working with the student should be trained.

If the team is able to obtain the device, however, those who will be working closely with the student must know how to use it. The time factor must be considered and is especially critical if the loaner comes with a limited time agreement. Some popular commercial devices are available for a limited time and may have a 30-day "try before you buy" program. Even simple-to-use devices take time and effort to learn the correct use of the device and the circumstances in which the student will use the device. Some students with cognitive disabilities who have problems with generalization may need to be shown how to use the device in all settings. During the training program, data should be collected to determine how the device meets the student's needs. These data can provide information for making meaningful decisions.

Step Four: Implementation of the Assistive Technology Device

After all the preliminary work and decision making based on the assessment, the time comes to purchase the device and implement it to meet the student's learning outcomes. (Funding and funding resources are found in Chapter 1.) Once the device has been procured for the student, additional training may be necessary if the device is different from the one used in the trial period. After any additional training is completed, the student may need short-term assistance and monitoring to ensure that the device is used correctly and appropriately. During the early stages, it is critical that the student, classroom teacher, and family receive support from related service personnel and other members of the IEP team. Related service personnel may include the assistive technology specialist, speech therapist, occupational therapist, and physical therapist. Depending on the individual needs of the student, other related service personnel and other agency personnel may be involved in the support.

The special education teacher has a significant role in the implementation of the device. This role includes making sure the support is there for the student and seeing that the student is a successful learner. The AT device should be assessed while the student is assessed to see if his or her learning goals are met. This ongoing assessment is necessary to confirm the effectiveness of the device.

Teachers and other related service personnel who are in frequent contact with the student are most likely to have a good overall picture of how the student is progressing in the general education curriculum. These personnel can use the checklist found in Table 3-3 to assess the AT device and the student's use of it. This informal assessment assists the IEP team in making future decisions regarding AT for the student. It is recommended that this checklist be used multiple times, and whenever the student is assessed, to determine if the student is progressing toward meeting IEP goals and other curriculum standards.

TABLE 3-3   Ongoing Assessment Assistive Technology Checklist

Assessment Items	Responses			Comments
1. Is the student using the AT device to meet IEP goals and/or curriculum standards?	Yes	No	Undecided	
2. Does the AT device allow accessibility to learning or demonstration of knowledge?	Yes	No	Undecided	
3. Is the AT device as unobtrusive as possible in the classroom environment?	Yes	No	Undecided	
4. Is the student able to generalize the use of the AT device to other environments?	Yes	No	Undecided	
5. Is the student receiving the necessary support from school personnel to use the AT device effectively?	Yes	No	Undecided	
6. Does the AT device appear to enhance the student's participation and interaction with peers?	Yes	No	Undecided	

Any items marked "no" or "undecided" should receive immediate attention to resolve the issue. This may include reconvening the IEP team or simply consulting with a team member. Any significant changes must be addressed by the IEP team. If issues and concerns are addressed immediately, student learning will not be interrupted, the student will continue to progress, and the probability of AT abandonment will be minimal.

How can the referral and assessment process enable the team to be proactive in making AT decisions?

ASSISTIVE TECHNOLOGY FOR STUDENT LEARNING

The first step in student learning must begin with a well-written IEP that provides the map for the student to be a successful learner. The following assessment tools feature specific components of the IEP that show the relationship between assessment, the student's goals, and AT.

Examples of Assistive Technology Assessment

POSITIONING AND MOBILITY FOR ERNIE

Please note: This is only a section of an evaluation that an AT specialist would conduct on a child.

AT Assessment for Positioning and Mobility

Does the child have limited range of motion?   _X_ Yes   ___No

If so, describe the range of motion and the motor control.

Ernie does have limited range of motion and problems with his muscle coordination due to spending a large amount of time in a stroller in earlier years and in a wheelchair that was not fitted for him in more recent years. Ernie has been kept in an upright position in the wheelchair with adapted supports to keep him upright. This has adversely affected his muscle development. Ernie's mother has fed him and given him little independence in learning to do basic skills such as reaching and grasping that would help to develop his muscle tone and would require more effort for this development on his part.

Describe the child's mobility.

Does the child walk independently?	__ Yes	X No
Does the child walk with aids?	__ Yes	X No
Does the child use a wheelchair?	X Yes	__ No
Does the child use the wheelchair and require the assistance of another person to aid in this process?	X Yes	__ No
Does the child use a power wheelchair?	__ Yes	X No

Ernie is unable to walk. He does wear leg braces—however, the braces are very heavy. His wheelchair was purchased at a yard sale. He has never had a wheelchair designed specifically for him. The current wheelchair has no footrests, which results in his feet not being supported. The wheelchair does not have a tray, which results in Ernie not being able to place objects on a tray to manipulate objects and play. This also results in isolation, which in turn results in developmental delays in social development. Ernie has never had the opportunity to use a power wheelchair.

Recommendations
- Ernie should have a wheelchair designed specifically for him.
- Ernie should achieve a level of independence by learning to manipulate the wheelchair within his classroom with the assistance of his teacher.
- The wheelchair should be fitted with a tray so Ernie can learn to feed himself, to play with objects, and to function within a group setting.

Individualized Education Program: Present Level of Performance and Goals

Present Level of Performance

Area Assessed: Position and Mobility

Present Levels of Performance: See notes under each section of questions.

Sources of Information: Teacher, parents, and observations of OT and PT.

Goals
- Ernie will maneuver his wheelchair within the classroom with the assistance of his teacher.

- Ernie will manipulate objects on his tray to complete tasks during organized play.
- Ernie will feed himself independently.

The preceding abbreviated assessment for AT positioning and mobility and the IEP show how assessment for AT and the IEP come together to provide appropriate programming for the child. For Ernie, the AT specialists might confer with the OT and PT on the assessment; however, the IEP team decides on the best possible programming for children with disabilities. Note that the school system is obligated to provide training within the home for a preschool child, such as Ernie. This ensures that parents are involved and play an active role in utilizing the AT for the child's education. Although AT devices are the property of the school system, children may take them home and use them there. This ensures that devices will be used across all environments and will help children continue to progress and properly use the AT device (Wright-Ott, 1998).

How is the RAAT model useful in writing IEP goals?

ASSISTIVE TECHNOLOGY SPOTLIGHT 3-1

Sample Referral Letter

August 23, 2009

Dear Sir or Madam:

My son Ernie is currently receiving special education services at Johnson Elementary School in the preschool program. His teacher reports that he is unable to access many of the center and learning activities due to his disability. This is causing Ernie to be frustrated, and he is communicating these behaviors in inappropriate ways. Although Ernie's Individualized Family Service Plan Team talked about Ernie needing technology when he entered preschool, it was decided that it would be best to wait until Ernie was in the preschool environment. Ernie is now in that environment and appears to need more help to participate in the activities in the classroom.

I would like Ernie's IEP team to reconvene as soon as possible. At that time I would like the team to consider an assessment to see if assistive technology might help Ernie in his classroom. I understand as a parent that this assessment will be completed at no expense to me. I would like a specialist to determine (a) what assistive technology would benefit Ernie and (b) what services Ernie, his teachers, and I would need to support this technology. I would like to have this assessment completed as soon as possible so that Ernie may benefit from this information in this current classroom.

I appreciate your assistance with this matter and look forward to hearing from you.

Sincerely,
Patricia Hill

Chapter Review

- Evaluation of AT use for the classroom is important if the student is to have access to the general education curriculum. The means by which the evaluation is achieved is through collaborative teaming.
- The three different models of collaborative teaming are multidisciplinary, interdisciplinary, and transdisciplinary.
- The multidisciplinary model involves the discipline-specific expertise of each member.
- The interdisciplinary model involves members of a collaborative team conducting their evaluations separately from each other and then planning and developing the student's IEP as a team.
- The transdisciplinary model has one professional serving as the coordinator of services and being responsible for the implementation of such services. The AT specialist provides the results for this type of team model, and a different individual serves as the primary service provider.
- While each team model is unique and has many good characteristics, it is recommended that each team serve the best needs of the student by utilizing the characteristics of each team that would be most appropriate in planning the student's IEP.
- Teaming is a process whereby each member can have several roles. Each must serve in the professional, personal, and team role for the planning of AT to be successful. In the professional role, each member contributes to the process based on expertise. In the personal role, each member contributes personal characteristics, which can have a positive impact on the teaming process. In the team role, each member decides what roles to assume based on the makeup and needs of the team. Roles include facilitator, timekeeper, recorder, and reader. The collaborative role of the family is of utmost importance and is also mandated by the Individuals with Disabilities Education Improvement Act.
- Following an evaluation for student service, the IEP team may need to consider related services so the student can receive FAPE. Related services can come in the form of AT and can assist the student in benefiting from special education.
- IEP teams must be proactive in anticipating what problems or barriers students, families, and teachers may face. Being proactive will help prevent many problems. Evaluating student outcomes is an ongoing role of collaborative teams.
- IEP teams should consider reasonable modifications and accommodations to ensure that students gain access to the general education curriculum.
- AT is a tool to help the student meet individual IEP goals and benchmarks. Student outcomes should be written first to help determine what type of AT device would be appropriate.
- The three considerations to keep in mind when looking at the individual needs of the student are (a) AT is used to help the student meet IEP goals and other curriculum standards, (b) AT is specialized and designed to assist the student in meeting the education goals, and (c) there is a continuum for AT usage.

- The evaluation of AT should provide the necessary data to support the IEP team in making decisions regarding specific AT devices and services. All team members are stakeholders and should have an understanding of the process. The information from an AT assessment should include input from a variety of sources.
- The RAAT is a four-step process that includes (a) referral and assessment, (b) conducting an AT assessment, (c) the IEP team, and (d) implementation of the AT device.
- The first step in using AT is the writing of the IEP. The IEP serves as a map for student outcomes. Ernie's IEP team decided that he should work on independence as a goal so he will be able to access activities in various locations within the classroom.

References

Best, S. J., Heller, K. W., & Bigge, J. L. (2005). *Teaching individuals with physical or multiple disabilities* (5th ed.). Upper Saddle River, NJ: Merrill/Pearson Education.

Friend, M., & Bursuck, W. D. (2002). *Including students with special needs: A practical guide for classroom teachers* (3rd ed.). Boston: Allyn & Bacon/Pearson Education.

Friend, M., & Cook, L. (2003). *Interactions: Collaboration skills for school professionals* (4th ed.). Boston: Allyn & Bacon/Pearson Education.

Individuals with Disabilities Education Improvement Act of 2004, Pub. L. No. 108-446. 118 STAT.2647.

Scherer, M. J. (January, 2008). Matching child and technology: Closer to a sure thing. FCDT News and Notes. Retrieved on July 20, 2009, from http://www.fctd.info/resources/newsletters/displayNewsletter.php?newsletterID=10055

Wright-Ott, C. (1998). Designing a transitional powered mobility aid for young with physical disabilities. In D. B. Gray, L. A. Quantrano, & M. L. Leiberman (Eds.), *Designing and using assistive technology: The human perspective* (pp. 285–295). Baltimore: Brookes.

4

Assistive Technology for the Young Child

CHAPTER VIEW

- Assistive Technology Snapshot
- Early Childhood Special Education
- Assistive Technology and Service Delivery
- Assistive Technology for Student Learning
- Assistive Technology Spotlight 4–1
- Chapter Review

CHAPTER FOCUS

1. What is early childhood special education?
2. Why is the family such an important element in providing assistive technology (AT) for young children?
3. How is an Individualized Family Services Plan (IFSP) different from an Individualized Education Program (IEP)?
4. How might AT enable a child to play?
5. How might AT support young children in the developmental domains?

Assistive Technology Snapshot
MEET BECKY CRAWFORD

Becky Crawford turns 3 soon. She has decided to have a princess birthday party to celebrate her special day with her friends at the Mom's Day Out program she attends for 4 hours, 3 days per week, sponsored by her local church. On the other 2 days of the week, Becky can be found at home with her mom, Tomika. Becky is the only child of Lorenzo and Tomika Crawford. Mr. Crawford owns a successful automobile repair shop, and Tomika serves as his accountant so she can be a stay-at-home mom with Becky. Becky's records indicate that she was born prematurely at 30 weeks. Shortly after her birth, Becky's pediatrician administered the Brazelton Neonatal Behavioral Assessment Scale (NBAS) to identify possible abnormalities in the central nervous system and in sensory abilities. At that time, no abnormalities were noted in either Becky's central nervous system or sensory abilities. Becky did not have any respiratory distress at birth and was able to leave the hospital at 36 weeks gestational age. Although it appeared that she was developing in a typical manner, Becky was evaluated by the early intervention (EI) program for a possible developmental delay. At that time, the family was assigned a service coordinator and the decision was made to assess again after her 6-month well-baby checkup. At that checkup, Becky's mother mentioned that she was worried that Becky had learned only to roll over and was not attempting to sit alone. Her pediatrician suggested that she and her husband schedule a meeting with their EI service coordinator. Using assessment data gathered from the parents, a physical therapist, and Becky's pediatrician, the multidisciplinary team determined that Becky was eligible to receive early intervention services.

A significant developmental delay was found in the physical or motor skills domain. An Individualized Family Services Plan (IFSP) was written that recognized the strengths and needs of Becky and her family. At that time, the physical therapist began working with Becky at home and taught Tomika how to work with Becky to help her with her physical challenges. The therapist used a corner seat to support sitting so Becky could play for short periods in a sitting position. She provided a schedule for utilizing the chair when Becky was not in the home, and she taught Becky's parents how to use the chair properly. Becky's parents also were taught how to provide meaningful and motivating activities for Becky while she was in the chair.

After 2 months of therapy, Becky began to sit independently and to attempt to crawl. When she was 1 year old, the family and the other team members met to assess Becky's progress. At that time, Tomika and Lorenzo both mentioned that they were worried about Becky's lack of expressive vocabulary. She appeared to understand what they said, but she only responded with gruntlike vocalizations, squeals, clicks, cries, and laughter. Becky was evaluated for a possible delay in the language domain. After interpreting the assessment information, the team felt that Becky was eligible for EI in the area of communication development. The IFSP was revised and, in addition to the services of a physical therapist, a speech-language pathologist was assigned to work with Becky and her family. At age 24 months, Becky began walking and using one-word utterances and a simple communication board to point to pictures of things she wanted.

When Becky was 30 months, the EI team suggested that Tomika and Lorenzo consider placing Becky in a part-time daycare setting so that she would have the opportunity to play with typically developing children and perhaps improve her communication skills. The family's local church program for young children seemed to meet Becky's special needs. Becky began attending a class in the Mom's Day Out program with other children her own age. Both the physical therapist and the speech therapist worked with the caregivers at the Mom's Day Out program, and at least twice a month they provided services to Becky in this setting, as well as in her home. At this time, the service coordinator, with the help of the multidisciplinary team, developed a transition plan and began transitioning Becky from the EI services to the preschool special education services provided by her local school system. Becky will continue to go to her current daycare setting, but the responsibility for her services will now be provided by the early childhood special education teacher, a speech-language pathologist (SLP), and a physical therapist (PT). Becky's parents are eagerly waiting for the time she turns 4 and can attend the program for 4-year-olds provided for all children in the school district. They believe that, with the right supports, Becky has a bright future.

EARLY CHILDHOOD SPECIAL EDUCATION

CW See the Companion Website for more about the Council for Exceptional Children Division of Early Childhood Recommended Practices.

Families like Becky's have the right to expect that their children can reach their full potential. Early childhood special education provides the outcome-based services that enable young children with disabilities to have a hopeful and promising future. It encompasses early intervention, preschool special education, and special education providing a seamless array of services for children from birth through 8 years of age. AT can be an important component of these services. Service providers for young children with disabilities must consider how evidence-based recommended practices may be combined with AT to provide effective and successful skill development (Dugan, Campbell, & Wilcox, 2006).

Early Intervention and Assistive Technology

Professionals and family members who work with young children with special needs should have an understanding of the programs available to meet the changing needs of the young child. Becky started receiving services for her developmental delay at a very young age. A **developmental delay** is a category of disability assigned to young children from birth through age 9 who have delays in their development. These services were provided by an agency that specialized in **Early Intervention (EI)** services for children birth to age 3. While these services are not mandated by the Individuals with Disabilities Education Improvement Act (IDEA; 2004), states are strongly encouraged by the federal government to provide services to infants and toddlers through grant incentives. In most states, the responsibility for early intervention services falls to an agency other than the public school system. (More about this part of the law may be found in Chapter 1.) For the multidisciplinary team working with this age group, it is important to know that the services, including AT services, may be delivered and funded differently from those services for children ages 3 through 21.

Young children from birth to age 3 may receive early intervention services if they qualify under certain conditions. The Individuals with Disabilities Education Improvement Act (2004) specifically mandates certain criteria for eligibility. These criteria include the need for services due to a developmental delay in one of five developmental domains: cognitive development, physical development, social or emotional development, communication development, and adaptive development. AT may allow access to learning and development in all these areas.

Another criterion that can lead to eligibility is established risk conditions. This relates to young children who may have a diagnosed physical or medical condition that may lead to a developmental delay. Examples of this include low birth weight, identified syndromes, and chronic illnesses. **Low birth weight** is when a baby is born with a birth weight of less than 3 pounds, 5 ounces (1,001 to 2,500 grams) and complications.

Many states also serve infants and toddlers who are at risk for experiencing a developmental delay if early intervention services are not provided. These children do not have a diagnosis of a disability, but because of environmental risk conditions such as parental substance abuse, extreme poverty, abuse and neglect, and parental cognitive impairments, they may develop a disability.

For the professional working with young children in early intervention, it is important to remember that it is essential to include the parents or caregivers as partners. Early intervention is family-focused and will not be effective if the parents are not actively involved in the entire process. Part of the process includes a voluntary family assessment to determine the strengths and needs of the family. This information, together with the evaluation of the child, helps the multidisciplinary team in planning reasonable and successful outcomes for the child and family.

Assistive Technology and the Individualized Family Service Plan

The team develops the Individualized Family Service Plan (IFSP) to meet identified needs and use family strengths. The IFSP is a document similar to the IEP. However, the focus of the IFSP is on interventions for the family as well as for the child. Each child is assigned a service coordinator to assist the family in navigating the services. It is in the development of the IFSP that the team decides what AT devices and services are needed, how to obtain them, and how the professionals and family will be trained to use these devices. AT abandonment is almost certain to occur if the family and other caregivers are not part of AT planning and training for the young child.

In the case of Becky, her early interventionist used a corner chair to enable her to support her sitting so she could manipulate objects in ways different from when prone and to promote her ability to sit alone. If the only time the corner chair were used was when the interventionist was in the home, then the AT device would not be as effective. In addition, Becky's parents were trained in how to position Becky in the chair and how to provide interesting and meaningful activities for her while sitting. In early intervention (EI), the IFSP is reviewed every 6 months because young children grow and develop rapidly and the needs of the child and the family may change.

Service Delivery

During the development of the IFSP, the multidisciplinary team decides where the young child should receive services. According to the 1997 Amendments to IDEA, services must be provided in the child's natural environment.

How is the use of AT in the natural environment different from AT use in the least restrictive environment?

The **natural environment** is any place where typically developing children may be found. Introducing AT in the natural environment requires parents, professionals, and caregivers to be trained in the use of any AT device.

TRANSITION

When Becky reached 30 months of age, her service coordinator developed a transition plan to help Becky make the move from EI to preschool special education. The **service coordinator** assigned to the young child and family is responsible for many aspects of program delivery, with the main role being to ensure that families have access to the services they need. This includes helping the family gain access to AT services and devices. The service coordinator addresses concerns such as whether the family can and will support the use of AT. As a young child moves from EI to preschool special education, it is the role of the service coordinator to ensure that the transition to preschool special education is successful for the child and family. Table 4-1 includes helpful information to share with families.

Preschool Special Education

Preschool special education is required by the Individuals with Disabilities Education Improvement Act for all children ages 3 to 5 with disabilities. The responsibility for providing these services falls on the local education agency (LEA), and the services are very similar to services provided for students ages 6 to 21. There are three exceptions to note. First, students may continue to be identified and reported as having a developmental delay instead of a categorical classification, such as mental retardation. Second, the IEPs must have a section of information and suggestions for the family. Third, services may be provided in a variety of natural environments just as they were in EI. It is important to know that the LEA is responsible for providing services but may contract with outside service providers. This may be true for the use of AT services and devices, so a teacher may be working with a service provider who is not an actual full-time employee of the LEA.

As Becky makes the transition, it will be important for the new service providers to be part of the multidisciplinary team so that her goals can be met. For example, when Becky moves from the church day program to the LEA 4-year-old program, her new caregivers should be trained in how to use her communication board and any other AT devices that she may need.

ASSISTIVE TECHNOLOGY AND SERVICE DELIVERY

Planning for Assistive Technology

When considering child development, we should realize that each milestone leads the child closer to independence. **Developmental Milestones** are specific abilities that children master during the growth process. A child **at risk** is a child who has a higher probability of developing learning problems because of environmental, biological, or established risk factors. Along those lines, the critical component of AT is to support the child's development by providing tools that

TABLE 4-1   AT Information for Families

Alliance for Technology Access: Family Center on Technology and Disability http://www.ataccess.org	Community-based network of resource centers that provide developers and vendors with information and support services for children and adults with disabilities to increase their use of standard, assistive, and information technologies.
Assistive Technology for Children with Disabilities http://codi.buffalo.edu/children.htm	U.S. government information on assistive technology for children with disabilities.
Family Empowerment Network http:///www.downsyndrome.com National Association for Down Syndrome http://www.nads.org/	Resources for families and others interested in Down syndrome and related disabilities.
Family Village http://www.familyvillage.wisc.edu	Global community that integrates information, resources, and communication opportunities on the Internet for persons with disabilities, their families, and those who provide services and supports.
Federation for Children with Special Needs http://www.fcsn.org	Offers services to parents, parent groups, and others who are interested in children with special needs.
National Early Childhood Technical Assistance Center (NECTAC) http://www.nectac.org	Technical assistance to programs and projects for children with disabilities. Ages: birth through 8 years.
Sibling Support Project http://www.siblingsupport.org/	National program for the interests of brothers and sisters of individuals with special health and developmental needs.
United Cerebral Palsy http://www.ucp.org/ucp_channel.cfm/1/11	The information at this website assists parents and families in obtaining the necessary support and services in childcare, supported living, education, health, employment, and health and recreational activities for their family members.
Parent Training and Information http://fcsn.org/pti/index.php	Supports nationally organized parent-to-parent programs, parent training, and information centers.

may be used to address the challenges that may limit the child's ability to explore and manipulate the immediate environment. For a child who either has a disability or is determined to be at risk of developing disabilities, the goal is to foster the greatest independence that can be achieved by enhancing the ability to interact with the environments in which the child is expected to function. Assistive Technology Spotlight 4-1 provides additional information when planning assessment for young children.

When a child with disabilities has difficulty meeting one or more of these milestones, more or different supports may have to be implemented. With AT becoming a means to help the child reach independence, the effectiveness of any

CW See the Companion Website for Milestone Charts.

particular AT device or service can be expected to change over time as the child grows, develops, and matures and strengths and needs change. Keep in mind at all times that the goal of AT use is to increase the child's independence in and access to life events. For example, AT goals for Becky would be to help her gain independence in her motor development and speech and **language skills**. Language skills relate to forming words and making words into sentences. The use of AT with infants and toddlers is currently under investigation because it is perceived to be primarily a high-tech tool for helping school-age children enhance their opportunities for learning, and thus more appropriate for older children. Adding to the lack of recognition is the fact that babies may not be regarded as having functions in life that compel the use of AT. AT for the very young population must be child- and family-centered, require minimal training for everyone involved in the implementation of the device, be readily available, and enhance the child's participation in effective interaction within his or her natural environments (Sullivan & Lewis, 2000).

It is also critical that the utility of the AT be reevaluated on a regular basis as an ongoing intervention to address family-stated outcomes. Becky developed language later than her typically developing peers. If AT had not been under evaluation, the team might have lost valuable time for helping her develop her communication skills. The primary goals of AT should be those that increase the independence and/or the participation of a child with disabilities in daily activities within natural routines. New options must be considered immediately when an intervention that has been used to address a particular family outcome is no longer working or the objective is not performing an essential task.

Functional capabilities begin with the child exploring a batting motion that causes objects to move and practicing it until the batting has become purposeful. This learned skill is then generalized, and the child begins to make other things move with other actions of his or her body (Solano & Aller, 2000). If a child with a disability is unable to bat objects or generalize such movements, he or she may never get to control these movements to manipulate the environment. If AT can be used to help a child make batting movements, that aspect of the child's development may be somewhat normalized. Thus, infants and toddlers with disabilities require AT supports that are responsive to their individual needs, along a continuum following general principles that include both light-tech and high-tech options. More about the assistive technology (AT) Continuum is found in Chapter 1.

GENERAL PRINCIPLES   The general principles (Oregon Vision Working Group, 2002) of the AT Continuum include the following:

How can the general principles serve as a guideline for the development of the IFSP?

1. Assistive technology allows the child access to acquire basic skills.
2. Assistive technology should be used as part of the assessment and the developmental process.
3. Assistive technology for children is not an instructional tool. It is a fundamental tool developed to help the student interact with various environments.
4. Children use assistive technology to access and use standard tools and participate on an equal basis with peers in their various environments.
5. Use of assistive technology does not automatically make educational and commercial software/tools accessible or usable.

AT should be a key component in the development of the IFSP. The IFSP team helps develop family goals and objectives that help the student better ameliorate disabilities and thus make a smoother transition from home to the educational environment. Therefore, the IFSP team must consider which type of assistive technology may be included and where in the IFSP the AT is to be included. AT can be a related service, a supplementary aid or service, or a life-skills service. Regardless of where AT is considered in the IFSP, it must be considered as a tool for the overall development of the child. In addition to the evaluation process of Referral and Assessment for Assistive Technology (RAAT) introduced in Chapter 3, it is recommended that the IFSP/IEP team consider the dynamics of the family, assistive technology, timelines, and the environment featured in Assistive Technology Spotlight 4-1.

In writing objectives, it is important that the objective address four components: the area of need, the direction of change, the level of attainment, and the evaluation component (Best, Heller, & Bigge, 2005). These components must also be related to the functional task or outcome that the AT will be used to help the child master. We must always relate the use of technology to the functional outcome of the objective.

To assist the child in meeting the functionality component, the "so what–who cares" test must be applied. When considering the areas of need, change, attainment, or evaluation, look at the overall functionality of the skill and ask "If the child does not learn this skill, so what–who cares?" Using the "so what–who cares" test will keep the focus of the AT on the child and not on the equipment. The AT is a means to an end, not the end itself (Best et al., 2005). Writing the AT into the IFSP is just the beginning of the team's work.

The placement of AT as a related service is probably more appropriate than trying to use AT as an educational service. At this point, we are more concerned with using AT to help the young child function within the family setting, not in the attainment of an education-related goal. When AT is used as a related service, however, elevated focus must be placed on the specificity of the amount, frequency, duration, and location of the AT (Best et al., 2005). Therefore, teams tend to include AT under the supplemental aids and services section of the IFSP.

AT is usually more appropriately included in the IFSP under supplementary aids and services when the AT is used to better help the child gain more independence in his or her immediate environment. AT devices that can control televisions, radios, CD or DVD players, or clappers for turning lights on and off are easily obtained and can help the child gain control over the environment.

Children at this age change very quickly. The IFSP should be reviewed at least every 6 months and rewritten annually to try to keep up with the developmental changes in the child. The IFSP is an evolving document. Both the IFSP and the AT must be assessed regularly to support the individual needs of the child. At the early stages of development, the child may quickly outgrow the device and could be without AT supports during a critical stage of development. Table 4-2 provides additional resources for families of young children.

TABLE 4-2 Assistive Technology and Young Children	
Lekotek http://www.lekotek.org	Lekotek has 34 locations nationwide that offer family play sessions, toy lending, libraries, Compuplay family computer centers, and other innovative community-specific programming.
Abledata http://www.abledata.com	Provides a substantial directory of thousands of resources for people with disabilities, including information on technology for infants and toddlers.
Funding AT http://www.nectac.org/topics/atech/funding.asp	AT funding information for infants, toddlers, and young children with disabilities.
Kids Together http://www.kidstogether.org	Provides helpful information and resources to enhance the quality of life for children and adults with disabilities, and communities as a whole. Good information for families.
National Center to Improve Practice in Special Education Through Technology, Media and Materials http://www2.edc.org/NCIP/library/ec/toc.htm	Information on the range of assistive and instructional technologies available for children with disabilities in preschool and early childhood settings.

Assistive Technology Funding Considerations

Due to the rapid growth and development of young children, as discussed previously in this chapter, the IFSP team must be reminded that children outgrow AT like they outgrow clothes, shoes, and toys. New technology may be developed that could better serve the needs of children as they grow. The cost of high-tech devices should not be a factor in providing the device. In reality, however, it is an important factor for the family and service provider. Service providers should be aware of the various funding options, as well as sources that will lend AT devices on a regular basis. Begin the search for AT sources at any state agency that provides early intervention or rehabilitation services. More information regarding how AT is funded may be found in Table 4-2 and in Chapter 1.

What considerations make AT funding for young children different from AT funding for older children?

ASSISTIVE TECHNOLOGY FOR STUDENT LEARNING

As discussed, learning environments for young children are varied. Many types of AT may be introduced to enable children to access their learning environments. As service providers consider how to provide access, they should look closely at switches. **Switches** are input and output devices that facilitate interactions with their environments. For example, joysticks, buttons, and sip-and-puff systems could allow a child to play with toys. Other switch systems are mentioned throughout this text.

Assistive Technology and Play

AT for the young child is and should be an integral part of the child's daily activities. AT facilitates the active involvement in activities that are developmentally appropriate in both the home and at school. AT for the young child should consist of devices that facilitate communication, socialization, and play and enhance functional daily living skills.

Play is an important part of the young child's curriculum and is incorporated into most activities at the preschool level. It is important that young children with disabilities be part of the same activities as their typically developing peers. To facilitate that involvement, the use of AT must be considered when planning activities and choosing toys.

Adapting Activities in the Environment

The adaptation of activities is a key for young children with disabilities. Preplanning on the part of the teacher and in conjunction with the family is vital to the success of young children with disabilities in any preschool setting. An important rule to remember is to adapt only as much as is needed for the child. With accommodations, young children with disabilities can be included with typically developing peers. Planning the schedule of events at both home and school to determine appropriate adaptations is important. To carry through with activities in the home setting, the family should review the child's schedule at home.

Young children with disabilities should be included with their typically developing peers in developmentally appropriate activities. A good preschool program has a developmentally appropriate curriculum in place yet focuses on the individual needs of each child. If tables are used for activities, make sure the table is at the right height for the child's wheelchair to fit underneath it or for the child to stand if needed. If the child needs toys to be stabilized, the use of Velcro on both the table and toy can help in this endeavor. Tape can also be used to stabilize an object on most surfaces. Children with visual impairments may need more tactile objects to facilitate their involvement in play activities. Marking an area with a rough surface, such as sandpaper strips, can help a child define the boundaries of the play area.

If board games are used, accommodations can be made for children to grasp pieces or objects that may be part of the process for play. Objects that must be manipulated can have parts affixed to them or they can be built up so children have an easier time gripping and moving them. Boards can be copied and enlarged to enhance visual perception. Oral instructions can explain the rules of a game or how to play with a toy. If children need to verbalize the same sentence in a game, voice output devices could record the sentence and children could push a button to activate the device. For children who need accommodations for communication, the communication board (described in Chapter 7) with pictures related to the game can be developed specifically for various games and activities. The child can point to the appropriate picture during the game, which would encourage language development and activities for daily living.

Why is proper positioning important for the inclusion of a young child in play activities?

Positioning and mobility issues should be addressed by the IFSP members to facilitate play among young children with and without disabilities with their typically developing peers. It is important to make sure each child is in the proper position to enjoy play activities and has the proper supports to be included and to enjoy participation. Supports such as wedges, corner chairs, and other adaptive seating help the child in a seated position to participate in an activity with ease. *Remember:* Supports should be addressed and made useful across all environments.

Children have a natural desire to explore their environments. Young children are curious about their surroundings. To explore an environment, they must have mobility. Young children with a disability have the same curiosity. AT devices that provide mobility for the child should be a consideration of the IFSP team. Walkers and wheelchairs provide mobility for children to move within their environments. Walkways within classrooms should be wide enough and free from items that may hinder a child from moving in an area. The environment should be structured to promote movement and support for all children. Desks, bookshelves, and door handles, in addition to tables, should be at the correct height for a student to stand and reach an object or for a wheelchair to fit underneath. Toys with wheels that the child can push are an excellent means of support and mobility for the child.

Assistive Technology and Toys

CW See the Companion Website for tips on selecting toys for young children with special needs.

Toys are an important part of play for a child. With a simple switch adaptation, young children can often play with a toy without the assistance of a caregiver. A switch interface, such as a battery adapter, a timer, or a computer switch interface, can be installed, and the toy can be modified for use with a single switch. Children can then press one button to operate the toy. Almost any caregiver can adapt any battery-operated toy in this manner. Toys adapted with switches can encourage all children to play together and can encourage everyone to take turns with the item during playtime.

Using Table 4-3, find a toy that would be appropriate for Becky.

Organizations that promote toys for young children with special needs are increasingly partnering with toy companies to adapt off-the-shelf toys to meet children's unique play needs. One such example is The National Lekotek Center, which partnered with Rokenbok Toy Systems and Crane Industries to make the Rokenbok Toy Systems accessible for children with disabilities (Lekotek of Georgia, 2004). See Table 4-2 for a link to The National Lekotek Center and for additional information. Table 4-3 provides toy resources for parents of children with disabilities.

Assistive Technology and Literacy

The process of literacy begins early in the life of a child. Children begin the process of becoming literate at birth, and they are exposed to a variety of materials that facilitate this process. Early language experiences through association with pictures, books, the arts, and verbalization are part of what is known as the *emergent literacy process.* DeCosta and Glennen (1997) believe children as young as 1 or 2 are in the process of becoming literate.

TABLE 4-3	**Toy Resources**
AblePlay http://www.ableplay.org/	A toy rating system and website that provides comprehensive information on toys for children with special needs.
Adaptivation Inc. http://www.adaptivation.com	Variety of products for young children with disabilities.
AssisTech http://www.assistech.com	Light-tech solutions for children with disabilities; includes accessories to promote fun, learning, and living.
Enabling Devices: Toys for Special Children http://www.enablingdevices.com	Adapted toys, switches, and communication and sensory devices, plus much more.
Guide to Toys for Children Who Are Blind or Visually Impaired http://www.nfb.org/nfb/NOPBC_Toys_for_Blind_Kids.asp?SnID=4#two	Suggestions for commercial toys for children who are blind or visually impaired.
Special Needs Toys http://www.specialneedstoys.com/usa/	Adapted toys and products for children with special needs, including multisensory rooms.
Toys R Us: Toy Guide for Differently-Abled Children http://www.toysrus.com/shop/index.jsp?categoryId=3261680	Provides toy guide with symbols.
Adapting Toys http://letsplay.buffalo.edu/toys/adapting-battery-toy.htm **At Access** http://www.ataccess.org/resources/wcp/enswitches/enadaptingtoy.html **Switch Toys** http://letsplay.buffalo.edu/toys/switch-toys-begin.htm	These websites teach how to adapt off-the-shelf toys, add switches, and make a battery interrupter.

Webquest 4.1

For sample AT devices for young children, go to: http://enablingdevices.com/AssistiveTechnologyIdeas.aspx?gclid=CKXIqofN2psCFRNinAod2lB_AA

For young children who have a disability, AT may be a key factor in this process. Caregivers of young children can begin the process of implementing many strategies to adapt material so children can be part of the group activities related to reading. These modifications provide practice, as well as motivation, for the young child with a disability (Beck, 2002).

Children who are language delayed or nonverbal can benefit from listening to stories. Teachers who read to a group of children can include a young child with a disability with little or no accommodation, depending on the child. If the child has a sensory disability, accommodations and modifications would need to be made accordingly. For a child with a visual impairment, text-to-speech software can provide multiple opportunities to hear the story within the group and to listen to it multiple times if necessary. For the child with a hearing impairment, visual feedback is important. Computer software programs designed to provide immediate feedback are effective for the child with a sensory loss. Writing stories utilizing symbols or pictures are great for children who are hearing impaired. An interpreter is also useful if the IFSP team feels this will help the child. Books may be converted into electronic format. Children can activate a single switch that will turn the page of a book on a computer screen. A teacher making many books available in electronic format would encourage the child not only to read but to read independently. This encourages the use of technology by all children in a given setting.

Children who are nonverbal can receive assistance through a picture communication system. Children often associate pictures with verbal cues. Using various types of commercial software, teachers can put together a communication system for the young child to communicate for functional and literacy activities. A daily picture schedule can be created for any young child who needs a visual representation of what will take place during the day. The schedule can be created so the child can clip the picture on completion of the activity. Teachers can create language activities and story-time activities using software that correlates directly with those being covered in the classroom, thereby giving the nonverbal child still another opportunity to participate with peers. Software that produces icons is an effective means for enhancing communication in the home by creating picture schedules, reading time, and functional communication. Students can be encouraged to learn the names of each child and to begin recognition of names in written context. Symbols and words can be used for the child's daily schedule in the same manner that exposes the child to print material.

Eye-gaze communication boards are another form of communication. This type of board is useful for children who may not be able to point. The child gazes at the symbol and the caregiver follows the gaze. This allows the child to communicate if he or she has difficulty pointing to a communication board. Words could be written below the symbol, thereby encouraging word association with the picture symbol.

For caregivers of preschool children, many components of the day are excellent sources for encouraging literacy. Some activities may require modifications and the use of both light tech and high tech for children with disabilities to participate. The following are a few light-tech suggestions to consider when arranging the preschool classroom to promote literacy:

- Label common objects in the room with the word or visual representation (e.g., chair, desk, door, sink, restroom).
- Provide an environment that promotes inclusion of all children so that young children will have the opportunity to interact with typically developing peers.
- Children with disabilities need repetition. Rereading a story several times may be necessary for the child to understand or learn the concept.
- Provide opportunities for the child to use the computer. E-books, text-to-speech tools, screen readers, and scanners provide the child with the opportunity to read, encourage independent reading, and enhance interaction with typically developing children.

- Provide universal design for learning (UDL) and a multisensory approach to learning with tactile, auditory, and visual feedback in all areas of the curriculum. (See Chapter 2 for more about UDL.)
- Allow the child to explore the keyboard of a computer. This will encourage the recognition of letters and numbers.
- Talk to the child about a story, a song, or a picture he or she has drawn. Even children who are nonverbal will learn to provide the teacher with feedback through facial expressions and body language.

How would you know what words to use to design a simple picture schedule for a young child with no verbal language?

Children need to be exposed to an environment that encourages literacy development in their natural settings. Inclusive settings are important for all children to interact with each other. Children should be given the opportunity to access and interact with all types of printed materials to encourage literacy development. AT allows this to happen.

Assistive Technology and Developmental Domains

The Individuals with Disabilities Education Improvement Act recognizes the five developmental domains of adaptive, cognitive, communication, physical, and social and emotional development. A child who has a significant developmental domain in one or more of the domains is eligible to receive early intervention services or preschool special education services. It is important to note that a delay in any one domain affects development in other domains. To illustrate, consider that a child between 1 and 2 years old should be using two-word questions such as "What's that?" These questions help children explore and learn about their environment and express their thoughts. A child who is unable to express his or her needs and curiosity about the environment may experience a delay in cognitive development or social and emotional development. Another illustration relates to an infant who has spastic cerebral palsy and is unable to reach, grab, grasp, or turn over. A young child who has such a physical disability may experience challenges in eating, playing, and other activities that affect the ability to become more independent.

AT can assist a child with a developmental delay so that the effect of the delay has minimal impact on other domains. For example, when a child is not mobile and thus cannot explore the environment, AT can bring the environment to the child. Toys can be adapted with switches that allow the child to experience the development of cause and effect. Feeding utensils can be modified to accommodate a disability so that the child can learn to self-feed. Augmentative communication devices allow children with communication problems to communicate with their caregivers, as well as with peers.

The multidisciplinary team must consider not only the domain in which the child has a delay but also the whole child. Children have developmental needs in all five domains. As the team considers AT devices and services, the IEP/IFSP should reflect how the AT will allow the child to overcome a delay in one domain *and* how it will affect the development of the entire child.

ASSISTIVE TECHNOLOGY SPOTLIGHT 4-1

The Family, Assistive Technology, Timeliness, Environment (FATTE) Model

When considering the use of AT with infants and young children with disabilities, a different model of evaluation may be helpful when looking at AT for educational purposes. When considering the AT for educational use, the focus is on the student. When considering AT for the infant and toddler, the family also becomes a focus. In the case of infants and toddlers, we use the FATTE model:

Family

Assistive Technology

Timeliness

Environment

1. Family
   a. What are the family goals and objectives?
   b. What are the needs of the family?
   c. What are the expectations of the family?
   d. What are the strengths of the family?
2. Assistive Technology
   a. What types of AT will help the child better interact with these environments?
   b. How does the child interact with the AT?
   c. How does the family interact with the AT?
   d. How will the AT help the child gain independence within the different environments?
3. Timeliness
   a. How current is the AT in relation to the child's current and emerging strength?
   b. How often are the child and the AT evaluated?
   c. How often is the AT updated?
   d. If the AT is no longer meeting the needs of the child, what plans are in place for transitioning to another device and for gaining independence from the AT device?
4. Environment
   a. What are the environments in which the family and child must function?
   b. How does the child interact with these environments?
   c. What is the transitional environment for which we are preparing the child?

Chapter Review

- Early intervention (EI) services are provided for children from birth to 3 years of age, although such services are not mandated by the Individuals with Disabilities Education Improvement Act. States are provided with grant incentives to provide services for infants and toddlers. Young children may receive EI services if there is a developmental delay in any of these five areas: adaptive, cognitive, communication, physical, and social or emotional. The use of AT can enhance both learning and development in these areas. Other criteria may include low birth weight, identified syndromes, and chronic illness.

- Caregivers must remember that working with the family or caregivers is important during the early intervention process. Early intervention is family-focused and can be very effective with the involvement and input of parents.
- The IFSP is developed by a team and identifies needs and builds on family strengths. A service coordinator assists the family in navigating these services. The IFSP determines what AT devices will help the child grow and have access to the same activities as the typically developing child. Including the parents and other caregivers during the planning and training lowers the risk of AT abandonment early in the development of the child.
- Services are usually provided in the child's natural environment. Using AT in the natural environments of the child requires that parents, professionals and other caregivers be trained to use it properly.
- Preschool special education is mandated by IDEA and must be provided to all children ages 3 to 5 with a disability. It is the responsibility of the LEA to provide these services. Children are still considered to have a developmental delay rather than a categorical classification. Services are provided in a variety of settings.
- The development of each milestone helps a child achieve a new level of independence. A child considered at risk is one who has a higher probability of developing learning problems because of environmental, biological, or established risk factors. AT can provide a child with supports that enhance development. AT for the young child must be both child- and family-centered. It must also be readily available and help enhance the child's interaction with the natural environment.
- AT, as it relates to both early intervention and preschool, should be used to increase the independence of the child and to aid in the participation of a child with disabilities in the daily routine.
- General principles that include both light-tech and high-tech options are (a) AT allows the child access to acquire basic skills, (b) AT should be used as part of the assessment and development process, (c) AT is not an instructional tool but rather a fundamental tool developed to help the student interact with various environments, (d) children use AT to access and use standard tools and to participate on an equal basis with peers in their various environments, and (e) use of AT does not automatically make educational and commercial software or other tools accessible or usable.
- The IFSP must consider which type of AT is appropriate for the child and where the AT is to be included. AT can be a related service, a supplementary aid or service, or a life-skills service. IFSP objectives must meet four components: area of need, direction of change, level of attainment, and evaluation.
- The focus is on the child rather than on the AT device.
- The placement of AT as a related service is appropriate when using AT as an educational service. When AT is used as a related service, there must also be an elevated focus on the specificity of the amount, frequency, duration, and location of AT.
- AT can be considered in the IFSP as a supplementary aid and service when it is used to assist the child in gaining independence in the immediate environment.

- Funding options should be addressed when the AT is discussed. Sources for various funding options, as well as lending agencies, are important for family and service providers to know about when the IFSP is designed.
- AT should enhance the child's active involvement in activities that are developmentally appropriate both at home and at school. Adaptation of activities is important for children with disabilities in a preschool setting. A rule of thumb is to adapt only as much as is needed for the child. Scheduling both at home and at school is important for planning and adapting activities. A good preschool program should focus on the development of the child and on the individual needs of each child.
- Tactile objects, rough surface areas, board games, and objects that can be manipulated all provide opportunities for young children with disabilities to be included in all aspects of the program if appropriate adaptations are made to accomplish this objective.
- Positioning and mobility issues should be addressed by the IFSP team to facilitate play for young children with disabilities with typically developing peers. Supports such as wedges, corner chairs, and sassy seats can be used to ensure that all children are included in various activities.
- Walkers and wheelchairs provide mobility for children and can help a child explore the environment independently. The environment should be structured to promote movement and supports for all children.
- Toys can be adapted with various types of switches so young children with disabilities can operate them in a very simple manner. Such adaptations can encourage all children to play together.
- AT can be a key factor in literacy development. With very little adaptation, teachers can read to young children. Children who are language delayed or nonverbal can benefit from listening to stories. Children with a visual impairment can benefit from text to speech. For children with hearing impairments, visual feedback is important. Writing stories and utilizing symbols are also good for children with hearing impairments. If the IFSP team decides an interpreter is needed, that service should be provided. Books can be in an electronic format so that children can activate them by a single switch. Children who are nonverbal can also use a picture communication system that associates pictures with verbal cues.
- Many components of a young child's day are excellent for promoting and encouraging literacy. Caregivers can enhance this process by labeling common objects in the room with both the word and a visual representation; providing an environment that promotes inclusion; providing repetition for the child to understand or learn the concept; allowing the child to explore a computer keyboard; providing opportunities for computer use during the day; providing a multisensory approach to learning; and talking to the child about a story, song, or picture that he or she has drawn.
- In considering the five developmental domains—adaptive, cognitive, communication, physical, and social/emotional—a significant developmental delay in one domain affects development in other domains. For example, a child who is unable to express needs and curiosities about the environment may experience a delay in cognitive development or social and emotional development.

- AT can assist a child with a developmental delay so that the effect of the delay has minimal impacts on the other domains. The multidisciplinary team must consider the domain in which the child has the delay and the child as a whole when designing an appropriate IFSP.

References

Beck, J. (2002). Emerging literacy through assistive technology. *Teaching Exceptional Children, 35*(2), 44–48.

Best, S., Heller, K., & Bigge, J. (2005). *Teaching individuals with physical or multiple disabilities* (5th ed.). Upper Saddle River, NJ: Merrill/Pearson Education.

DeCosta, D. C., & Glennen, S. L. (1997). *Handbook of augmentative and alternative communication.* San Diego, CA: Singular Publishing Group.

Dugan, L., Campbell, P., & Wilcox, J. (2006). Making decisions about assistive technology with infants and toddlers. *Topics in Early Childhood Special Education, 26*(1), 25–32.

Individuals with Disabilities Education Improvement Act of 2004. Pub. L. No. 108-446. 118 STAT.2647.

Lekotek of Georgia. (2004, May). The Capable Commander. *Lekotalk.* Retrieved from http://www.lekotekga.org/lekotalk/may04.htm#commander

Oregon Vision Working Group, Oregon Department of Education, Office of Special Education, Oregon School for the Blind. (February 2002). *Providing Assistive Technology for Students with Vision Impairments.* Retrieved July 23, 2004, from http://www.ode.state.or.us/pubs/tech/sped/vtechtap.pdf#search='Oregon%20Vision%20Working%20Group'

Solano, T., & Aller, S. K. (2000). Tech for tots: Assistive technology for infants and young children (Part 1). *Exceptional Parent Magazine, 30*(6), 44–47.

Sullivan, M., & Lewis, M. (2000). Assistive technology for the very young: Creating responsive environments. *Infants and Young Children, 12*(4), 34–52.

5

Assistive Technology for Students with High-Incidence Disabilities

CHAPTER VIEW

- Assistive Technology Snapshot
- High-Incidence Disabilities Defined
- Assistive Technology and Academics
- Assistive Technology for Student Learning
- Assistive Technology Spotlight 5-1
- Chapter Review

CHAPTER FOCUS

1. What are the high-incidence disabilities?
2. Why is it useful to study the high-incidence disabilities together?
3. What are the academic and organizational demands of school that students must meet to be successful learners?
4. How can assistive technology devices and services enable students to meet these academic and organizational demands of learning?

Assistive Technology Snapshot
MEET MIKE SANTOS

Mike Santos is a sixth-grader who has been identified as a student with a learning disability. As the team meets to plan Mike's individualized education program (IEP), it must consider how his learning disability affects his academic progress in the general education curriculum. The team must also address behavioral issues that appear to stem from his lack of academic progress. As part of the planning, the team will develop goals and short-term objectives; determine any accommodations and/or modifications needed; and select any related services, such as assistive technology, that will enable Mike to be successful in the general education curriculum. As with many students with learning disabilities, Mike's academic performance is most seriously affected by his difficulties in reading and written expression. Learning differences in reading and written expression may have negative effects on Mike's performance in mathematics in the areas that require connections through written communication for reading and reflective tasks. The local school board has adopted the National Council of Teachers of Mathematics (NCTM) standards, which require writing through problem solving, reasoning, and problem formulation within the mathematics curriculum.

According to the recent evaluation data conducted for eligibility, Mike's difficulties in reading are his inability to read grade-level material and comprehend what he has read. The data suggested that Mike is reading at least three grade levels below his peers. When the material is read to him, however, he can answer questions with a high degree of accuracy. Mike's teacher reported that when she asks Mike to read aloud in class or respond verbally to written directions, Mike is often verbally abusive to her and to his classmates. In the area of oral expressive language, Mike demonstrated the ability to describe scenes, give directions, and explain steps as one might expect of a sixth-grader. However, in written expression, Mike scored significantly below his peers in his ability to spell words used in everyday writing and to compose and write an organized, complete letter. Although his mathematics scores were of concern, the team believes that difficulties in reading and written expression may account for Mike's poor performance.

The team is concerned with Mike's lack of academic progress in the general curriculum and the behavioral issues that appear to be a direct result of his lack of progress. As Mike is nearing high school, it is apparent that he is in need of options to assist him in being a successful learner. The team feels that it should consider the general curriculum first in developing the IEP and that Mike should participate in the statewide assessment.

The IEP team reviewed all of the available data and made the following decisions: (a) Mike should be able to participate in the general education curriculum with his peers with appropriate supports and related services; (b) the support will consist of learning strategy training, assistive technology training, and direct reading instruction by the special education teacher; and (c) related services will use assistive technology to assist Mike with his reading, spelling, and written expression. In addition, Mike will attend counseling for his behavioral issues with the school counselor for 1 hour per week. The special education teacher will train the general education teachers how to use the assistive technology to provide support in reading, math, and written expression.

HIGH-INCIDENCE DISABILITIES DEFINED

Understanding the needs of a student like Mike will help you apply the information found in this chapter. Mike is a student with a more mild form of a disability. In fact, the majority of students being served by special education are in the mild range of disability. Most students with mild disabilities receive most, if not all, of their education within the general education setting. These disabilities are often referred to as **high-incidence disabilities** because of the large numbers of students included and the three categories defined in the Individuals with Disabilities Education Improvement Act (IDEIA) of 2004: mild learning disabilities, mental retardation, and emotional or behavioral disorders. In this chapter, the term *high-incidence disabilities* is used because many of the characteristics are similar and, as stated previously, many students with such disabilities are educated in the general education classroom. A large number of these students are being served by special educators with a noncategorical-type of license.

Although a degree of disability may be described as mild, it is a serious disability. Students with a mild disability may not have the stigmatizing physical characteristics of students with moderate and severe forms of disabilities, but that usually means they do not elicit empathy, sympathy, or assistance. A Student with a mild disability may approximate age-appropriate behaviors and appear physically similar to his or her typically developing peers. However, without academic, social, and emotional support, the consequences of the disability can have profound effects on the student's self-esteem and academic success. A mild level suggests that the student is more similar to typically developing students but that the student must have accommodations, modifications, and related services to access the general education curriculum successfully.

Students with Mild Disabilities

Students with mild disabilities account for 85% of the students with disabilities receiving services for special needs (U.S. Department of Education, 2009). Approximately 78% of students with disabilities received at least part of their education in general education classrooms during the 2003–2004 school year. This includes approximately 52% who were served in general education classrooms and 26% who received some services in the resource classroom. The vast majority of these students are considered to have mild disabilities.

The Individuals with Disabilities Education Improvement Act of 2004 authorizes the team to consider the general education curriculum first in developing the IEP and that students must be educated with their peers to the maximum extent appropriate. Special classes, separate schooling, or other removal occurs only when the nature or severity of the disability is such that education in general education classes, with the use of supplementary aids and services, cannot be achieved satisfactorily. The use of assistive technology for a student like Mike enables him and other students with a mild disability to be educated with peers and to become a successful learner.

Students with mild mental retardation, specific learning disabilities, and mild emotional disturbance often have difficulties meeting the academic and organizational demands of school independently (Friend & Bursuck, 2002). The

How does understanding the characteristics of students with high-incidence disabilities affect decisions related to assistive technology (AT)?

ability to work independently, both academically and organizationally, is an essential factor in being successful as students like Mike move through the grades. Ellis and Lenz (1996) suggest key areas in which students must perform to be successful learners. Those areas include gaining, expressing, and organizing information. Assistive technology can provide the tools necessary for student success in these areas.

ASSISTIVE TECHNOLOGY AND ACADEMICS

Gaining Information

Gaining information involves many skills. Students with mild disabilities lack many of the skills needed to gain information to be a successful learner. These skills require the student to be a listener and a reader, to follow written directions, and to interpret textbooks and other media. Students who experience difficulty with reading have difficulty gaining information, and without accommodations and modifications, they are unable to access the general education curriculum.

READING   Reading is an essential part of life. It is a receptive language process that uses visual and auditory abilities to derive meaning from the language symbols found in written text. It is also an interactive process between the reader and the text for the purpose of deriving meaning (Raymond, 2004). Individuals must have a mastery of basic reading skills to succeed at the most fundamental level. Reading is an important skill for academic success across the curriculum in the United States. Clearly the process of learning to read involves various methods, materials, and strategies that reflect the student's individual learning style. Developmentally appropriate practices to enhance literacy skills are a must in any reading program. Students with mild learning disabilities often struggle with reading, and difficulty with reading affects nearly all areas of academics.

The IEP team must identify goals and objectives designed to promote progress in reading. The general educator and the special educator must implement appropriate instructional strategies to improve the literacy skills of students with special needs. Students with learning disabilities who experience reading difficulties must have appropriate supports to meet these needs, such as accommodations allowing access to the curriculum, modifications of existing curriculum standards, and supplemental aids and related services. Intervention strategies to meet the needs of all students should be incorporated into any reading program to ensure success.

Technology provides visual and auditory supports in various software programs and packages to help the student with mild learning disabilities become a better reader. Teachers can match various software packages that help such students to each student's individual needs.

For the student who has difficulty with visual discrimination, certain parts of the text might be highlighted with various colors. Changing the background on the computer screen can help emphasize certain parts of a text. For some students, pairing pictures and written words can serve as a very basic reading aid.

Students who have difficulty with auditory discrimination could benefit from talking storybooks and electronic books. For students like Mike, uploading assigned texts and allowing the students to listen to it with headphones would be less distracting for the students and might provide the needed support. Wireless reading devices (WRDs) can provide a student with the ability to upload large quantities of reading materials. WRDs are handheld and have extended battery life. Some WRDs hold over 1,500 titles and have screens that mimic paper. Many WRDs allow the user to upload word-processing documents, magazines, newspapers, and documents in portable document format (PDF), in addition to books. Some WRDs have keyboards and touchscreens for input devices.

One of the most useful features for a student like Mike is the text-to-speech feature. This form of assistive technology can be very powerful for struggling readers and writers. Text-to-speech programs, sometimes referred to as screen-reading programs, can use a digitized voice to read typed text aloud. Text-to-speech software systems can scan and read printed text to create digitized speech. Features may include the ability to regulate speed, spell words, and choose language and voices. This can reduce fatigue in students who struggle with reading. Grade-level material can be scanned and read by the computer for the student who reads below grade level. Students can also use text-to-speech programs to download and read electronic texts, often referred to as e-books, from the Web with screen-reading programs. Table 5-1 provides a list of assistive technology (AT) resources for reading. As with any program, the varied needs of students should be taken into account prior to deciding what to purchase.

What technology skills does a teacher need for successful use of software programs for reading?

For students with mild disabilities, trying to gain information from reading print materials is a major deficit and a continuing struggle. For the teacher, assisting the struggling reader to gain information is a continuing challenge. Converting curriculum materials to digital form to make them more flexible so they can be used by diverse learners is one way to meet this challenge. Teachers may use technology to convert these materials themselves or they may find existing sources in digital form or on audiotapes.

Digital text, known as ASCII text, is a pliable medium that can be represented in the computer in a variety of ways. ASCII can appear as letters on the computer screen or as spoken words through speech synthesis. The appearance of ASCII text (font, font size, color) can be easily modified and edited.

Converting printed text to digital form requires a scanner and special software. Three main types of scanners are available: single page, flatbed, and handheld. The computer creates a picture of the text when the text is scanned. That picture must be converted to American Standard Code for Information Interchange (ASCII) text through the use of optical character recognition (OCR) software. After this is done, the text is ready to be used in a word processor, on a webpage, or in a program that supports learning by reading text aloud.

Teachers may also find literature available in digital format. Books delivered as electronic files or e-books may be purchased from many publishers. Some e-books can be downloaded and read by programs that read text.

For a light-tech approach, teachers may use books on tape, such as those from Recordings for the Blind and Dyslexic (RFB&D) in Princeton, New Jersey. Anyone with a documented disability that makes reading standard print difficult or impossible is eligible to use audio textbooks. To access the RFB&D library, readers must first become members on their own or through their schools. The RFB&D website can be found in Table 5-1.

TABLE 5-1   Assistive Technology and Reading Resources

Edmark Reading Program http://www.donjohnston.com	This software uses a whole-word, multisensory approach to teach comprehension and recognition. Users of this software learn sight recognition and the meaning of a word, practice comprehension, and use the word in story content. Repetition and short instructional steps are used.
JAWS for Windows http://www.freedomscientific.com/products/fs/jaws-product-page.asp	Screen Reading Software
IntelliTools Reading: Balanced Literacy http://www.intellitools.com	This is a nine-unit program that provides literacy instruction at the first-grade skill level. It incorporates reading, phonics, and writing. Included are 142 lessons, nine full-color storybooks, 212 phonics activities, a CD with more than 500 activities, and 27 structured writing exercises. This program uses a mouse and IntelliKeys.
Key Skills for Reading: Letters and Words http://store.sunburst.com/Search.aspx?	Five multilevel activities provide animated practice. Students learn the order of the alphabet, how to organize words and objects by initial consonant sounds, how to identify short and long vowel sounds, and lots more. The program has clear auditory support to help in reading success.
Kurzweil 3000 http://www.kurzweiledu.com	Kurzweil offers printed or electronic text for the computer screen with visual and audible assistance. The program includes many features to help with study skills, writing, and test taking. It adapts to each learning style. Kurzweil 3000 offers an audible assistant to help with spell checking and word prediction as students type.
WYNN 3.1 Freedom Scientific's Learning Systems Group http://freedomscientific.com	This software solution transforms printed text into understandable text and reads it aloud while simultaneously highlighting it.
Let's Go Read http://www.sunburst-store.com/cgi-bin/sunburst.storefront/EN/Catalog/1244	This software helps students learn to read through lessons with interactive stories and sequencing. Vocabulary skills are expanded, as is comprehension.
Picture It http://www.slatersoftware.com/pit.html	This software includes more than 6,000 pictures that can be incorporated with text so that the reader can see picture-supported material to better understand the text. Students can listen to stories and read along with highlighted words.
Readingpen http://www.donjohnston.com	A handheld scanner that allows users to simply scan over a word that is not understood. The word is then read out loud back to the student and the dictionary definition is provided.

(Continued)

TABLE 5-1   *(Continued)*

ScreenReader http://www.brighteye.com/texthelp.htm	Allows a PC to read out loud words that appear in any Windows-based application.
Recordings for the Blind and Dyslexic (RFB&D) http://www.rfbd.org	RFB&D's audio library contains titles available in every subject area and at any grade level.
Text Readers Read Outloud http://www.donjohnston.com/products/read_outloud/index.html ClassMate Reader http://www.donjohnston.com/products/portables/classmate/index.html	Text-to-speech readers for nonreaders or students reading below grade level.
TextHelp Read and Write Gold http://www.brighteye.com/texthelp.htm	This software offers a range of helpful tools for special education in reading and writing. Some of these tools include word prediction, a dictionary, a spell checker, RealSpeak (providing a humanlike voice), and a pronunciation tutor.
Recorded Books http://recordedbooks.com/index.cfm?fuseaction=rb.playaway&school	Publisher of audiobooks
UDL Book Builder http://www.cast.org	Use this site to create, read, and share digital books that build reading skills for students.

As we discussed in Chapter 1, AT funding is an issue. One free resource for IEP teams is open source software. Open source refers to a set of principles that guide the development of software. It means that the source code enables users to use the applications for free and to modify the applications for their own purposes. Open source AT software installs and runs on a standard flash drive, thus providing a portable option for the user (Jacobs, 2007). Service providers can use open source code for free AT device trials. If the AT device does not meet the needs of the students, then it can be discarded in favor of another device. In the case of Mike, free speech-to-text applications can be used to see if they help him become a more successful learner. These applications can be downloaded to a flash drive, and Mike can carry it to different environments such as the classroom and library.

Expressing Information

Expressing information includes many tasks that may be difficult for students with mild disabilities. AT devices range from light-tech devices, such as writing-surface adaptations, to high-tech devices, such as auditory support through talking word processing. Understanding the complexity of the writing process will help you understand the variety of AT devices available to assist the student with mild disabilities in accessing the general education curriculum.

WRITING AND ASSISTIVE TECHNOLOGY   Writing is the process of encoding thought into graphemes, or phonograms, so that communication can occur across time and space (Raymond, 2004). Students with mild disabilities exhibit problems with written expression. To be an effective writer, students must have skills in three areas: handwriting, spelling, and composition. Students with mild disabilities usually have difficulty in all three of these areas.

Students who experience difficulty with handwriting may need additional assistance with motor development. Sometimes simply adapting the writing surface, for example, by stabilizing the paper with a clipboard or providing an angle to the writing surface with a slanted board, will lead to improved handwriting. Providing tactual boundaries with raised lines, puffy painted lines, or wax lines on paper provides additional support for handwriting. Adding pencil grips to the writing tool or using other adaptations may become necessary for those students who need additional support. For students who have dysgraphia—severe disabilities in written expression and in performing the motor functions associated with handwriting—alternate types of keyboards and portable word processing might substitute for handwriting.

Mike (from the chapter-opening Assistive Technology Snapshot, has problems spelling. What AT device in Table 5-2 might help him?

SPELLING   One of the areas Mike has problems with is spelling. This is not uncommon for many students with mild disabilities. Knowing how to spell is an important link to writing composition. If a writer is bogged down with spelling, the writing progress becomes a struggle. Numerous light-tech as well as high-tech devices can help Mike be a better speller. Light-tech devices include highlighting tape, colored acetate overlays, and personal dictionaries. For example, Mike can use the highlighting tape to focus on important words. He can write the word on the tape and then transfer the tape to his personal dictionary. Personal dictionaries can be made easily or purchased. Table 5-2 has examples of light-tech AT spelling devices.

TABLE 5-2   Assistive Technology and Spelling Resources

Crystal Springs Books http://www.crystalspringsbooks.com/7852.html	Highlighting tape
EZC Reader http://www.reallygoodstuff.com/results.aspx?keyword=reading%20helper	Each sturdy EZC Reader is fitted with a transparent plastic edge that acts as a movable highlighter and that can be used to focus the reader's attention to important vocabulary.
Personal Dictionaries Curriculum Associates http://www.curriculumassociates.com/	QUICK–WORD Handbooks feature more than 1,000 high-frequency writing words and space for adding personal words.
Spell Correctors Franklin http://www.franklin.com/	Spelling Ace. Improve spelling and vocabulary skills with this 110,000-word. phonetic spell corrector. It also includes 500,000 synonyms and antonyms.

Students like Mike may benefit from high-tech AT spelling devices. Examples range from personal computers with spell-check features to portable word processors. These portable or mobile computers feature text to speech, word prediction, spell checkers, and connectivity to other technologies. In addition to features that assist with spelling, the student would have access to additional writing tools that support successful writing. Pairing AT spelling devices with research-based spelling strategies can be effective in assisting students in overcoming deficits in spelling. However, the IEP team must remember that students, as well as teachers and caregivers, must have instruction in how to use the devices. Failure to provide instruction may lead to AT abandonment. AT spelling resources may be found in Table 5-2.

WRITTEN EXPRESSION   Expressing information in the form of a written composition is a struggle for many students with mild disabilities. The computer offers a plethora of options in this area. From standard word processing to software and hardware, the student with mild disabilities can find assistance with written composition.

The Cut, Copy, and Paste functions in most word-processing programs can help students with mild disabilities reorganize an entire document. The thesaurus, grammar, and spell checker provide additional support as the student composes. Students can view their documents prior to downloading them for editing. They also can view their documents before printing final versions.

Comprehensive **concept-mapping** software allows students who have problems with written expression to develop ideas and organize thoughts into an outline or an idea web prior to beginning to write. This allows students to see the connections among related concepts and ideas before translating them into coherent text. Many of these programs allow students to export an outline to popular word-processing or even to presentation programs. Even with the support of AT devices for writing, students must be explicitly taught the multistep process of writing. If word-processing software is used, then the student must be taught keyboarding skills. Students who are fluent in keyboarding increase their speed of producing text. Writing programs and AT devices can be found in Table 5-3.

ASSISTIVE TECHNOLOGY FOR STUDENT LEARNING

Other areas that students with high-incidence disabilities find challenging are content areas such as math, history, and science. Math requires some reading and also abstract thinking. Content areas often require large amounts of reading, a high level of comprehension skills, and basic organizational skills. AT can assist the student with mild disabilities in accessing the general education curriculum.

Mathematics and Assistive Technology

Students with mild disabilities have problems with mathematics for a variety of reasons. These students typically score below their chronological peers on measures of mathematics achievement (Scruggs & Mastropieri, 1986; Zentall & Smith, 1993). In the Assistive Technology Snapshot at the beginning of this chapter, the IEP team determined from the assessment data that Mike's difficulties in mathematics resulted from his reading difficulties and his struggle with mathematics

Webquest 5.1

Use the speech-to-text option in Windows XP or VISTA to teach your computer to recognize your speech patterns. Go to http://support.microsoft.com/kb/306901 for directions.

TABLE 5-3	**Assistive Technology and Writing Resources**
Co:Writer http://www.donjohnston.com/products/cowriter/index.html	This program adds word prediction, grammar, and vocabulary to word processors. FlexSpell helps students who spell phonetically by recognizing and predicting words consistent with the actual letters and sounds of the letters. Grammar support helps correct errors such as subject-verb agreement, spelling, customary word usage, and proper noun usage.
EZ Keys http://www.freedomofspeech.com	Uses dual word prediction by displaying a table of the six most frequently used words that begin with the letters that the student types when beginning to type a word. EZ Keys provides alternatives to using a mouse, such as an expanded keyboard, joystick, and single and multiple switch scanning.
Gus! Word Prediction http://www.enablemart.com/Catalog/Word-Prediction/Gus-Word-Prediction	Improves typing speed by offering word completion and word prediction. Offers a list of words based on what keys the user has already typed. The list changes according to the keys that the user types and then predicts the current and the subsequent words. This helps slow or two-finger typists. Abbreviation expansion, speech output, and a dictionary are also provided.
WordQ 2Writing Aid Software http://www.enablemart.com/Catalog/Word-Prediction/WordQ-2	This writing tool is used with standard word processors. It provides spoken feedback and suggests words to use through word prediction. Students can hear each word spoken so that it is easier to differentiate words. It is simple to use and transparent to all Windows applications.
Write:Outloud http://www.donjohnston.com/products/write_outloud/index.html	Immediate speech feedback is given as students type words, sentences, and paragraphs. Students can listen for proper word usage, grammar, and misspellings. Students with disabilities can correct their work independently because they hear and see what they write. Demo on publisher homepage.
Draft:Builder http://www.donjohnston.com/products/draft_builder/index.html	This tool leads students through three key steps in creating a first draft: organizing ideas, taking notes, and writing the draft. The display gives students a framework to generate, manipulate, and connect ideas and information.

standards within the mathematics curriculum that require writing through problem solving, reasoning, and problem formulation. While learning computation continues to be part of mathematics instruction, the NCTM strongly recommends that the primary emphasis should be on problem solving and activity-based learning. NCTM standards state that mathematics should include methods of reasoning and methods of communicating mathematically (National Council of Teachers of Mathematics, 2010).

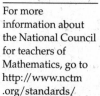

Webquest 5.2

For more information about the National Council for teachers of Mathematics, go to http://www.nctm.org/standards/default.aspx?id=58.

What skills might
a student with a
mild disability need
to master to use
a calculator
successfully?

The implications for students with disabilities are clear: If students have difficulty with written composition, they will need support not only in the language arts but also in mathematics. Other reasons for difficulty relate to understanding or being able to read math problems. In other cases, students may not have the computation skills needed to adequately complete problems. In other instances, the factors may be related not to knowledge of math but to other factors such as motivation and ineffective teaching strategies (Ginsburg, 1997; Vaughn, Bos, & Schumm, 2000).

AT can play a primary role in assisting the student in mathematics to access the general education curriculum and be a successful learner. The NCTM recommends that computer applications and the use of calculators be taught to all students. Using computer spreadsheets and databases can be helpful to students in organizing data and providing visual pictures of data. Students can then display concepts in presentation format, or they can print the data.

Students who have difficulties with paper-and-pencil tasks (i.e., keeping numbers and problems aligned) may benefit from electronic number processors and math worksheets. These programs allow students to work arithmetic problems directly on a computer.

Calculators assist students with mild disabilities in acquiring mathematics skills, and, for many, calculators improve their attitudes toward mathematics (Vaughn, Bos, & Schumm, 2000). A variety of calculators are available for students. Speaking and nonspeaking handheld models are available with varying functions. Some are equipped with scientific functions, while others are designed for younger students. Conventional calculators often cannot help students with visual discrimination or reading problems. Talking onscreen calculators can provide math support by letting students work according to their preferred learning styles. Font size and colors can be adjusted. Auditory cues can help students who reverse numbers. Calculators, whether conventional or onscreen, prevent frustration due to memory and information retrieval problems, and they allow students to focus on problem solving.

Students with mild disabilities may find they have few or no problems learning computations in mathematics. However, in portions of the mathematics curriculum that require the results of problem solving, reasoning, and problem formulation to be expressed in reflective, organized written form, AT devices may be considered useful by the IEP team for mathematics, too. Table 5-4 provides a list of AT devices for mathematics.

Other Content Areas

Students with mild disabilities often have difficulties learning in the content areas, for many reasons. Vaughn, Bos, and Schumm (2000) suggest that the level of conceptual complexity and density in some content areas may be overwhelming for many students, learning in the content areas requires basic skills that many students lack, and classes require homework assignments and long-term projects. AT devices may allow students with mild disabilities who are not successful learners in content areas to experience success as they access the general education curriculum.

TABLE 5-4 Assistive Technology and Mathematics	
MathPad Plus (IntelliTools) http://store.cambiumlearning.com	MathPad enables students to do arithmetic directly on the computer. The program is ideal for students who need help organizing or navigating math problems or who have difficulty doing math with pencil and paper.
ViewPlus Accessible Graphing Calculator http://www.abledata.com/	An audible graphing calculator program designed for use by individuals who are blind or have low vision or visual dyslexia. This onscreen graphing calculator is capable of displaying graphs or other sets of y-versus-x data both visually and audibly as a tone graph. The audio tone plot gives users access to plots comparable to that on standard graphing calculators.
Portable Calculator with Talking Multiplication Table http://www.independentliving.com	This small folding calculator performs standard arithmetic functions. When the key is pressed, followed by the number of the multiplication table the user wants to hear, it speaks the entire table.
GTCalc Scientific Calculator http://www.independentliving.com	This software offers a comprehensive range of scientific functions in logical groups for easy accessibility. Accessibility features include input via keyboard or mouse with input and output spoken, large number display, a Mouse Talk feature that speaks the button captions, and four levels of screen magnification.
Talking Pocket Calculator http://www.independentliving.com	A small, thin, folding calculator with clear numbers on the number pads and on the monitor. All the setting functions speak, except the calendar, which is visual. Says numbers in units or digital.
Talking Texas Instruments Scientific Calculator http://www.independentliving.com	The features of this small scientific calculator include a learning mode for key identification that does not affect calculations. The key is announced when pressed. There is a choice of silent or talking operation. Tactile, large, functionally zoned keys; volume control; and an earphone are included.

Preparing students to learn is one strategy a teacher can use to activate students' prior knowledge. Preteaching concepts and vocabulary using semantic mapping and concept maps is one way to do this. Software is available to enable the student to use graphic organizers such as concept and semantic maps. These strategies are good for organizing content, making presentations, and writing reports.

Because lecturing is a common method of teaching in the content area class, note taking is a challenge for many students with mild disabilities. Teachers can provide light-tech writing outlines, advance organizers, or a copy of the teacher's notes. Students can use recorders paired with note-taking learning strategies. High-tech note-taking devices include portable word processors, handheld computers, personal digital assistants and smart pens. Bauer and Ulrich (2002) indicated that students already use handheld devices for entertainment and are comfortable with the technology. They found that lecture notes and the content of overheads could be beamed directly from the teacher's handheld device, so a note taker was unnecessary.

Content-area teachers often rely heavily on the textbook as the primary medium of instruction (Alvermann & Moore, 1991). A textbook's level of difficulty is gauged by its readability and is expressed as a grade level. Students who are reading below grade level often experience difficulty in reading material from texts that are written on grade level. Students like Mike need access to the same material as their peers. AT can give them access to the general education curriculum. Substituting for the textbook is one method of making information accessible for the content-area classroom. The textbook can be obtained on a CD or downloaded tot a personal reader that has audio capability (see Table 5-1), or portions of it can be scanned. Scanning was described earlier in this chapter.

Assistive Technology and Organization

Out-of-class assignments in the content areas, such as homework and long-term projects, are often a challenge for many students with mild disabilities. Successful learners must have the academic and organizational skills to complete homework independently. AT can assist students in this endeavor by helping with the organization component. Electronic organizers, content-area/subject-matter notebooks and file systems, and software-based calendars help students keep track of the demands of outside assignments. Handheld and portable computers help students keep up with the increasing demands of middle school and high school. Activity task assistants such as activity notebooks, tape players, voice diaries, reminder software, and even mini video cameras help students with short-term memory and retrieval problems. Table 5-5 has a list of AT devices to assist the student with organization.

Look at Table 5-5 and review the Assistive Technology Snapshot at the beginning of this chapter. How might an organization device be helpful to Mike during the school day?

TABLE 5-5 Assistive Technology for School Organization	
Day Timer http://www.daytimer.com	Daily and weekly formats give one full year of organizing power.
Palm Pilot http://www.palmpilot.com	Handheld Palm Pilots can be used for organization, business, and education.
Quarter Hour Watch http://www.zygo-usa.com	Augmentation communication systems for persons with profound mental and physical disabilities.
Plan Your Day http://www.attainmentcompany.com	Organize daily schedule with pictures.
Voicemail to Text www.jott.com	Turns voicemail into text and delivers it as text messages to email. Users can use telephones to leave reminders of events.

ASSISTIVE TECHNOLOGY SPOTLIGHT 5-1

Assistive Technology Inclusion Tips

When using AT for students with high-incidence disabilities, consider the following:

1. Consult the student's IEP.
2. Understand the student's specific strengths and needs.
3. Collaborate with the special education teacher and other professionals.
4. Determine how the use of AT will enable the student to access and progress in the general education curriculum.
5. Determine if the AT device is isolating the student from his or her peers.
6. If the AT device proves to be ineffective for the student, reconvene the IEP team and consider the options.

Chapter Review

- Students with high-incidence disabilities receive most, if not all, of their education within the general education setting. Such disabilities include learning disabilities, mild mental retardation, and emotional or behavioral disorders. These students are served by both general educators and special educators who have a noncategorical certification.
- Without academic, social, and emotional support, a disability can have profound consequences on the student's self-esteem and academic success.
- Students with mild mental retardation have deficits in intellectual functioning, adaptive behavior, and developmental abilities. Students with a diagnosis of mild mental retardation usually have test scores that fall within the second and third standard deviations below the mean. They learn at a much slower rate and usually have deficits in cognitive functioning.
- Students with specific learning disabilities exhibit unexpected differences in ability and achievement. A learning disability is pervasive across the life span.
- Students with a diagnosis of emotional disturbance exhibit one or more of the following characteristics over a long time: inability to learn that cannot be explained by intellectual, sensory, or health factors; inability to build or maintain satisfactory interpersonal relationships with peers and teachers; inappropriate types of behavior or feelings under normal circumstances; a generally pervasive mood of unhappiness or depression; and a tendency to develop physical symptoms or fears associated with personal or school problems. Educational performance is markedly and adversely affected by these characteristics.
- Students in the mild disabilities category account for 85% of students with disabilities receiving services for special needs. AT can provide students with mild disabilities with the tools necessary to be successful in gaining, expressing, and organizing information.

- Students with mild disabilities who have trouble gaining information have difficulty accessing the general education curriculum without modifications and accommodations. The skills needed to gain information to be a successful learner include listening, reading, following written directions, and interpreting textbooks and other media.
- Reading across the curriculum is vital for success in academics. When students struggle in reading, they struggle in all academic areas.
- Accommodations allow access to the curriculum. Modifications provide strategies for changing the material so the student can be successful.
- Technology provides both visual and auditory supports to enhance the probability of the student becoming a better reader. Highlighting certain parts of the text, changing backgrounds on the computer screen, electronic storybooks, and converting curricular material to digital format are means of modifying materials so students can access the general education curriculum.
- Expression can take many forms and is essential for the student's success. Writing and spelling are two expression areas where AT devices can be helpful.
- Students must develop handwriting, spelling, and composition skills to be successful writers. Students who experience difficulty with handwriting may need assistance with motor development. For students who exhibit difficulty with spelling, word-processing software can provide a spell checker. Handheld AT devices can speak and translate and even define written words.
- Students who have difficulty with composition can use the Cut, Copy, and Paste, features of word-processing software to construct a document. Students can also preview a document prior to printing. This provides a visual picture to help the student understand and see what documents look like prior to printing.
- Concept mapping provides opportunities for students to organize their thoughts and outline ideas before writing.
- AT can assist a student who has difficulty in the area of mathematics. Computer applications and calculators are recommended by the NCTM.
- Concept mapping and semantic mapping are useful for students engaged in learning activities outside the classroom, such as developing presentations and writing reports.
- Advance organizers provide students with outlines, copies of notes, and so on, to assist during lectures. Portable word processors and recorders are also useful during lectures for students with high-incidence disabilities.
- Handheld and portable computers can assist students with organization. Students with high-incidence disabilities have difficulty at times with organization skills. A personal digital assistant is also useful in this area.

References

Alvermann, D. E., & Moore, D. W. (1991). Secondary school reading. In R. Barr, M. L. Kamil, P. B. Mosenthal, & P. D. Pearson (Eds.), *Handbook of reading research: Vol. 2* (pp. 951–983). New York: Longman.

Bauer, A. M., & Ulrich, M. E. (2002). "I've got a Palm in my pocket": Using handheld computers in an inclusive classroom. *Teaching Exceptional Children, 35*(2), 18–23.

Ellis, E., & Lenz, B. K. (1996). Perspectives on instruction in learning strategies. In D. Deshler, E. Ellis, & B. K. Lenz (Eds.), *Teaching adolescents with learning disabilities: Strategies and methods* (2nd ed., pp. 9–60). Denver, CO: Love Publishing Company.

Friend, M., & Bursuck, W. D. (2002). *Including students with special needs: A practical guide for classroom teachers* (3rd ed.). Boston: Allyn & Bacon.

Ginsburg, H. P. (1997). Mathematics learning disabilities: A view from developmental psychology. *Journal of Learning Disabilities, 30*(1), 20–33.

Individuals with Disabilities Education Improvement Act (IDEA) of 2004. Pub. L. No. 108-446, 118 Stat. 2647.

Jacobs, S. (December, 2007). A man and his mission: Bringing free AT to those who need it and can't afford it: An Interview with Steve Jacobs. FCTD News and Notes. Retrieved on July 21, 2009, from http://www.fctd.info/resources/newsletters/displayNewsletter.php?newsletterID=10054

National Council of Teachers of Mathematics. (2010). National Council of Teachers of Mathematics: Process standards. Retrieved January 15, 2010, from (Report No. SE-050-418 http://www.nctm.org/standards/content.aspx?id=322

Raymond, E. B. (2004). *Learners with mild disabilities* (2nd ed.). Boston: Allyn & Bacon.

Scruggs, T. E., & Mastropieri, M. A. (1986). Improving the test-taking skills of behaviorally disordered and learning disabled children. *Exceptional Children, 53,* 63–68.

U.S. Department of Education. (2009). *Twenty-eighth annual report to Congress on the implementation of the Individuals with Disabilities Act, 2006.* Washington, DC: Author.

Vaughn, S., Bos, C. S., & Schumm, J. S. (2000). *Teaching exceptional, diverse, and at-risk students in the general education classroom* (2nd ed.). Boston: Allyn & Bacon.

Zentall, S. S., & Smith, Y. N. (1993). Mathematical performance and behavior of children with hyperactivity, with and without coexisting aggression. *Behavior Research in Developmental Disabilities, 10,* 225–240.

6

Assistive Technology for Positioning and Mobility

CHAPTER VIEW

- Assistive Technology Snapshot
- Orthopedic Impairment
- Positioning for Access to the General Education Curriculum
- Assistive Technology for Mobility
- Assistive Technology for Student Learning
- Assistive Technology Spotlight 6-1
- Chapter Review

CHAPTER FOCUS

1. What are physical disabilities?
2. Why is positioning important for academic success?
3. How can wheelchair design help the student with a physical disability access the general education curriculum?
4. How can assistive technology devices and services enable the student with a physical disability meet the academic and organizational demands of the general education curriculum?

Assistive Technology Snapshot
MEET JOAN RUTHERFORD

Joan Rutherford is a fifth-grader who has **spastic cerebral palsy** in its most severe form, **spastic quadriplegia**. At its spring annual review, the team plans Joan's Individualized Education Program (IEP) for next year. As they meet, the team members must consider reevaluation data and how the disability affects Joan's academic progress in the general education curriculum. The team members must also address communication and behavioral issues that have been brought to their attention by Joan's resource teacher, Mr. Adonis. The team will complete a behavior plan based on a functional assessment to address Joan's behavioral issues. In addition, the occupational therapist has contributed information from an ecological assessment of Joan's environment. This information will allow the team to engage in planning and developing goals and short-term objectives; determine any necessary accommodations and/or modifications; and select any related services, such as assistive technology (AT), physical therapy, occupational therapy, and speech services, that will enable Joan to participate in the general education curriculum. As with many students with physical disabilities, Joan's progress in the general education curriculum is affected by her ability to communicate effectively and by her physical disabilities, which are typical of someone with her medical diagnosis.

According to the reevaluation data gathered for the annual review, Joan is functioning well below average intellectually. In all academic achievement areas, she is performing on a pre-primer level. She has limited mobility due to her dependence on a wheelchair. The occupational and physical therapists reported that her physical disabilities continue to affect her ability to participate in many classroom activities and to produce written products. Joan has made some progress in toilet training and feeding herself. The speech-language pathologist indicated that Joan communicates her basic needs verbally; however, her speech is difficult to understand if the person is not familiar with her speech patterns. The resource teacher presented data collected on Joan's behavioral issues. These data indicate that Joan has tantrums frequently during the day and often strikes her classmates for no apparent reason. Consequently, Joan is socially isolated due to her inappropriate behavior. Joan's mother reported that the medication Joan is taking for her seizure disorder had been successful in preventing her seizures. The team members are concerned that Joan is currently spending more than 60% of her time outside the general education classroom in a resource room. The team would like to determine ways in which Joan could be included in more general education class curriculum activities.

The IEP team reviewed all the available information and makes the following recommendations: Joan's time in the general education classroom should be increased to 50% of the day, with support and related services provided in both settings. The support will consist of a paraeducator to assist with Joan's self-care skills, positioning, and mobility issues. Other support will be provided to the general education teacher to provide accommodations and modifications in the curriculum so that Joan may participate. Related services will include the use of assistive technology for communication, mobility training, and wheelchair positioning so that Joan can participate with her peers. The team has requested that the speech teacher explore and evaluate different types of augmentative and alternative communication that will enable Joan to communicate more effectively with her teachers, caregivers, and peers. The team believes that the source of Joan's tantrums may be her challenges with communication. Most 11-year-olds have a lot to say!

ORTHOPEDIC IMPAIRMENT

Educators typically use the term *physical disabilities* when referring to students who have orthopedic impairments. The term *orthopedic impairment* was defined by the Individuals with Disabilities Education Improvement Act (2004) and its regulations as follows:

> **Orthopedic impairment** Orthopedic impairment means a severe orthopedic impairment that adversely affects a child's educational performance. The term includes impairments caused by a congenital anomaly, impairments caused by disease (e.g., poliomyelitis, bone tuberculosis), and impairments from other causes (e.g., cerebral palsy, amputations, and fractures or burns that cause contractures). (34 C.F.R., Sec. 300.8[c][8])

Educators and agencies serve students with traumatic brain injury, severe and multiple disabilities, and other health impairment as they would serve students having any physical disabilities. In fact, the term *physical disabilities* may refer to a large number of students who have different characteristics. The primary focus of this chapter is students with physical disabilities, like Joan, who have an orthopedic impairment that involves the skeletal system or neuromotor impairment that involves the central nervous system and the ability to move, feel, and/or control parts of the body. The commonalities within this heterogeneous disability group include (a) orthopedic or neuromotor impairment that affects the student's educational performance, (b) the need for pervasive support to access the general education curriculum, and (c) the need for assistive technology to be successful in the general education classroom.

Where are these students receiving services to ensure progress in the general education curriculum? More than 90% of students with physical disabilities are in schools with their general education peers. Only 52% of students with orthopedic impairments are educated in the general education classroom. Nineteen percent are in resource rooms, and 26% are educated in separate classrooms for the entire school day (U.S. Department of Education, 2009).

What related services and service delivery personnel would be included on the IEP team for a student with physical disabilities?

To make progress within the general education curriculum, many students with physical disabilities require related services for accessibility to the school's physical environment, general education curriculum, and extracurricular activities. In collaboration, the IEP team provides the plan for the student with physical disabilities to access all these areas successfully. This chapter focuses on three areas that make the general education curriculum accessible: (a) positioning, (b) wheelchair design, and (c) mobility aids.

POSITIONING FOR ACCESS TO THE GENERAL EDUCATION CURRICULUM

AT for positioning can range from simple to the most complex. It may mean adjusting the height of a table to accommodate use of a standing frame or a wheelchair. It can require custom-designed high-tech equipment to address a very specialized need, such as standing. When AT must be considered, it is important to determine how the student will be positioned. Students cannot be expected to use their hands and arms effectively unless they are positioned correctly. Proper positioning helps with muscle tone, visual efficiency, postural support, and compensation for physical deficits. When the body is properly positioned, the student will have an easier time accessing the curriculum in an inclusive setting.

Issues regarding proper positioning should be addressed with the student's physical therapist (PT) or occupational therapist (OT). If a student with a physical disability needs AT, the OT or PT should be a member of the IEP team. This assessment helps the team make decisions regarding the types of AT devices and services to use for the most efficient assistance. The student with physical disabilities will be placed in varied positions throughout the school day. The AT device or devices that are used for positioning should be chosen with the comfort and functionality level of the student in mind. The student must be positioned comfortably to maximize student participation, and the device must be as functional as possible. Proper positioning can improve student performance in many different school environments, if it is done correctly.

It is vital to ask the following question: "How will the student be positioned throughout the school day?" Then the student's IEP team must consider several additional issues when making decisions regarding positioning the student for inclusion: (a) How will appropriate positioning help the student participate in the general education curriculum? (b) Does the position allow the student mobility within the classroom and building? (c) What is the most useful, least obtrusive AT device that will enhance the student's participation? (d) What is the best position for muscle development and alignment? (e) Will positioning help the student's circulatory, digestive, and respiratory functions (Westling & Fox, 2004)? Good data and input are needed from all IEP team members, including the student, for positioning to enhance the student's participation.

Positioning a student to feel part of any classroom is of the utmost importance. Students are in seated positions for much of the school day. Thus, a student in an appropriate wheelchair would be positioned well for participation in almost any classroom activity. As noted, Joan could access learning and social activities better with appropriate positioning.

Arrangements should be made to ensure that tables, doorways, and desks are the proper height and width to allow the student with an orthopedic impairment to move around the classroom. All students are not the same size, so they need desks and chairs of various sizes. A student utilizing a standing frame, mobile stander, or prone stander to enhance muscle length and development could participate in certain cooperative learning groups, games, and activities that require standing. A mobile stander or wheelchair makes it possible to access other parts of the building and thus to participate in activities scheduled outside

Webquest 6.1

Check out wheelchair accessories at http://www.ncaonline.org/index.php?q=taxonomy/term/68

Webquest 6.2

Check out the different prices of wheelchairs at http://www.1800wheelchair.com/asp/view-category-products.asp?category_id=373

the classroom, such as art, music, physical education, and other extracurricular activities, as well as library and lunch.

When determining AT for positioning within the classroom, consider where the equipment will be used. Teacher observation of the student during the initial phases of AT use will aid in making any necessary adjustments. Issues such as how AT affects the student's academic success, socialization with peers, and mobility within the classroom should be addressed during the first few days of student use.

Alignment

Alignment of the head, neck, and trunk are important considerations for positioning the student. A student's circulation, digestion, and respiration will improve with proper head, neck, and trunk positioning. Proper postural support will help the student feel better and can result in improved self-concept. Proper positioning can also help maintain postural alignment and muscle tone. Students can be positioned properly without the use of extensive adaptive equipment (Snell & Brown, 2006).

Adaptive Equipment

Adaptive equipment should allow students to socialize in a normal setting with their peers. Students should not feel isolated or be isolated due to any AT device. All devices should have as normal an appearance as possible while allowing the student to feel included. In addressing Joan's needs, the IEP team might consider AT devices, in addition to her wheelchair, that would enhance her participation with peers. The IEP team might also consider (a) what positions peers occupy and use when they engage in classroom activities, (b) what positions allow the student the most mobility, (c) whether the equipment meets the needs of the student and helps him or her to be a better learner, and (d) whether the equipment provides a means by which the student can feel part of the class and not isolated from the group.

Webquest 6.3
Examine the differences between power chairs and manual chairs at http://www.wheelchair.net/?adv=google&tar=wheelchair-b&gclid=CPb0473V6ZsCFQQVswodUws36g.

When equipment is needed, it should be as unobtrusive as possible to foster the student's involvement with classmates. A student in a side-lying position would most likely not be appropriate in a general education classroom. However, an activity chair or wheelchair with a lap tray attached to it would be an appropriate AT device. Depending on the nature of classroom activities, a standing frame could be an appropriate option. For some classroom group games and activities on the floor, a side-lying position or positioning with a wedge would help the student to feel part of the group. Such unobtrusive AT devices would allow for full inclusion of students with disabilities.

Participation with peers is essential if inclusion is to be successful. Classroom layout should incorporate the principles of Universal Design for Learning (UDL) (see Chapter 2). In Joan's situation, the IEP team should look at UDL guidelines that would help design the classroom for easy student mobility.

All students have certain abilities and talents that can be emphasized in any lesson within the classroom. Students with physical disabilities have the capacity most of the time for high academic performance. Such students can and

TABLE 6-1 Assistive Technology Devices for Seating and Positioning

Disability Products http://www.disabilityproducts.com	Assistive devices and daily living aids that support independent living for handicapped and disabled seniors or those with a medical condition or injury.
Varilite http://www.varilite.com	Seating and positioning devices.
Invacare Comfort-Mate Extra Cushion http://www.invacare.com	A cushion that is anatomically designed to provide long-term sitting comfort and promote correct seating posture.
PleezrElite Gel Foam Cushion http://www.allegromedical.com/cushions-covers-backs-c544.html	Pressure-relieving gel and memory foam cushion. Supports the pelvis and the lateral and medial thigh areas.

should take part in school activities with their peers. The strengths of all students should be considered when planning any activity. If teachers plan accordingly, they can get most, if not all, members of the class involved.

Specialized toys and games and switches are considerations for students with physical disabilities. Alternative keyboards, keypads, and touchscreen monitors offer much in the way of AT for students with physical disabilities.

ASSISTIVE TECHNOLOGY FOR MOBILITY

Self-directed mobility expands students' opportunities to interact with their physical and social environments and promotes integration into society at an earlier age than for students without self-directed mobility (Kermoian, 1998). Many students, especially those with severe physical disabilities, need aids to move from one location to another and from one environment to another. When mobility is impaired, opportunities for learning are limited and social interactions are impaired. Students with decreased mobility must have their mobility needs met at the earliest possible opportunity to maximize their learning (Butler, 1986; Deitz, 1998; Thiers, 1994).

Many mobility aids are available, but one size does not fit all students, so to speak. Many factors must be considered, including the student's age, abilities, endurance, home life, social and work environments, funding abilities, school

Using Figure 6-1 and the Assistive Technology Snapshot at the beginning of the chapter, determine what positioning aid might improve Joan's written products.

Beanbags	Conforms to the individual for positioning
Bolsters	Pillowlike objects to support various positions
Mobile stander	Upright positioning; allows for mobility
Prone stander	Upright positioning; enhances use of arms and hands
Wedges	Lying position; enhances use of arms and hands; enhances head control

FIGURE 6-1 Assistive Technology for Positioning and Mobility

placement, and individual preferences. In some environments, speed of mobility may be more of a consideration than in other environments. A student may need to get to a location under time constraints (changing classes in school) but may not be under similar constraints in another environment (at home, for instance, when being called for supper). A person might use a motorized wheelchair for speed of mobility, but she or he might use a reciprocal walker in environments where speed is not essential.

Selection of the most appropriate mobility aid must begin with input from the student and the PT, OT, physicians, parents, siblings, and teachers. Then the mobility aid selection can begin. Selection must consider age appropriateness. Young children may achieve mobility by crawling or scooting or with scooter boards, tricycles, strollers, walkers, or other age-appropriate devices. As a student ages, however, he or she may need new, more age-appropriate devices. Older students may need a wheelchair for rapid locomotion but may choose crutches when in familiar environments that do not present time constraints.

The primary goal of mobility aids is to provide the student with the most independence and the best quality of movement in the most efficient manner possible (Bigge, Best, & Heller, 2001). Efficiency includes not only the ability to move from one point to another but also issues such as physical maintenance, physical exertion, and the time required to recover from exertion. Body alignment and proper positioning must also be considered when selecting mobility aids.

A key point to remember about mobility aids is that the primary objective is to enable the student to move as efficiently and independently as possible (Best, Heller, & Bigge, 2005). However, no mobility aid should be considered as the primary seating system for anyone unless all other possibilities have been exhausted. When choosing a seating device, several tenets must be explored. For example, general physical management, such as seating and positioning, should be assessed for all students in the classroom, not just for students with disabilities. All students should reach either the floor or foot pedals with the feet and ankles at 90 degrees, the knees should be relaxed at a neutral position (also at 90 degrees), and the hips should be pushed back in the chair to relieve strain on the lower back.

Another important rule of thumb is that the student's position must be changed every 20 minutes. When a person sits on one part of his or her body with no change of position, the skin can experience breakdown, and decubitis ulcers can form. These potentially serious ulcers can be largely prevented by careful attention to good physical management. The IEP team should address these issues for any student who uses a mobility system.

Mobility Systems

When the members of the IEP team consider the factors and issues related to mobility, they must have a thorough working knowledge of the type of mobility system that the student is using. Mobility systems come with many variations, but there are two basic types: manual and power. Each type has advantages and disadvantages. The team must determine which type best matches the student's needs and must assess the prerequisite skills necessary for use of a mobility system.

Determining the student's skill level enables the team to choose the best and most appropriate mobility system. For example, students must have the proper sensory skills to operate a chair. It is important that they be able to locate any obstacles (including other students) that may appear in their paths. Students must have adequate visual and auditory skills so they can locate environmental hazards. They must have appropriate cognitive skills to be able to follow directions and understand environmental dangers. (Health and safety issues for each type of mobility system are discussed later in this section.) Using the assessment of the student's present level of performance, the IEP team can decide the most effective mobility system for access to learning.

MANUAL WHEELCHAIRS   Manual wheelchair design and construction continue to improve. Made now of lightweight materials, wheelchairs have become more durable but also more expensive. Generally constructed of a cloth or vinyl seat and back and a lightweight frame, these chairs are light enough for transport, are relatively durable, and are easily maneuverable. However, the sling-back design tends to offer little support for the student's back. Therefore, many students may also require support for seating and positioning. The correct seating and positional support may prevent the development of certain orthopedic disorders of the spine.

Supports are usually made of plywood covered with a firm foam and washable cover. Inserts can also be constructed of molded plastic or rubberlike substances. These inserts are usually lightweight and easily cleaned, but they tend to be hot and uncomfortable for the student. Again, the OT and PT can offer assistance in making mobility systems more supportive and can teach the caregivers proper positioning.

Manual wheelchairs require the student to push with both hands to make the chair move. Certain hemi-driven chairs allow the student to use only one hand for movement. The effort required by the student to propel the wheelchair should be considered. For many students, the manipulation of the wheelchair may be equal to strenuous exercise (Best, Heller, & Bigge, 2005). For that reason, it might sometimes be appropriate for another person to push the wheelchair or for the student to use a power wheelchair.

POWER WHEELCHAIRS   Power wheelchairs are electric and motorized. They are available in three basic models: (a) conventional power wheelchairs, (b) power-based systems, and (c) scooters. Power wheelchairs are operated by a variety of control devices. See Table 6-2 for links to examples. Control devices allow the user to control speed, direction, and even access to environmental needs. The type of control device is determined by the student's abilities. For example, a student who cannot use his or her hands may operate a joystick with a foot.

Conventional power wheelchairs look like manual wheelchairs. The attached motor makes this chair heavier to manipulate for transport. As with the manual wheelchair, the student may need supports for seating and positioning.

Power-based units have a smaller wheelbase with heavier wheels. Users may choose from a variety of seating systems to meet their individual seating and positioning needs. The heavier, wider, and smaller wheels provide mobility options in a variety of environments. Advances in technology have created high-tech mobility system options that allow the student to go from a sitting to a standing position, to climb up and down stairs, and to traverse the roughest terrain.

Scooters represent another motorized mobility system option for students with physical disabilities. Scooters are designed with three or four wheels and in varying sizes. They can be used indoors or out. They are controlled by handlebar steering and have seats that swivel and elevate. In addition, they can be disassembled for easy storage during transport.

While the high-tech aspects of the power-based mobility systems provide more options and efficiency than the manual wheelchair, power systems also have limitations. In particular, they are costly and more complex, requiring skill for maintenance and repair.

When considering a mobility system for a student, the IEP team must address health and safety considerations. Health issues include factors that can help students using mobility systems to protect their joints and muscles from overuse, underuse, and injury. A mobility system is not exercise equipment. Students will have to keep fit, including a daily regimen of stretches and toning exercises to keep their muscles strong and flexible. They must remember to exercise all the muscle groups so that all muscles are equally strong. The student should be encouraged to eat a healthy diet that helps to maintain strength and to control weight. Extra weight adversely affects joints, mobility, and transferability. Students using mobility systems benefit from extended rest periods. The OT and PT can assist in providing a beneficial and safe exercise routine that can perhaps be incorporated into the student's physical education activities.

MOBILITY SAFETY ISSUES   Teachers and peers must understand the safe use of any mobility system and take a proactive approach. When a student with a manual system requires assistance pushing a wheelchair, the student's (and the helper's) hands should be kept away from the spokes. Speed should also be managed appropriately. Students who operate their own wheelchairs may wear gloves for better traction and protection.

Other safety issues include the use of seat belts. For example, a seat belt must be available for the student and the belt must fit low on the hips. If the belt has a web design and a buckle, the belt must be inspected regularly for wear and the buckle must release easily.

The classroom teacher can collect important information for the IEP team about a student's mobility. How will this information enable the student to access the general education curriculum?

For students who operate a power mobility system, the controls must be accessible but not so easily that the mobility system becomes accidentally engaged during transfers to or from the chair. When appropriate, the speed of the chair must be adjustable and, if necessary, governed. Time and attention must be given to ensuring that both the teacher and student are well trained in the operation of any chair. Appropriate etiquette related to students who use mobility systems should be observed by the teacher and taught to the student's peers. (See Assistive Technology Spotlight 6-1 for wheelchair etiquette tips.) The teacher should have a plan in place for emergency events, such as fire and natural disasters.

Chair width	18"
Seat upholstery depth	16"
Seat height from floor	20"
Distance between arms	16"
Arm height from seat	10"
Arm height from floor	30"
Back upholstery height	17"
Overall length (without rigging)	32"
Overall length (with rigging)	43"
Overall height	36"
Overall width (open)	24"
Overall width (closed)	11"
Gross weight (with rigging)	42 lbs.
Overall weight (without rigging)	39 lbs.
Front wheels	8"
Rear wheels	24"

FIGURE 6-2   Dimensions of a Standard Manual Wheelchair

WHEELCHAIR SPECIFICATIONS   Most chairs have standard measurements. Figure 6-2 and Table 6-2 provide additional details on this topic.

ASSISTIVE TECHNOLOGY FOR STUDENT LEARNING

Students with physical disabilities can be successful learners in general education classrooms, but the IEP team must consider AT for access to curriculum, teaching and learning strategies, and proper supports. Position and mobility are support issues that affect academic success for students with physical disabilities. Peer acceptance, AT, physical management routines, and proper positioning for learning are essential for social and academic success.

Peer Acceptance

As we saw in the Assistive Technology Spotlight about Joan, the student with a physical disability has a disability that is difficult to conceal. Either because of a physical difference or because of equipment, peer interactions may be negatively affected. Unfortunately, the very device that enables communication often creates a difference in the classroom. These visible disabilities and the required supports make it necessary for teachers to consider how AT may enable the student with a disability to interact in positive ways with his or her peers.

Whenever possible and with the knowledge and permission of the parents, information should be given to peers to help explain the student's use of AT. This may be done by the teacher, parent, or student. For example, many students with

TABLE 6-2 Mobility	
Tilt-in-Space Manual Wheelchair http://www.invacare.com http://www.sunrisemedical.com	Manual and power chairs and accessories.
MVP Manual Wheelchair http://www.invacare.com	Described by the manufacturer as versatile, growable, and designed with performance in mind. Three rear-frame options available are needs-responsiveness (curved frame), stability (square frame), and growth (extended frame).
Pediatric Wheelchairs http://www.sunrisemedical.com	A variety of manual pediatric wheelchairs can be found at this website.
Standard Trays http://www.sunrisemedical.com	Trays for wheelchairs come in extra small, small, medium, large, and extra-large. These trays allow the student to have a workspace to meet his or her individual needs.
The Garaventa Evacu-Trac http://www.evacutrac.com	A lightweight, compact, and easy-to-use evacuation chair. Designed for people with limited mobility to transfer from their wheelchair to the Evacu-Trac without assistance.
The Model 1900 Emergency Rescue Chair http://www.rescuechair.com	This rescue chair is designated specifically for use in buildings and emergency vehicles. It is 20" wide and can be used in all regular stairwells and hallways. The rescue chair transforms a stairwell into a safe, usable escape route. Two locking bars secured by a Velcro-webbing strap make this a safe and secure chair for transporting a person up or down a flight of stairs.
Safety First Tips http://www.easterseals.com	How to prepare an evacuation plan for students who use mobility aids.
Accessibility Guidelines and Standards http://www.access-board.gov	The Access Board is an independent federal agency devoted to accessibility for people with disabilities. Teachers will find this a helpful resource for resolving accessibility issues.

physical disabilities communicate either through nonsymbolic communication or symbolic communication. Nonsymbolic communication consists of a menu of behaviors, such as verbalizations, physical gestures, or object manipulations (Best, Heller, & Bigge, 2005). Helping classmates understand the meaning of these expressions facilitates communication. If there is no explanation, then others may perceive that the student is acting inappropriately.

The same is true when a student uses symbolic communication to interact. Symbolic communication is the use of communication that represents something else (Best, Heller, & Bigge, 2005). For example, a student may use a communication board, an eye-gaze system, or another electronic communication device. These devices rely on symbols to convey meaning. Classmates who understand the use of the AT device communicate more successfully with the student with a disability.

Assistive Technology Devices for Students with Physical Disabilities

Students with physical disabilities often have various types of equipment that support daily living and learning. The IEP team must evaluate the school environment to determine what changes must be made for safety and for learning. Efforts should be made to normalize the visual effects of the equipment (Snell & Brown, 2006). Taking the time to explain the purpose of the equipment may help students without disabilities accept and understand the student with disabilities. Also, devices that are commonly used in the environment can be used for positioning. For example, in the early grades, the OT or PT may use a colorful bean-bag chair for positioning when the student must be out of a wheelchair. For older students who use computer equipment, it may be possible for an AT device to blend with other computer equipment in the classroom. Teachers must determine how to integrate the AT in the most unobtrusive manner possible so that students with physical disabilities are more alike than different from their peers.

Physical Management Routines

The proper physical management of the student with a physical disability is important for maintaining proper alignment, relieving stress points on the body, using daily living skills, and participating in class activities. An assessment of the classroom, both the physical aspect and the class routines, enables the IEP team to make recommendations for a routine of physical management. The routine should include the health and safety of the student as he or she is lifted, repositioned, and carried in the most efficient manner possible. Although the physical management routine is individualized for the student, some general considerations should be noted. Stremel et al. (1990) suggested the first four in the following list, and we added a fifth:

1. Verbally or physically make contact with the student.
2. Help the student to understand what you are going to do and why. For example, "Joan, I want to move you to the beanbag so you can have circle time."
3. Get the student ready physically for the move. For example, remove the shoulder harness before lifting.
4. Enable the student to participate as much as possible in the routine.
5. Make sure any AT device the student may need in the new position is moved and working properly.

Establishing a routine for the physical management of the student is imperative in helping the student become a successful learner.

Proper Positioning

The OT and PT work closely with the family and teacher to assist in the delivery of the right programming for the child. Strengthening muscles through proper positioning and exercise can help the child begin to develop these areas. Wedges, balls, corner chairs, and mats are used to position a child so he or she can be included in all activities with peers. Teachers should reposition children every 20 minutes.

Adaptable toys with switches can enhance the student's ability to play with peers when positioned on a mat, on a beanbag, or in a corner chair. Chapter 4 provides more information about switches for young children.

As children progress into the elementary grades, accessibility must still be a consideration with positioning. The IEP team must consider what positions the student needs, as well as what positions will be advantageous for the student to participate in activities with peers. If the student uses positioning aids, such as pillows, wedges, specialized corner chairs, mats, and the like, how can they help the student access the general education curriculum? The teacher must also

ASSISTIVE TECHNOLOGY SPOTLIGHT 6-1

Wheelchair Etiquette

The following 10 tips enable better communication with students who use wheelchairs.

1. These steps should be incorporated into a lesson for all students.
2. Focus on the student, not the disability.
3. Prepare the physical environment of the classroom to allow maximum accessibility and safety for all students.
4. Before jumping in to help, always ask the student who uses a wheelchair if he or she would like assistance. Your help may not be needed or wanted.
5. Speak directly to the student who uses the wheelchair, not the caregiver or paraeducator who is nearby.
6. When working with a student who uses a wheelchair and the like, consider sitting down to get at eye level with the student. It will keep both of you from getting a stiff neck!
7. When taking the student to an unfamiliar location, such as on a field trip, be proactive. Think about possible issues like travel distance, location of curb cuts and ramps, weather conditions, and physical obstacles that may hinder travel or access to the site.
8. When a student who uses a wheelchair transfers out of the wheelchair to a chair, desk, or toilet, do not move the wheelchair out of reach. If you think for some reason it would be best to move it, ask the student who uses the wheelchair for the best option.
9. Remember that the wheelchair is an expensive and important piece of equipment. Learn how to operate and care for the wheelchair so that you are ready to help when the student needs assistance.
10. Prepare an emergency evacuation plan for all students, including those who use wheelchairs or other mobility aids.

arrange the classroom for positioning of the student while at the same time considering inclusion.

IEP teams must consider both positioning and mobility issues, as well as which AT devices support both these areas. Students who need AT devices to access the general education program must have the support of both teachers and parents to be successful. Teachers, parents, and—in some cases—classmates must be trained to use AT devices so the student can have access to the general education curriculum and so everybody can understand the safety issues for the student.

Students with physical disabilities comprise a relatively low percentage of the student population. These students require modifications and/or accommodations to ensure their inclusion in the general education curriculum and, ultimately, to live independently.

Chapter Review

- The term *physical disability* may refer to a large number of students who have different characteristics. As defined by the law, students with physical disabilities often have a severe orthopedic impairment that adversely affects educational performance. It can include impairments induced by congenital anomaly, disease, and other causes.
- More than 90% of students with physical disabilities are in schools with their peers and are receiving services in the general education classroom. Many of these students require related services to access the school's physical environment and general education curriculum and to participate in extracurricular activities.
- AT for positioning ranges from simple to very complex. It can mean adjusting the height of a table in a classroom or providing a custom-designed stander. Proper positioning helps with muscle tone, coping with deformities, and postural support.
- The physical therapist or occupational therapist should address issues regarding positioning. AT devices used for positioning should account for the comfort and function of the student. The AT device must be as functional as possible.
- With input from members of the IEP team, good positioning should enhance student participation in an inclusive setting. A student in a wheelchair is in a good position for participation in almost any classroom activity. Tables, doorways, and desks should be the proper height and width to allow for mobility. Students using a standing frame, mobile stander, or prone stander can enhance muscle length and development. Such devices help the student to participate in certain cooperative learning groups, games, and activities.
- Observation of AT in the initial phases will aid in making adjustments for AT use.
- Alignment of the head, neck, and trunk are important considerations regarding positioning and AT usage. Proper positioning can help maintain posture and muscle tone.

- Adaptive equipment should provide students with opportunities for socialization. Students should not feel isolated because of reactions to an AT device. Equipment should be as unobtrusive as possible to aid in the student's involvement with peers. Consideration of how and where the AT device is used should factor into decisions regarding AT usage.
- Classroom teachers should consider UDL when designing the classroom.
- Mobility expands students' opportunities to interact with their physical and social environments. The student's age, ability level, physical health, home life, social and work environments, funding abilities, school placement, and preferences should be factored into the selection of an AT device.
- The goal of a mobility system is to provide the student with the most independence and best quality of movement in the most efficient manner. Body alignment and proper positioning must be considered when selecting mobility aids.
- No mobility system should be considered as the primary seating system until all other options have been explored.
- Students who depend on a mobility system should change positions frequently. This prevents breakdown of skin tissue.
- Mobility systems come with many variations, but they come in two basic types: manual and power. Each type has advantages and disadvantages. The IEP team must determine which type best matches the student's needs and assess the prerequisite skills necessary for use of a mobility system.
- To operate a chair, the student needs adequate sensory and cognitive skills to follow directions and understand environmental dangers.
- Students with physical disabilities need services beginning with early intervention and continuing through adulthood.
- Children with physical disabilities benefit from early childhood intervention and preschool programs that focus on motor development. This involves proper positioning across all environments to ensure the success of the child in an inclusive setting. The multidisciplinary team works closely with teachers and families to provide training that meets the needs of the child for motor development across all environments.
- As children move from preschool programs to elementary settings, it is important for IEP teams to consider positioning and mobility issues and how each can facilitate student involvement with peers in academics. The team must consider what positions will be advantageous and must ensure that the classroom and building are barrier-free.
- Ergonomically designed workspaces with appropriate software provide opportunities for individuals with physical disabilities to access the general education curriculum.
- Robotics can assist in the development of motor skills and provide a level of independence across all environments.
- IEP teams must consider positioning and mobility issues and what AT devices and supports will allow and assist the student in accessing the general education curriculum.

References

Best, S. J., Heller, K. W., & Bigge, J. L. (2005). *Teaching individuals with physical or multiple disabilities* (5th ed.). Upper Saddle River, NJ: Merrill/Pearson Education.

Bigge, J. L., Best, S. J., & Heller, K. W. (2001). *Teaching individuals with physical, health, or multiple disabilities.* Upper Saddle River, NJ: Merrill/Pearson Education.

Butler, C. (1986). Effects of powered mobility on self-initiated behaviors of very young children with locomotor disability. *Developmental Medicine and Child Neurology, 28,* 472–474.

Deitz, J. C. (1998). Pediatric augmented mobility. In D. B. Gray, L. A. Quantrano, & M. L. Leiberman (Eds.). *Designing and using assistive technology: The human perspective* (pp. 269–284. Baltimore: Brookes.

Individuals with Disabilities Education Improvement Act of 2004. Pub. L. No. 108-446, 118 Stat.2647.

Kermoian, R. (1998). Locomotor experienced psychological functioning. In D. B. Gray, L. A. Quantrano, & M. L. Leiberman (Eds.). *Designing and using assistive technology: The human perspective* (pp. 251–268). Baltimore: Brookes.

Snell, M. E., & Brown, F. (2006). *Instruction of students with severe disabilities* (6th ed.). Upper Saddle River, NJ: Merrill/Pearson Education.

Stremel, K., Molden, V., Leister, C., Matthews, J., Wilson, R., Goodall, D. V., et al. (1990). *Communication systems and routines: A decision making process.* Washington, DC: U.S. Office of Special Education.

Thiers, N. (May, 1994). Hope for rehab's forgotten child. *OT Week,* pp. 16–18.

U.S. Department of Education. (2009). *Twenty-eighth annual report to Congress on the implementation of the Individuals with Disabilities Education Act.* Washington, DC: Author.

Westling, D. L., & Fox, L. (2004). *Teaching students with severe disabilities* (3rd ed.). Upper Saddle River, NJ: Merrill/Pearson Education.

7

Assistive Technology for Communication

CHAPTER VIEW

- ▪ Assistive Technology Snapshot
- ▪ Communication
- ▪ Communication Disorders
- ▪ Augmentative and Alternative Communication
- ▪ Assistive Technology for Student Learning
- ▪ Assistive Technology Spotlight 7-1
- ▪ Chapter Review

CHAPTER FOCUS

1. Define communication.
2. What is a communication disorder?
3. What is the purpose of augmentative and alternative assistive technology (AT) devices?
4. How are AT devices and services for communication disorders delivered within the AT Continuum?
5. How can teachers encourage and promote communication during instructional time?

Assistive Technology Snapshot
MEET BETSY TAYLOR

Betsy Taylor is a 6-year-old, first-grade student attending Northside Elementary School. Betsy lives with her mom, Amy Downing, who works at a local fast-food restaurant as a server. Betsy's father is not active in Betsy's life. Betsy has a younger sister, Carolyn.

Ms. Downing reported that Betsy had been slow in beginning to speak, but at that time Ms. Downing believed that her daughter was slow because of prematurity and low birth weight. She also reported that Betsy began making cooing and comfort sounds, but beginning around age 2, Betsy began communicating with a series of grunts and pointing. Ms. Downing became worried, however, when Betsy's behavior became bizarre, especially around strangers. If Betsy was introduced to a stranger, she would scream loudly, and if the stranger didn't leave, she would begin to strike out or bang her head on any available object. Ms. Downing further reported that Betsy rarely made eye contact with anyone and, on the rare occasions that she did make eye contact, she seemed to stare right through the other person as if he or she were not there. After seeing two different pediatricians, Betsy was diagnosed with **pervasive developmental disorder**, characterized by limited social interactions, communication impairments, and stereotypic behavior patterns, when she was 3. When Betsy was 4 years old, this diagnosis was changed to **autism**.

Due to the late diagnosis, Betsy did not receive early intervention services but did begin to receive speech and language services through early childhood special education. The local school district provided these services to Betsy in the home of her maternal grandmother, who was Betsy's caregiver

when her mother was at work. At age 5, Betsy entered a kindergarten class. She continued to receive speech and language services for 30 minutes twice a week within a group setting. In the kindergarten setting, Betsy exhibited behaviors such as tantrums, aggression toward students and adults, perseveration, and self-abuse. In addition to behavioral excesses, Betsy exhibited deficits in speech and language, social, and academic skills. In the middle of the school year, Betsy's kindergarten teacher requested an individualized education program (IEP) meeting to arrange having a paraeducator to assist in Betsy's education. The paraeducator was assigned 2 months before school was out.

Although Betsy made limited progress in kindergarten, the IEP team felt that, with the assistance of the paraeducator, Betsy should be placed in first grade. After entering first grade, Betsy's behavioral deficits became more pronounced; her behavioral excesses intensified and interfered with productive learning. Betsy's first-grade teacher, Mrs. Dawson, requested an IEP meeting to provide support for Betsy's continued inclusion in the general education classroom. The teacher reported that Betsy did not get along with her classmates. She had no productive speech, and some of her more challenging behaviors included rocking and perseverating on certain speech sounds. Mrs. Dawson felt that these behaviors were the reason that Betsy had no friends and was often physically abusive to her classmates. She indicated that Betsy was especially disruptive during language activities, especially the activities that required her to respond to verbal directions. Mrs. Dawson reported that Betsy was below grade level in all academic areas, but especially in areas that involve language skills. Betsy's mother and teacher reported that Betsy's behavioral excesses were significant challenges in the classroom and at home.

The IEP team met and decided on a full reevaluation of Betsy. In addition to the typical assessments, the team requested that Betsy be assessed by the school's behavior and AT specialists. Based on the results from the evaluation, the IEP team made the following recommendations: Betsy's areas of strength included fine-motor skills. As the team hypothesized and the evaluation confirmed, Betsy's language skills were significantly below average. The AT specialist reported that Betsy would benefit from the use of AT for her expressive language skills. The IEP team felt that, if Betsy could express herself in meaningful ways, her level of frustration might decrease and she would become a more productive learner. Behavioral objectives in this area were defined as follows: (a) Betsy will point to desired objects when asked what she wants, (b) Betsy will respond to yes or no questions, (c) Betsy will spontaneously point to desired objects, and (d) Betsy will pair appropriate speech sounds with her responses. The AT specialist prescribed a simple **fixed-display communication board**

with photos of desirable objects such as food items, a restroom, and so on, as the starting point. The speech-language specialist and the special education teacher were assigned to teach Betsy how to use the communication board. The AT specialist would also make a duplicate board for Betsy to use at home. The IEP team envisions a time when Betsy will progress from a fixed-display board to a more complex **dynamic-display communication board**.

The team felt that a picture schedule might help provide predictability, stability, and structure within the general education classroom for the teacher and Betsy. The AT specialist would work with the classroom teacher, the paraeducator, and Betsy to create a picture schedule to outline the daily classroom activities. The team believes that this will provide a sense of security for Betsy and prevent some of her behavioral excesses.

The team requested that the behavior specialist work closely with Betsy's mother, general education teacher, and special education teacher to develop a behavior plan to handle and decrease Betsy's behavioral excesses. The team decided to reconvene in 6 weeks to follow up implementation of the AT and behavioral plan.

Webquest

7.1

To learn more about pervasive developmental disorders, go to http://www.ninds.nih.gov/disorders/pdd/pdd.htm

See the Companion Website for additional information on milestone charts for speech and language development.

COMMUNICATION

Communication is a complex process. The development of communication skills begins in the prenatal stage and continues throughout the developmental period and beyond (American Speech-Language-Hearing Association, 2004). The exchange of information is a reciprocal process of expressing and receiving information, feelings, ideas, wants, and desires by encoding, transmitting, and decoding information (Heward, 2003).

Communication occurs through seeing, hearing, speaking, reading, writing, signing, and gesturing. For a successful exchange of information to take place, a message must be sent, with a sender expressing the message and a receiver responding to the message. Most communication, with the exception of when we communicate with ourselves, involves at least two participants. This creates a social dimension to communication. Thus, communication skills are critical for successful student learning.

Students who have adequate and appropriate communication skills are able to meet the demands of the general education curriculum. These demands include narrating, explaining or informing, requesting, and expressing (Heward, 2003; Lindfors, 1987; Owens, 2001). For students like Betsy, a deficit in communication creates barriers to successful learning and living. Understanding communication

TABLE 7-1   Speech and Language Resources

American Speech-Language- Hearing Association http://www.asha.org	The American Speech-Language-Hearing Association (ASHA) is the professional, scientific, and credentialing association for more than 114 members and affiliates who are audiologists; speech-language pathologists; and speech, language, and hearing scientists.
Speech, Language and Swallowing http://www.asha.org/public/speech/swallowing/default.htm	Information packets on speech, language, and swallowing disorders.
Language Development http://www.asha.org/public/speech/development/chart.htm	Typical language development.
Index of Information http://www.asha.org/topicindex.htm	Multiple topics on communication disorders.
Activities for Speech/Language Development http://www.asha.org/public/speech/development/Parent-Stim-Activities.htm	Activities to encourage speech and language development.
Pragmatic Disorders http://www.asha.org/public/speech/development/Pragmatics.htm	Language tips for pragmatic disorders.

requires that professionals comprehend the components of typically developing speech and language and the components of communication disorders. Often, students who have autism appear to develop typically for the first few years of life, as Betsy did, but then they do not progress through the developmental milestones as typically developing children do. See Table 7-1 for more information on speech and language development.

We met Betsy in the Assistive Technology Snapshot at the beginning of the chapter. What characteristics does she have that illustrate her communication disorder?

Language

Language is the formal code of abstract symbols used by a group of people to communicate. These symbols consist of sounds, letters, numbers, and manual signs. In addition, language includes a system of rules for combining those symbols into larger units (Hulit & Howard, 2002). This complex system contains five components: phonology, morphology, syntax, semantics, and pragmatics.

- **Phonology** is the form or linguistic rules of the sound system of a language. Each individual speech sound is called a *phoneme*.
- **Morphology** is the form of language. This system governs the structure of words. Morphology allows for the recognition of meaning by hearing. The smallest meaningful unit of sound is a *morpheme* (Heward, 2003).
- **Syntax** is the component that provides the meaningful structure of words into sentences.

- **Semantics** is the content or meaning of a word or a combination of words. Language learners must have knowledge of vocabulary, contextual word meaning, concept development, and the relationships among words.
- **Pragmatics** is the social use of language.

The development of these five components is critically influenced by social interaction (Heward, 2003; McLean & Synder-McLean, 1988; Turnbull, Turnbull, Shank, Smith, & Leal, 2004).

The set of rules governing how spoken language is used to communicate involves three kinds of communication skills (American Speech-Language-Hearing Association, 2001): (a) using language for different functions—such as greeting, informing, demanding, promising, and requesting; (b) following rules for dialogues and narrative accounts—such as conversational rules, telling a story, appropriate use of nonverbal signals, personal space between speaker and listener; and (c) adapting or monitoring language according to the expectations or needs of a listener or situation—such as speaking differently to a teacher than to a peer. The rules governing language may differ across languages and cultures.

Speech

Webquest
7.2

To learn how to make a talking communication board, go to http://atmac.org/making-communication-boards/

Speech is primarily the forming and production of oral language. Oral speech may be replaced or enhanced by gestures, manual signs, picture symbols, or written symbols. Learning speech begins early in life and usually follows a sequential pattern of development. Typically developing children have learned to produce nearly all of the vowels and consonants that make up their language by the age of 8 (Turnbull, Turnbull, Shank, Smith, & Leal, 2004). Speech sounds are produced by four separate but related physiological processes: (a) **respiration**, which powers speech; (b) **phonation**, which produces sound in the larynx; (c) **resonation**, which shapes the sounds; and (d) **articulation**, which forms the specific speech sounds.

COMMUNICATION DISORDERS

Students may have a speech or language impairment, or both, as illustrated in the Assistive Technology Spotlight you read at the beginning of this chapter. The American Speech-Language-Hearing Association Ad Hoc Committee (1993) defines a communication disorder as follows:

> An impairment in the ability to receive, send, process, and comprehend concepts or verbal, nonverbal, and graphic symbol systems. A communication disorder may be evident in the processes of hearing, language, and/or speech. A communication disorder may range in severity from mild to profound. It may be developmental or acquired. Individuals may demonstrate one or any combination of communication disorders. A communication disorder may result in a primary disability or it may be secondary to other disabilities. (p. 40)

For students to receive special education services for communication disorders under the Individuals with Disabilities Education Act (IDEA) (2004), the disorder, speech impairment, or language impairment must have an adverse affect on the child's learning. Speech or language impairment is defined as "a communication disorder, such as stuttering, impaired articulation, language impairment, or a voice impairment that adversely affects a child's educational performance" (34 C.F.R. Sec. 300.7(a)(c)(11)).

Many of the students receiving services for speech and language impairments, like Betsy, also have concomitant disabilities, or co-occurring disabilities, such as mental retardation, specific learning disabilities, multiple disabilities, traumatic brain injuries, or hearing impairments. For example, Betsy had a diagnosis of autism and speech and language impairments. Students with these disabilities typically receive services within the general education classroom setting.

Language Impairments

Students who have language impairments have difficulty with comprehension or use of spoken, written, or other symbol systems, such as gestures (American Speech-Language-Hearing Association, 1993). One of the most severe types of language impairment is **aphasia**, a debilitating disorder that results from damage to the language centers of the brain. Although the most common cause of aphasia is stroke, children who experience traumatic brain injury may also experience it (American Speech-Language Hearing Association, 2004b). Other disorders that result in language impairments in children are childhood **apraxia** (the inability to execute learned movement), language-based learning disabilities, traumatic brain injury, cerebral palsy, and autism. Children like Betsy who have serious language impairments also experience difficulty being successful learners.

Speech Impairments

As defined by the American Speech-Language-Hearing Association (1993), a speech impairment is a disorder that affects the articulation of speech sounds, fluency in speech, or voice. Articulation disorders include the atypical production of speech sounds characterized by substitutions, omissions, additions, or distortions. A student with a fluency disorder exhibits an interruption in the flow or fluency of speaking. This may be characterized by atypical rate, rhythm, repetitions of sounds, syllables, words, and phrases. Voice disorders are the abnormal production or absence of vocal quality, pitch, resonance, loudness, or duration that are inappropriate for the student's age or gender (American Speech-Language-Hearing Association, 1993). Examples of disorders or conditions that cause speech impairments are cerebral palsy, cleft lip or palate, and stuttering. Significant hearing loss can also contribute to disorders of speech. (Hearing loss is discussed in Chapter 8.)

Students who exhibit severe language and speech impairments may be taught to use an augmentative or alternative communication system. These systems provide students with a means to communicate ideas when communication through speaking is not an option. The AT specialist and speech-language pathologist (SLP) play vital roles in the referral and assessment process by creating supports for successful learning. Chapter 3 describes this process more fully, and Table 7-1 provides additional resources for speech and language.

Webquest 7.3

To turn text to speech, go to http://text-to-speech.imtranslator.net/speech.asp?dir=ko

Using Table 7-1, find a communication milestone chart that shows the communication skills of children who are developing typically.

AUGMENTATIVE AND ALTERNATIVE COMMUNICATION

One of the greatest teaching opportunities and challenges is experienced by teachers who are working with students who have both severe speech-language impairments and physical disabilities. A speech-language impairment can hinder the student's ability to interact with the immediate environment, but when one is coupled with a physical disability, it becomes difficult, if not impossible, for the student to interact. When a person is unable to interact, basic needs can go unmet and social interactions become strained to the point of isolation and personal frustration.

It is imperative that communication skills be developed so students can interact with their environments. This involves enhancing the abilities the student has while developing a system with the greatest utility. Making the student a more effective communicator across various environments is the primary goal of language programs. Augmentative and alternative communication (AAC) can be used to facilitate this process.

Augmentative and Alternative Communication Defined

AAC is defined as the combination of communication tools available to an individual, including any speech, vocalizations, gestures, and communication behaviors related to specific methods and devices. This method may supplement, enhance, or replace conventional communication methods (Belson, 2003). However, augmentative communication and alternative communication are different. Augmentative communication systems help the student use the communication the student has; an alternative communication system is one in which the oral system is bypassed altogether. In the case of Betsy, we learned that the multidisciplinary team decided that an alternative communication device would offer the best solution for her communication disorder because she has no useful language. The fixed-display communication board was chosen as the way to initially introduce using a communication device to Betsy. As she masters this device, the team can suggest the use of a more complex dynamic-display communication board.

Augmentative and Alternative Communication Choices

As illustrated by Betsy's team, the type and method of AAC depend on the student's physical, cognitive, sensory, and receptive communication skills. Another factor in the choice and development of the AAC system is the consideration of how well others can understand the student. When developing AAC systems for students with disabilities, assessment information should be gathered from numerous sources. The primary source is the individual who needs the system, but the secondary source is the individual(s) in the immediate environment who interact with the student on a regular basis. Also to be considered are questions about financial feasibility, other financial resources, student and family support for the system, and the system's usefulness across all environments.

The selection of the best communication method for the student is not a simple task. Language development is complex, even though it is used in our everyday lives. The evaluation process for the selection of the right communication system for a student with a severe speech-language deficit consists of an evaluation by many professionals. These professionals must help the student and individuals involved daily with the student to learn to use the AT device so that they can facilitate better communication skills. The selection of the AAC device can be one of the most important decisions made in the student's educational career. Teaching students to communicate effectively across environments, both social and educational, is the primary goal for the student and the IEP team. The multi-disciplinary team should evaluate not only the student but also the student's environment. The team must consider numerous factors when developing and utilizing AAC. Chapter 3 has more information on this evaluation process.

Indications

When developing systems for the student, especially the nonverbal student, it is important to address indications. An *indication* is the technique by which the student can make the message known. Indications are subdivided into *scanning, encoding,* and *direct selection* (Schmidt, Weinstein, Niemic, & Walberg, 1986; Vanderheiden, 1984).

Scanning is any technique whereby choices are offered to the student in a predetermined order and the student indicates which of the choices he or she wishes to make. The strength of scanning lies in its simplicity. Many students with significant disabilities can use scanning. It can be as simple as a yes or no response or a game of 20 questions. However, the simplicity of scanning is also its main weakness. A certain cognitive ability is assumed for the receiver. In addition, it is very difficult for the sender to ask questions about the environment, thus making it difficult to use a scanning device to learn about the environment or initiate communication with another party.

Encoding is any technique whereby parts of the message are communicated separately by a pattern. The code and the parts must be interpreted by the receiver. Encoding is used when a sender selects a series of signals to send a message using communication devices such as manual signing and spelling.

Encoding has some built-in strengths. It is much quicker than scanning and allows for interactions because the sender can ask questions. Encoding is also much more abstract than scanning. It requires the sender and receiver to chain concepts together, and a higher cognitive level is required before encoding can be used effectively.

The third type of indication is **direct selection**. Direct selection is used when the student is allowed to choose directly parts of the message he or she wants to make known. Direct selection allows a choice of vocabulary elements. When appropriate, using direct selection is preferable for the student. Direct selection allows the student to communicate partial or whole messages in less time than either encoding or scanning takes. Direct selection is usually tied to an output device such as a printer, monitor, or synthesized/digitized speech tool.

Implementations

Implementations are the devices used to help students with communication. They are divided into five areas: (a) unaided, (b) fundamental, (c) simple electronic, (d) fully independent, and (e) fully electronic and portable. Typically, as the level of a device goes from light tech to high tech, so do the sophistication and cost of the device.

Unaided implements are devices or techniques for which no device is present. The student uses body language, head nods, or manual signs for yes and no to make parts of a message understood. Generally, the sender has no way to ask questions and little interaction takes place.

Fundamental devices are generally supplements to communication. An example of a fundamental device is a picture board, where students can point to pictures or symbols in a certain order to make parts of the message understood.

Simple electronic devices are aids that interpret motion. The device usually scans selections for the student, and the student stops the scanner at the appropriate choice. The message generally becomes self-evident.

Fully independent devices allow output to be auditory, visual, or both. These devices are connected to a monitor, printer, or speech output device and to a DC power source. They are generally quite bulky. And their utility is limited due to the dependency on a power supply.

Fully independent and portable devices can have all the properties of independent devices, but they are not connected to a DC power source. Some are run on batteries, and some can be run on solar power supplies.

When examining the different levels of indications and implementations, the team should not lose sight of the primary reason for doing this work: the student. The goal is to produce the most effective device to aid the student in accessing the general education curriculum and being a successful learner. The device itself must be examined based on financial needs, portability, environmental utility, and future expandability.

The Technology Continuum for Augmentative and Alternative Communication

AAC systems use symbols that represent the message the student is communicating. The symbols range from one word to a full sentence or to several sentences. As we discussed in Chapter 1, AT can range from no tech to light tech, to high tech (Vanderheiden, 1984). (Chapter 1 has additional information on the AT Continuum.) This technology continuum allows for greater selection of the type of communication device that a student needs. However, all types of AT use some kind of symbol for communicating the message. The following section focuses on the technology continuum for AAC systems.

NO TECH   In some cases, students can indicate wants and needs without the use of an AAC device. For example, if a student can nod his head to indicate yes or shake his head no, the student may not need a high-tech device to meet his needs at that particular time. It is important to remember to look at current student needs initially and long-range goals eventually.

LIGHT TECH   A light-tech device is a communication system usually designed by the general or special education teacher or member of the school staff. It can be made from various materials within a classroom. A light-tech device requires no power source. A few examples of light-tech devices are gestures, necklace photos, communication boards, eye-gazing objects, choice boards, props, and voice output devices. More light-tech devices are also available.

Gestures are an unobtrusive way of making a request of the student. Gestures, such as pointing, making eye contact, or nodding the head, can provide students with direction in a classroom setting. Gestures draw less attention to the student and provide the student with a visual cue to perform a certain task.

Necklace photos are a means of putting together pictures that are symbols of certain tasks the student is expected to perform. The pictures can be laminated, put in a ring binder, or attached to a cord and worn by the student. The images can range from depictions of functional tasks to academic subjects. When the student is asked to perform a certain task, such as washing hands, the teacher holds up a picture representative of the activity. This type of light-tech AAC device can be devised for any subject area. The pictures can be photos or drawings and can be taken from magazines, books, or the Internet. This is a simple aid for students who may be nonverbal or who have auditory issues.

Communication boards may take various forms or be of various styles, depending on the disability of the student and the environment in which the boards will be used. Communication boards may be used for each activity the student will take part in at school and elsewhere. Pictures, objects, letters, words, or sentences can be made for use on multiple boards and placed in several locations around the classroom so they will be accessible to the student. Picture sources can be photos and icons, commercial software, the Internet, or hand drawings. If a student needs a visual schedule for the day, photos of the student performing each task can be organized sequentially. Students can mark each task (e.g., by attaching a clothespin to the picture as the task is completed so they know what to do next. Words can be used for those students who can read and sequence them in the correct order. Teachers can also have a set of students' symbols so they can show students the task they are requesting. Visual schedules and communication boards can be constructed by using pictures downloaded and printed from websites.

Eye gazing is used by students to make their needs known. Eye gazing can be very simple because a student can look at an object long enough for another person to understand the student's choice. Another way this method is used is to put two or three symbols on a surface and allow the student to gaze at one symbol long enough for another person to understand the choice made.

Choice boards made of heavy cardboard with Velcro strips are another good means of communication. Several symbolic objects are placed on the Velcro strip, and the student can point to or gaze at what is appropriate for the situation. This method provides the student with a certain sense of choice. For an example of symbolic objects, such as pictures, see Assistive Technology Spotlight at the end of this chapter.

Props within a classroom help a student be successful within the academic environment. Props are a good means to stimulate language development with young students and enhance vocabulary development with older ones. Props can be tactile markings added at the measure to graduated cylinders, beakers, and flasks for an experiment in the science lab. Puff paint can be used for tactile markings in math, science, chemistry, or physics. Timers can be used to indicate transition times or the end of an activity. Props are good AAC devices and are unobtrusive.

Voice output devices can be considered either light tech or high tech. Small handheld devices record one or two messages that the student may use several times during the day. The devices are activated by pushing a button. Many of these devices use digitized speech.

Tape players can be adapted with a switch. A message can be recorded on a loop tape that the student can activate as needed by pushing the switch. Tape recorders are usually standard in the typical classroom, so the cost for adapting them should be minimal. Newer auditory devices, such as a CD player may need to be adapted with switches to meet the needs of the student.

Other suggestions for light-tech AAC devices include audiotaping lectures; extra time for the completion of an assignment; translation of materials into whatever form the student might need (e.g., braille, adaptive electronic media); allowing students to manipulate objects, models, and various materials where appropriate; and assigning a peer to assist the student when necessary. These suggestions are all easy to incorporate with little financial expenditure.

HIGH TECH   A high-tech AAC device is a high-level communication device that usually requires a power source. However, the term is not indicative of a device that is difficult to use. High-tech devices may require a large financial commitment; therefore, it is imperative that the IEP team weigh the options when selecting a high-tech device. Some examples of basic high-tech devices include, but are not limited to, text-to-speech devices, single-level voice output devices, multiple-level voice output devices, and screen display devices. Manufacturers provide various options for the basic devices. The options are updated in a very timely manner that coincides with technological advances.

A text-to-speech device allows the student to type in a word or phrase, and the device displays it on a monitor that will speak the word or phrase on command. A computer is not always needed for text-to-speech software, which can be used with a more portable device.

Single-level voice output devices use digitized speech and allow the user to record one message. The message can be used over and over within a classroom. More than one device can be used for accessibility. If only one device is available, the message will have to be changed as the student transitions from one activity to the next.

Multiple-level voice output can provide the same functions as single-level voice output devices, but they have multiple levels. Multiple keys can provide multiple messages. The student activates each message by pressing the key associated with that message. Depending on the software, the user can record multiple messages.

Communication overlays are placed on top of the communication board. The overlays can be categorized so the students can use them during several different activities. The teacher can keep these in file folders and categorize each so the student or someone working with the student can change them as needed.

Screen display devices are activated through a touchscreen. The student touches a symbol on the screen, and the computer either speaks or brings up a different screen that relates to the picture that was touched. This system is designed for use on the computer. This type of system should be planned carefully so the student will not be overwhelmed initially. Symbols can be added as the student becomes more familiar and more comfortable using the system.

Many computers come with built-in accessibility options that are designed to help students change the layout of computer keyboards. One of these options includes **filter keys**, a function that allows students with disabilities to use a single key for access to functions on the computer keyboard that normally require use of two keys, such as the Shift key or the Control key. Another option, the **sticky key**, allows the computer either to slow down repeated keystrokes or to ignore repeated keystrokes altogether. This is especially useful for students with physical disabilities who have limitations in their abilities to press and release computer keys. Some mouse options slow down the mouse pointer or give it a trail, making it easier to track, enlarge, change the color of, or change the shape of the pointer.

Layout changes can also be used to change the order of the keyboard. The keyboard can stay in the traditional **QWERTY** layout or can be changed to a **Dvorak** layout, in which the keyboard is laid out with keys arranged more by their use than they are on the standard QWERTY keyboard. These options can be downloaded easily and saved to your computer (Bigge, Best, & Heller, 2001).

Variations are also available for the design of the entire keyboard. When typing, it is important that the student hold his or her hands in as neutral a position as possible, with the hands extended and without significant bending at the wrist. Standard keyboards sometimes force users to rotate their forearms and bend their wrists outward at an unnatural angle. This position not only decreases the speed of typing, it also increases stress on the wrist joints and can contribute to repetitive stress injury. **Ergonomic** devices reduce or relieve some of these problems. Ergonomics is the principle behind the design of alternative computer input devices such as special split keyboards, curved keyboards, and other alternative input devices.

Many such redesigned keyboards are available. One of the more popular designs is a split and rotated keyboard with a wrist support. This design has a keyboard that is split down the middle, with either the space between the right and left side of the keyboard increased or the space angled so that the student's wrists are held in a neutral position and stress on the wrist joints is relieved.

A variation is when the keyboard is split and tented, meaning the two sides of the keyboard are elevated to form a tent. This design reduces significantly the rotation in the forearms and wrists and in some cases can relieve stress on the elbows.

Key positioning and keyboard slope are two additional considerations. Some keyboards come with concave wells where the keys are placed so that the keys to be pressed by the longer fingers are slightly lower than the other keys. Other specialized keyboards have curved keys that feel more natural for the shape of the human fingertip. Slope can be adjusted on many keyboards for the individual comfort and preferences of the student. One student may prefer a flat keyboard, but another may need a sloped keyboard to communicate. Adjust the slope by raising or lowering the legs underneath the keyboard. Some keyboards already have a negative slope that raises the front of the keyboard. Always remember that slope, positioning, and keyboard design are all individual decisions, and such decisions should be made in conjunction with the student.

Several considerations are important when choosing a keyboard. Figure 7-1 serves as a guide to help with that decision. See Table 7-2 for resources for alternative keyboards for users of AAC.

1. Is the keyboard compatible with the existing hardware?
2. Some keyboards are wider than standard keyboards. Will the selected keyboard fit on the keyboard tray?
3. If a tented keyboard is used, is the tray tall enough to allow the keyboard to slide under the desk?
4. If the student uses the hunt and peck method for typing, are the keys visible?
5. What are the specifications for the job? Some alternative keyboards change the function of certain keys or, in some cases, eliminate some keys altogether.
6. How much time will it take for the student to learn to use the keyboard?

FIGURE 7-1 Guiding Questions for Keyboard Considerations *Source:* U.S. Department of Health and Human Services, Public Health Service, Centers for Disease Control and Prevention, National Institute for Occupational Safety and Health (n.d.).

TABLE 7-2 Alternative Keyboard Resources

OrbiTouch Keyless Keyboard http://www.keybowl.com	The OrbiTouch creates a keystroke when two domes slide into one of eight positions.
Ergonomic Keyboards http://www.ergodirect.net	Split, trackball, and touchpad styles.
FrogPad http://www.frogpad.com	One-handed keyboard used with universal serial bus (USB) keyboard-compatible PDAs, pocket PCs, tablets, and wearable PCs.
IntelliKeys http://store.cambiumlearning.com	IntelliKeys USB plugs into the computer's USB port and provides access for anyone with physical, visual, or cognitive disabilities who has difficulty using a standard keyboard.
Cirque Glidepoint Wave Keyboard http://www.cirque.com	The keyboard's design fits the natural angle of arms and hands, allowing wrists and fingers to meet the keys in a more natural position.
Cirque Smooth Cat Keyboard http://www.cirque.com	Similar to the Microsoft Natural Keyboard but with enlarged Backspace and Enter keys.
Comfort Keyboard www.comfortkeyboard.com	Addresses the issues of awkward posture, discomfort, and fatigue experienced by computer users.
Darwin Smartboard http://www.datadesktech.com	Engineered to encourage typing in a more natural position.
Data Hand http://www.datahand.com	Comprised of two ergonomically designed keyboards (one for the left hand and one for the right hand).
ErgoLogic Keyboard http://www.alimed.com	A customizable keyboard. Compatible with all PC software.
Freestyle Convertible Keyboard http://www.kinesis-ergo.com	Ergonomically designed to reduce the negative effect of keyboard use by allowing the user to align hands, arms, and shoulders while keying.

TABLE 7-3   Touchscreen Resources

APOGEE http://www.cybertouch.com/ LCDOPENFRAM.html	Open-frame touch LC screen system supported by a metal bracket.
Magic Touch http://www.abilityhub.com/mouse/ touchscreen.htm	Patented external add-on touchscreen kit. Good where user-friendly input device is needed.
Micro Touch 5-Wire Resistive Touch Screen http://www.3m.com/3MTouchSystems/ Products/PDFs/5-wire.pdf	Solution application that requires input flexibility and fast response time.
MicroTouch PL Analog Resistive Touch Screen http://www.3m.com/3MtouchSystems/ Products/PDFs/ PL.pdf	Specially formulated optical-grade adhesive creates a shatter-resistant touchscreen to withstand temperature and humidity extremes.

A number of both light-tech and high-tech devices are available for students with communication disorders that enhance the student's participation in the general education curriculum and improve student outcomes. Spending time gathering information ensures that the student has the right AAC device. This will help eliminate AT abandonment. Information on touchscreens for users of AAC is provided in Table 7-3.

In the Assistive Technology Snapshot at the beginning of this chapter, the AT specialist initially prescribed a fixed-display communication board for Betsy. Where does this appear on the AT continuum?

ASSISTIVE TECHNOLOGY FOR STUDENT LEARNING

Preparation for Augmentative and Alternative Communication Use

The selection of the AAC device is a very important factor for the success of the student. The right device must meet the needs of the individual student. Following the assessment process, it is important that the individual learn to use the device across all environments. Teachers, parents, and paraprofessionals who work with the student on a day-to-day basis should also be trained to use the device.

STRATEGIES   The following are helpful strategies for using AAC devices:

1. *Provide a supportive environment.* Teachers, parents, and service providers should all work together to evaluate the student's needs on a regular basis. This facilitates the student's communication.
2. *Challenge the student.*   Adults who work with the student should challenge the individual to use the device. A system of gentle reinforcement should also be used when the student succeeds.
3. *Keep communication open among team members.*   Common goals and consistent strategies should be developed by members to implement the AAC device.

4. *Take an active role.*   All team members must be knowledgeable about the system the student is using to make sure the student is successful.

5. *Check the IEP, the individualized family services plan (IFSP), and the transition plan language.*   Make sure the IEP, the IFSP, and the transition goals are followed. The IEP, the IFSP, and the transition plan guide the process that allows for various strategies and devices as the student develops communication skills. (The transition plan will be covered in more depth in Chapter 9.)

6. *Try simple strategies first.*   Try light-tech devices first and get into the more sophisticated devices later (Jaehnert, 2005).

It is important that those involved with the student understand that progress may not be as smooth as anticipated. Several different AAC devices may have to be tried before one is found that the student can use successfully. Also, the student may take longer than anticipated to become comfortable with the device and to use it correctly. Flexibility is the key to success here. Given time, the student will eventually learn to use the device successfully. Table 7-4 provides a partial list of AAC resources.

TABLE 7-4 Resources for Augmentative and Assistive Communication Devices	
Mrs. Riley Picture Cards http://mrsriley.com/introduction	Inexpensive site for making, sharing, and printing picture cards. Free trial is available.
Tufftalker Convertible http://www.words-plus.com	Communication system that blends form and function into one easy-to-use AAC device.
SpringBoard Lite http://www.prentrom.com	Speech output device for use as a starting point for beginning augmentative communication.
Boardmaker Plus! http://www.mayer-johnson.com	Features more than 4,500 picture communication symbols (PCSs) in both color and black and white, all in 44 languages. Boardmaker Plus! is a drawing program combined with a graphics database that also has the ability to talk and play recorded sounds and movies. This interactive component allows users to create talking activity boards, worksheets, schedules, books, writing activities, games, and more. It also has the ability to adapt all materials to each student.
Tango http://www.dynavoxtech.com/products/tango/	Communication device with multiple options.
M3 http://www.dynavoxtech.com/products/m3/	The **M3** by DynaVox is a dynamic display AAC device for emergent communicators of all ages and physical abilities.
Palm3 http://www.dynavoxtech.com/products/palm3/	The **Palm3** is a handheld AAC device with enhanced message composition and accessibility options for fast and powerful communication.

Assistive Technology and the Speech-Language Pathologist

The SLP has a background rich in phonic skills and can be an important support to the classroom teacher in the development of language and early literacy skills. The SLP can assist the classroom teacher in the development of lesson plans that focus on sound–word relationships. The SLP can co-teach lessons within specific content areas that are language-based. Good teachers understand that students must have a means for language development within the classroom. The SLP can help them adjust their teaching styles to assist students with any type of speech impairment.

ROLE OF THE SPEECH-LANGUAGE PATHOLOGIST The role of the SLP is significant for students who require the use of an AT device for communication. As students continue to grow, language use becomes more complex. Thus, it is important for the SLP to assist the student and those who come in direct contact with the student daily to understand and use the appropriate AT device correctly and consistently.

A student must have good communication skills for the educational experience to be successful. The role of the SLP can encompass four different aspects within an educational setting, including:

1. Providing speech-language therapy to the student on a one-to-one basis. The SLP can schedule time to work with the student on an individual basis. If the student requires the use of an AT device, a more intense session may need to be scheduled so the student can learn to use the device across all environments. This type of session can be subject to change as the student becomes more comfortable and learns to use the device effectively.

2. The SLP should be part of the student's IEP team that selects the appropriate AT device. The SLP can work with the family as part of the IEP team to develop appropriate goals and benchmarks that can be used across all environments. The SLP should stay in contact with the family to ensure that the AT device is used correctly within the home. This will help decrease the chances of AT abandonment.

3. The SLP can work in the inclusive setting to assist the student in accessing the general education curriculum.

4. The SLP can serve as a consultant to the general education teacher so that the student's use of the AT device is enhanced within the general education classroom.

The role of the SLP in student learning should not be overlooked. The SLP should be a major part of the student's daily routine to facilitate better communication skills across all the environments in which the student will use the AT device.

Assistive Technology Strategies for Language

Strategies for language development with the AAC user can be as simple as a gesture or as sophisticated as text-to-speech software for a notebook computer. Everything depends on the needs of the individual user. The classroom environment should be structured to maximize the AAC user's potential. If the student has any language ability, the teacher should encourage the use of it. If the student can use AAC through gesturing, eye gazing, or sign language, these techniques should be incorporated into the daily schedule and academic content areas to facilitate language development.

For the student who can use symbols for words, the student, teacher, and SLP can devise a communication system based in large part on symbols specific to the student. The SLP can work with the student in the general education classroom to facilitate use of the system, which can coincide with the curriculum covered within the class.

Assistive Technology Strategies for Speech

The development of speech is as important as the development of language. As discussed in the beginning of this chapter, speech is primarily the forming and production of oral language. The individual should be encouraged to use oral speech to the maximum extent possible, even if he or she is using an AAC device. The teacher is the role model other students will turn to in class, so the teacher should encourage the student to respond verbally whenever possible. Through the strategies previously listed for language, the teacher can also encourage verbalization through pictures, symbols, gestures, and eye gazing. If the student uses a picture of silverware to mean he or she is ready to eat, the teacher could respond to the student with "What would you like to eat?" While the student may be unable initially to respond, the teacher should keep encouraging the student by asking the same question each time the student uses the picture. If the student can vocalize, eventually the student may be able to respond to the question verbally. However, the IEP team should decide whether the student is capable of some verbal responses prior to any initiation on the part of the teacher.

As discussed previously, a student who uses e-books can break the words into syllables to stimulate pronunciation of the word. The student may vocalize some sounds more easily than others. If lectures are recorded for audio playback, students can be encouraged to vocalize certain words on the tape when cued to do so by the person doing the recording. Teachers may opt to videotape or put a lesson on DVD, making it possible to cue the student to pronounce a certain word by repeating it very slowly and asking the student to say the word with them. The student should have the option of stopping and starting any multimedia form of delivery, thus enhancing the number of times he or she can practice vocalizing the word or phrase.

Teachers, family members, support personnel, and peers should encourage student independence through communication. Instruction should facilitate communication and independence throughout the school day. Projects, assignments, working as part of a group, or taking part in class discussions can be encouraged through the use of any AAC device. The teacher is vital in providing instruction that enhances the student's ability to communicate within the classroom. This ability will also increase the student's self-concept and foster a sense of independence.

Assistive Technology Strategies for Reading

For students to be successful in any content area, they must be successful in reading. The development of literacy skills can be incorporated with the use of AAC. Teachers can capitalize on communication through literacy. Pairing the text with pictures or other appropriate symbols can stimulate language development along with reading. Materials presented through videotapes or DVDs allow the student to replay the lesson until he or she has mastered the content. This can also stimulate speech development because the student can vocalize various parts of the content through visual representation of the lesson being delivered. This also provides the student with time to work at a comfortable pace. In addition, e-books can be used for language development and to provide motivation for reading. (Wireless reading devices [WRDs] were discussed in Chapter 4.) Through e-books, the student can develop an interest in a certain subject area, which can stimulate language development.

Students who use AAC devices typically have fewer opportunities to practice literacy skills than do their peers. Teachers should look at literacy strategies for students in the general education curriculum and adapt these strategies to meet the needs of students who use an AAC device. Teachers should have a wide range of activities designed for students who have severe communication impairments.

PHONEMIC AWARENESS *Phonemic awareness* is an area students must develop to become more proficient readers. Recording books on tapes with emphasis on specific sounds can assist the student in recognizing a sound. Pictures with certain sounds programmed into an output communication device can be part of a communication board for a reading lesson. Letter games programmed on an output device can help a student learn to distinguish certain letter sounds. Many software programs can be programmed with various letter sounds to assist in the development of phonemic awareness during the early stages of reading.

For emergent readers, certain letters of the alphabet can be put on index cards. When two letters are held up, the teacher can make the sound of one letter. The student can gaze or point to the correct letter. These cards can also be used with a high-tech device or voice output with a touchscreen display.

Scan/read systems combine the use of a scanner, optical character recognition (OCR) software, and speech output to read printed material aloud. The computer monitor has a visual display of what is being read aloud. Scan/read systems are effective tools to support reading for AAC users within the classroom.

GUIDED READING Guided reading can be used to foster enjoyment of reading and to develop comprehension. A teacher can select a story, introduce vocabulary prior to reading the story, and relate certain vocabulary to symbols familiar to the AAC user. Graphic organizers can be used to highlight and organize information in the story. Teachers can stop at various points in the story and ask the student to summarize some of the information using vocabulary developed specifically for the story. This can be programmed on the communication board, recorded on audiotape, or reproduced as multimedia text with speech. AAC users can see themselves as readers when given the opportunity for as much independent reading as possible with appropriate accommodations and modifications.

Assistive Technology Strategies for Writing

Writing is an important part of any student's education. Many students utilizing an AAC device have various types of physical disabilities that limit their ability to write. Students with poor motor coordination experience difficulty

ASSISTIVE TECHNOLOGY SPOTLIGHT 7-1

A Daily Schedule for a Student Communication Board

Come into the room.

Sit down.

Begin working.

When you have a question, raise your hand.

Put things away.

with written expression and thus are unable to deliver hard-copy products to a teacher.

It is important for the teacher to make accommodations or modifications for students with poor motor skills who are unable to write. In the classroom, note taking and formal writing assignments are important components of the curriculum. With the use of a computer, many students are able to develop good written expression and can participate with peers in these assignments. The computer has excellent editing capabilities that can be tailored to meet the needs of an AAC user. Formal writing should be done on a computer adapted for use by the AAC user.

Students who need to take notes can use abbreviations, which may be understood only by them. Notes can be stored on the computer and then downloaded after class for the student's personal use.

Many text modification functions, including Delete, Print, and Insert, can be used within an AAC device. These editing features are standard on most computers and can be adapted to meet the needs of almost any AAC device.

What is the role of the SLP in assisting a student to access the general education curriculum?

Chapter Review

- Communication is a major part of successful independent living. Communication involves the exchange of information, feelings, ideas, wants, and desires by encoding, transmitting, and decoding information. Communication occurs through seeing, hearing, speaking, reading, writing, signing, and gesturing.
- Language is the code of abstract symbols used by people to communicate. These symbols consist of sounds, letters, numbers, and manual signs.
- The complex system of language involves phonology, morphology, syntax, semantics, and pragmatics.
- The set of rules governing how spoken language is used to communicate involves three kinds of communication skills: (a) using language for different functions, such as greeting, informing, demanding, promising, and requesting; (b) following rules for dialogues and narrative accounts; and (c) adapting or monitoring language according to the expectations or needs of a listener or situation.
- Speech is the forming and production of oral language. Speech sounds are produced by four separate but related physiological processes that include (a) respiration, (b) phonation, (c) resonation, and (d) articulation.
- A communication disorder is an impairment in the ability to receive, send, process, or comprehend concepts or verbal, nonverbal, or graphic sound systems. It may range from mild to profound in severity.
- Many students with speech disorders have additional disabilities. When this occurs, it is known as *concomitant disabilities.*
- Language disorders may consist of aphasia, which results from damage to the language centers of the brain, or apraxia, which results from language-based learning disabilities, traumatic brain injury, cerebral palsy, and autism. A speech impairment is a disorder that affects articulation of speech sounds, fluency in speech, or voice.

- Students with severe language or speech impairments may be taught to use an augmentative or alternative communication (AAC) system. These systems are designed to provide students with a way to communicate when communication through speaking is not an option.
- AAC is defined as the combination of communication tools available to an individual, including any speech, vocalizations, gestures, and communication behaviors related to specific methods and devices. This method can supplement, enhance, or replace conventional communication methods. The type of AAC used depends on the student's physical, cognitive, sensory, and receptive communication skills. The selection of an AAC device must be made with the input of many professionals. The multidisciplinary team must evaluate not only the student but also the student's environment in selecting the most appropriate AAC device for the student.
- Indications should be addressed when considering and developing an AAC device for the student. An indication is a technique by which the student can make a message known, and it consists of three areas: scanning, encoding, and direct selection.
- Implementations are the devices used to help students with communications. They are divided into five types: unaided, fundamental, simple electronic, fully independent, and fully electronic.
- The technology continuum for AAC consists of no tech, light tech, and high tech. No tech involves a student indicating wants and needs without the use of an AAC device. Light tech is usually designed by the general or special education teacher and is made from materials within the classroom. High tech is a high-level communication device that requires a power source.
- AAC devices should be used by the student across all environments. Six strategies can help a student learn to use the AAC device: providing a supportive environment, challenging the child, keeping communication open among team members, taking an active role in ensuring that the child is successful, checking the IEP and/or IFSP to make sure that it is being followed, and trying simple strategies first.
- The role of the SLP is very important for the student who uses an AAC device. As the student grows, so does the use of language. It is important for the SLP to assist the student and those who come in direct contact with the student daily to ensure that the appropriate device is used correctly and consistently. The role of the SLP includes four aspects within an education setting: providing speech-language therapy in a one-on-one setting, serving on the student's IEP team, working with the student in an inclusive setting, and serving as a consultant to the general education teacher to enhance the student's use of the AT device within the general education classroom.
- AT strategies for language with the AAC can be very simple to very sophisticated, depending on the needs of the individual student. Strategies such as eye gazing, sign language, and utilizing symbols for words can assist the student and be incorporated into the student's daily schedule at school and at home.
- The teacher should encourage the student to respond verbally to a question or directive whenever possible. Through the use of language strategies, the teacher can encourage verbalization through pictures, symbols, gestures, and

eye gazing. Teachers, family members, support personnel, and peers should encourage independence on the part of the student through communication.

- The development of literacy skills should be included in the use of AAC. Teachers should look at literacy strategies for students in the general education curriculum and adapt these strategies to meet the needs of students who use the AAC devices.

- It is important for students who use an AAC device to use the editing capabilities on the computer when they produce their own writing. These capabilities can be tailored to meet the needs of the AAC user.

References

American Speech-Language-Hearing Association Ad Hoc Committee on Service Delivery in the Schools. (1993). *Definitions of communication disorders and variations. ASHA, 35*(Suppl. 10), 40–41.

American Speech-Language-Hearing Association. (2001). Pragmatics, socially speaking. Retrieved May 18, 2004, from http://www.asha.org/public/speech/development/Pragmatic-Language-Tips.htm

American Speech-Language-Hearing Association. (2004a). Roles of speech language pathologists in the neonatal intensive care unit: Technical report. ASHA Supplement October, 2003.

American Speech-Language-Hearing Association. (2004b). Aphasia. Retrieved May 21, 2004 from http://www.asha.org/public/speech/disorders/Aphasia_info

Belson, S. (2003). *Technology for exceptional learners.* Boston: Houghton-Mifflin.

Bigge, J. L., Best, S. J., & Heller, K. W. (2001). *Teaching individuals with physical, health or multiple disabilities.* Upper Saddle River, NJ: Merrill/Pearson Education.

Heward, W. L. (2003). *Exceptional children: An introduction to special education* (7th ed.). Upper Saddle River, NJ: Merrill/Prentice Hall.

Hulit, L. M., & Howard, M. R. (2002). *Born to talk: An introduction to speech and language development* (3rd ed.). Boston: Allyn & Bacon.

Jaehnert, K. (2005). Selecting an augmentative and alternative communication (AAC) device for your child. Retrieved May 25, 2005, from http://www.ucp.org/ucp_general.cfm/1/129

Lindfors, J. W. (1987). *Children's language and learning* (2nd ed.). Boston: Allyn & Bacon.

McLean, J., & Snyder-McLean, L. (1988). Applications of pragmatics to severely mentally retarded children and youth. In R. Schiefelbusch & L. L. Lloyd (Eds.), *Language perspectives: Acquisition, retardation, and intervention* (pp. 255–288). Austin, TX: PRO-ED.

Owens, R. E. (2001). *Language development: An introduction* (5th ed.). Boston: Allyn & Bacon.

Schmidt, M., Weinstein, T., Niemic, R., & Walberg, H. (1986). Computer assisted instruction with exceptional children. *Journal of Special Education, 19*(4), 493–501.

Turnbull, R., Turnbull, A., Shank, M., Smith, S., & Leal, D. (2004). *Exceptional lives: Special education in today's schools* (4th ed.). Upper Saddle River, NJ: Merrill/Prentice Hall.

Vanderheiden, G. (1984). High and light technology approaches in the development of communication systems for the severely physically handicapped persons. *Exceptional Education Quarterly, 4*(4), 40–56.

8

Assistive Technology for Sensory Impairments

CHAPTER VIEW

- Assistive Technology Snapshot
- Sensory Impairments
- Assistive Technology Devices for Sensory Impairments
- Assistive Technology for Student Learning
- Assistive Technology Spotlight 8-1
- Chapter Review

CHAPTER FOCUS

1. List the types of sensory impairments.
2. What supports are needed for the student with a sensory loss to have access to the general education curriculum?
3. What kinds of assistive technology devices are appropriate for students with visual impairments?
4. What kinds of assistive technology devices are appropriate for students with hearing impairments?
5. How is age of onset of a sensory disability related to learning?
6. What role does assistive technology play in allowing a student with a sensory impairment to succeed with partial participation?

Assistive Technology Snapshot

MEET KAY GRIGGS

Kay Griggs is a teacher of students with visual impairment (TVI) in a small rural school district. As a TVI, Ms. Griggs is specially trained in the program area of visual impairment and is certified by her state department of education to teach special skills to students with visual impairments. She is an itinerant teacher and travels to four school sites within her system to provide services for the seven students currently among her caseload. Her caseload is determined by the number of hours she spends (a) providing direct and indirect services to students with visual impairment, (b) meeting related professional responsibilities, and (c) traveling from school to school.

Within the itinerant teacher model, Ms. Griggs serves students who are assigned either to the general education classroom or to a special educator in a self-contained classroom for students with multiple disabilities. She travels to each school site to address the special educational needs described in the student's Individualized Education Program (IEP). Her time with each student varies according to the individual needs of the student. It is Ms. Griggs's responsibility to bring to the student any special materials that might be needed. She also assists in any training for the use of assistive technology (AT) devices. Ms. Griggs spends time consulting with the students' teachers and with other service providers, such as the Speech-Language Pathologist (SLP) and the assistive technology specialist.

While visual impairment is a low-incidence disability, Ms. Griggs's students are a heterogeneous group. Two of her students have low vision, one has deaf—blindness, and four students have low vision with additional disabilities. Miranda and Josh, two of her students, are good examples of how diverse students with sensory impairments can be.

Miranda has **low vision**, which is a severe visual impairment after correction, but she has increased visual functioning through the use of AT. She is a 9-year-old student in the third grade. Shortly after birth, Miranda was diagnosed with **congenital cataracts**, a disorder of the eye that occurs when the lens of the eye becomes cloudy, and later with **retinopathy of prematurity**, a retinal disorder, leaving her with limitations in her far vision (**myopia**) and near vision (**hyperopia**) in both eyes. Her cataracts were removed at age 6 months. She received early intervention services for visual impairment and a developmental delay in language. When evaluated in the first grade, Miranda scored within the average range of intelligence. Prior to entering first grade, Miranda was seen at a low-vision clinic to help determine what, if any, accommodations and modifications needed to be made for her to be a successful learner. At that time, recommendations from the low-vision clinic included the use of magnification, large-print materials, and a **closed circuit television (CCTV)** for magnifying objects placed on the viewing platform for viewing on a large-screen monitor.

Miranda had successful first- and second-grade years. She received special education services to support her access to the general education curriculum, including consultation by the teacher of students with visual impairment and speech-language services for visual impairment and developmental delay in language. Miranda's most recent report from her **ophthalmologist**, a physician who specializes in the diagnosis and treatment of diseases of the eye, indicated that her best-corrected vision was 20/200 in both eyes with a minor field of vision loss in both eyes. He also prescribed extended-wear contact lenses to replace the surgical loss of her lenses when her cataracts were removed at age 6 months.

During the summer before her third-grade year, Miranda was reevaluated at the low-vision clinic. The recommendations from the assessment included the following:

1. Any materials presented or projected from the walls should be individually produced in large print for Miranda to use at her desk.
2. Whenever possible, large print should be 24-point Tahoma font.

This is an example of the 24-point Tahoma font.

3. Continue using the CCTV.
4. Use an illuminated handheld magnifier with a prescription lens.
5. Use a computer-based reading system that uses an optical recognition system.
6. Avoid moving desks, chairs, and tables within the classroom environment.
7. Adjust light sources so that no glare is on Miranda's workstation.

Ms. Griggs arranged for the AT specialist to teach Miranda, her parents, and her general education teacher how to use the magnifier and the computer-based reading system. It is Ms. Griggs's responsibility to provide large-print classroom materials for Miranda.

Josh, Ms. Griggs's other student with low vision, is a 5-year-old attending a general education kindergarten class. Josh lives with his grandmother. According to information from his grandmother and his medical records, Josh's birth mother contracted **cytomegalovirus (CMV)** during the early stages of her pregnancy. CMV is a virus that can be contracted by the fetus at the prenatal stage (before birth), perinatal stage (during birth), or

through breast milk. Shortly after birth, Josh was diagnosed with glaucoma. He was promptly treated to slow down the progression of the disease. According to Josh's grandmother and his pediatric records, Josh's mother haphazardly administered the required treatment that consequently caused his glaucoma to damage his eyes. Because he has visual acuity of 20/200 or less in the better eye after the best correction or vision restricted to 20 degrees or less, Josh was declared **legally blind** and was fitted with corrective lenses.

In addition to his low vision, Josh was diagnosed at age 3 with a mild bilateral sensorineural hearing impairment and a developmental delay in speech and language due, it was thought, to his prenatal exposure to CMV. Shortly after this diagnosis, Josh's mother abandoned him, and he was placed with his frater paternal grandmother. At the age of 4, Josh began to receive preschool special education services from Ms. Griggs.

Josh entered Ms. Mobley's general education kindergarten class at age 5. He received special education services for visual impairment and developmental speech and language delay. Ms. Griggs worked with Ms. Mobley to provide support for Josh in the general education classroom. Josh left Ms. Mobley's classroom three times per week for 30 minutes each time to work with the speech-language pathologist. During the third month of school, Josh's grandmother had his hearing retested. The results showed that Josh's hearing loss had progressed from a mild hearing loss to a moderate bilateral mixed hearing loss. The hearing specialist recommended in-the-ear hearing aids to amplify environmental sounds and perhaps help with his comprehension of sounds. Josh chose a bright green color for his ear molds.

After receiving the new assessment of his hearing, Ms. Griggs arranged for Josh's multidisciplinary team to review this new information. The team reclassified Josh as having *deaf–blindness*. The team also understood that now both his vision and hearing losses are unstable and progressive. As a result, they developed goals, objectives, and supplemental aids and services to allow Josh access to the general education curriculum. Josh's teachers and grandmother were trained in how to take care of his hearing aids. Josh will receive special education services for deaf–blindness and speech and language impairment. The team also recommended that, in addition to oral speech, Josh should begin to learn tactile finger spelling and to pair tactile sign language with tactile symbols in his environment. Ms. Griggs will also work with Josh's grandmother to learn how to finger spell by touch and to use sign language. In addition, the team suggested that the AT specialist assess Josh and his kindergarten environment to see what devices might be appropriate. At this time, Josh is able to read print materials with a 16-point font. The computer screen will be adapted to meet this need, and Ms. Griggs will provide large-print materials for Josh.

In spite of Josh's challenges with sensory impairments, he remains an active, engaged student with a natural curiosity about his environment. He is well accepted by his classmates and is included in all activities.

SENSORY IMPAIRMENTS

Sensory impairments, such as those that Miranda and Josh exhibited, are considered to be **low-incidence disabilities** because they occur relatively infrequently in the general population. For this reason, many general education teachers may have limited experience with students who have visual impairments, hearing impairments, or deaf–blindness.

All sensory impairments have the potential to affect how a student learns. The impairments may range from mild to severe. The age of onset is a major factor in determining how the student communicates and learns. This chapter defines and describes visual impairment, hearing impairment, deaf–blindness, and the assistive technology (AT) that may allow the student with such a disability to succeed in the general education curriculum.

Webquest
8.1

To see a video of screen readers, go to http://www.doit.wisc.edu/accessibility/video/intro.asp

Visual Impairments

Visual impairment among children is a low-incidence disability. Only about 0.4%, or 1 in 200, of children ages 6 to 21 who have IEPs under the Individuals with Disabilities Education Act (IDEA) received services for visual impairment (U.S. Department of Education, 2009). Like Miranda and Josh, the population of students with visual impairments is also a very diverse group. All have individual characteristics and all differ in ability, developmental rate, and social skills. The one commonality of these students is that they all have less than fully functional visual systems, which can interfere with access to the general education curriculum and prevent them from being successful student learners. All these students require individualized and specialized instruction. Children learn from seeing, and no two children with visual impairment see in the same way (Huebner, 2003). Thus, it is important that teachers have an accurate understanding of a student's vision and individual learning needs, as well as the legal and educational definitions of visual impairment.

Teachers and other related service professionals must know the age of onset of the vision impairment and whether the student ever had useful vision. This information affects learning and instructional strategies that can be used by the teacher for the student (Huebner, 2003).

Miranda's vision loss was **congenital**, meaning that the loss occurred before or at birth. Other students, like Josh, have an **adventitious** loss of vision, usually the result of an accident or disease. This term often refers to loss of vision after visual memory is established, generally by the age of 5. Students who possessed some vision until age 5 will likely have some visual memory that they can use to learn.

Although Josh was diagnosed as legally blind, that does not mean he is totally blind. The term *legally blind* has very little use in the educational environment, but it is sometimes helpful in determining eligibility for some government-funded resources. The definition of *visual impairment* in the Individuals with Disabilities Education Improvement Act of 2004 emphasizes the relationship between the student's vision and learning and how the student's visual disability affects educational performance.

For educational purposes, it is better to use the term *low vision* to describe the visual impairments exhibited by Miranda and Josh. They continue to be able to use their vision as a primary means of learning, but they supplement this learning with input from their other senses.

Others who may be classified as *functionally blind* have very little vision and learn primarily through auditory and tactile senses. These students may be able to use their remaining vision to support information received from other sources (Heward, 2009). Other students may be diagnosed with total blindness, which is the inability to see and technically refers to individuals with only light perception or no vision at all. These students receive no useful information through vision and must rely on tactile and auditory input for learning. For many, the term *visual impairment* encompasses all these terms.

Many states determine that a student is eligible for special education services when the student does not use his or her vision as a primary sensory channel for learning. Across the United States, state departments use specific terminology to determine if students are eligible for special education services. Therefore, a teacher should be familiar with the terminology that is specific to his or her state and local school district. In addition, parents, teachers, and special education service providers should determine as much as possible about each student's vision. Table 8-1 contains a list of Web sites for more information on visual impairment.

Both Miranda and Josh received special education services for their visual impairments. In addition to the required members of collaborative teams listed in Chapter 3, the student with a visual impairment may have several additional specialists as members. A professional who works very closely with the student, the caregivers, and the student's teachers is the TVI. The TVI is trained and certified specifically to teach special skills to students with visual impairments. This professional, like Ms. Griggs, is a key member of the student's multidisciplinary team and contributes information and insight to other team members regarding the individual learning needs of students. In addition, the TVI has the qualifications to address the students' assessment and instructional needs. For Miranda and Josh, Ms. Griggs consulted with their teachers to provide instructional resources and materials and to evaluate assessment data specific to visual impairments. The TVI is often responsible for ensuring that the team includes the student's parents and caregivers and other professionals who are needed to develop the student's IEP, goals, and supports. (For more information, see Chapter 3.)

Other specialists that might be part of a student's multidisciplinary team are the (a) orientation and mobility specialist, (b) adaptive physical education teacher, (c) SLP, (d) occupational therapist (OT), (e) low-vision specialist,

Look at Table 8-1. How might a parent of a student with a visual impairment benefit from an organization such as NAPVI?

TABLE 8-1 Information about Visual Impairment	
Assistive Technology Assessment Texas School for the Blind and Visually Impaired http://www.tsbvi.edu/technology/ vieval.htm	A downloadable checklist summary of technology skills achieved by students with visual impairments.
National Association for Parents of Children with Visual Impairments (NAPVI) http://www.spedex.com/napvi	The National Association for Parents of Children with Visual Impairments (NAPVI) is a nonprofit organization of, by, and for parents and is committed to providing support for children who have visual impairments. The site has a list of NAPVI chapters, publications, a parent directory, and useful links.
American Printing House for the Blind http://www.aph.org	The mission of the American Printing House for the Blind is to promote the independence of persons who are blind and visually impaired by providing specialized materials, products, and services.
Lighthouse International http://www.lighthouse.org	A leading resource worldwide on vision impairment and vision rehabilitation. The Lighthouse distributes free information regarding vision loss. Links include research, products, publications, and vision resources.
National Braille Factory http://www.braillefactory.com	Produces braille documents, including coloring books and greeting cards.
Nemeth Code of Braille Mathematics and Science Notation http://www.tsbvi.edu/math/ math-resources.htm	Computer-based interactive tutorials for learning the Nemeth Code.
Universal Design for Internet Access http://www.cast.org	"Bobby" s a Web-based tool that examines webpages for accessibility.
National Center for Accessible Media (NCAM) http://ncam.wgbh.org	NCAM provides examples of accessible webpages.
DO-IT http://www.washington.edu/doit	DO-IT provides a list of Internet resources for accessible webpage design.

(f) AT specialist, and (g) paraeducator. These professionals help the team make the decisions necessary to provide an appropriate education for the student with visual impairments (Topor, Holbrook, & Koenig, 2003).

In addition to developing goals for the students, the multidisciplinary team must make decisions regarding special education services, related services, and supplementary aids and services. This includes the use of AT for access and for accommodations and modifications. (See Assistive Technology Devices for Students with Visual Impairments later in this chapter.)

Hearing Impairments

As with visual impairment, a hearing impairment is also considered a low-incidence disability. Students with hearing impairments make up about 1.2% of all students ages 6 to 21 who receive special education services, or about 0.11% of the total student population (U.S. Department of Education, 2009). It is not uncommon for a student with a hearing loss to have additional disabilities. This is the case for Josh, who has a moderate bilateral mixed hearing impairment in addition to his visual impairment.

Terminology is important to understand so that the individual needs of the student with a hearing loss can be identified and the student can receive an appropriate education. The definition of hearing impairment found in the Individuals with Disabilities Education Improvement Act (2004) is an educational definition and specifies that a student's hearing loss must adversely affect his or her educational performance. Most special educators use the terms **deaf** and **hard of hearing**. Deaf refers to those students who have a hearing impairment so severe that they are unable to understand speech even with amplification. Hard of hearing refers to those students who have hearing impairments that affect educational performance but allow some linguistic information to be processed aurally, with or without amplification (Heller, Alberto, Forney, & Schwartzman, 1996; Heward, 2009).

Other terms are necessary to explain the types of hearing impairments students may have. In the Assistive Technology Snapshot at the beginning of this chapter, Josh was described as having an adventitious hearing loss. Although his is a progressive hearing loss caused by a disease his mother passed to him early in the prenatal stage of development, his hearing was normal at birth, so he developed speech and language. Some students have congenital hearing loss and, depending on the degree of loss, will have varying difficulties developing speech and language. Many students who have **prelingual deafness**, a hearing loss occurring before language develops, do not develop speech and language. The multidisciplinary team should identify age of onset so that the proper instructional strategies and AT devices can be used.

As with Josh, students who have a **postlingual hearing impairment** have developed speech and language, so they have learning needs that are very different from those of students who have never developed speech and language. According to Heward (2009), the educational program for a student who is prelingually deaf must emphasize language and communication skills, while the postlingually deaf student must focus on the maintenance of existing speech and language patterns. Students who exhibit either a postlingual or prelingual loss will most likely benefit from AT.

Hearing impairment is measured on a continuum from normal hearing to severe hearing loss. A student may have a **unilateral** (one ear) or **bilateral** (both ears) hearing loss. Hearing impairment is either caused by a **conductive hearing loss** or a **sensorineural hearing loss**. A conductive hearing loss occurs when sound waves cannot pass from the outer ear or inner ear to the other structures within the ear (Heller et al., 1996). A sensorineural hearing loss oocurs when sound waves travel normally through the outer ear and middle ear but are

Webquest 8.2

To see some of the hearing devices that are available, go to http://www .hdhearing.com/

TABLE 8-2 Information about Hearing Impairment	
Alexander Graham Bell Association for the Deaf and Hard of Hearing http://www.agbell.org	Founded in 1890 by Dr. Alexander Graham Bell, the Alexander Graham Bell Association is a lifelong resource, support network, and advocate for listening, learning, talking, and living independently with hearing loss. The association promotes the use of spoken language and hearing technology for those persons with hearing impairment. The association serves as the nation's largest information and support center for pediatric hearing loss and oral/deaf education.
American Society for Deaf Children http://www.deafchildren.org	This website provides information specifically for children who are deaf or hard of hearing. It features services, events, and resources.
American Speech-Language-Hearing Association (ASHA) http://www.asha.org	Provides information about speech, language, and hearing. Research is disseminated through this highly respected organization.
Deaf Resource Library http://www.deaflibrary.org	This website contains mailing lists, newsgroups, research, and online magazines about and for people who are deaf or hard of hearing.
Hearing Aid Care http://www.healthyhearing.com/articles/31575-hearing-aid-care-made http://www.nidcd.nih.gov/health/hearing/hearingaid.asp	Information educators need to know about caring for a hearing aid.

impeded in the inner ear or along the auditory nerve (Heller et al., 1996). For many types of sensorineural hearing losses, a hearing aid is not recommended because the problem is not with conducting sound but with the mechanisms in the ear that are damaged. The combination of both a conductive and sensorineural loss is called a **mixed hearing loss**. Josh has a mixed hearing loss and was fitted with hearing aids to enhance his remaining hearing and assist with his comprehension of environmental sounds. Resources for learning more about hearing impairment are found in Table 8-2.

At this time, Josh does not have a teacher of the hearing impaired to work with him. Ms. Griggs, the TVI, was also trained to work with students who have deaf–blindness. As Josh's hearing loss progresses, however, the multidisciplinary team will have to address the issues related to providing additional support for his hearing loss. This may include the services of a deaf educator or may necessitate that Josh be considered for services at a special school for students who have severe disabilities or who are deaf, hard of hearing, or deaf–blind. Teachers of the hearing impaired are specially trained and certified to provide services to students who have hearing impairments.

Deaf–Blindness

Josh actually represents a small but challenging group of students who have dual sensory impairments. According to the Individuals with Disabilities Education Improvement Act of 2004, these children have such severe communication, developmental, and learning needs that they cannot be educated in special education programs solely for visual impairment, hearing impairment, or multiple disabilities due to the nature of the dual, concurrent disabilities. Estimates suggest that less than 0.1% of children who received special education services are categorized in the disability category of deaf–blindness (U.S. Department of Education, 2009).

The majority of children categorized as having deaf–blindness have some functional hearing and/or vision (Heller et al., 1996). The impact of having dual sensory loss is felt in the areas of communication, orientation and mobility, functional skills, concept development, academic skills, and social skills. For these reasons, instruction for students with deaf–blindness requires specialized instructional strategies.

Factors that must be considered by the multidisciplinary team when designing an IEP for a student who is deaf–blind are the degree of sensory loss and the age of onset of each component of the sensory losses (Heller et al., 1996). These factors will help the team choose the best instructional strategies and AT devices to promote access to the general education curriculum. Table 8-3 lists several resources to gain a better understanding of students with deaf–blindness.

Webquest 8.3

To see examples of orientation and mobility devices, go to http://orientationandmobility.org/

TABLE 8-3 Information about Deaf–Blindness	
DB-Link http://www.tr.wou.edu/dblink	DB-Link is a federally funded information and referral service that identifies, coordinates, and disseminates (at no cost) information related to children and youth (birth to 21) who are deaf–blind.
Helen Keller National Center for Deaf–Blind Youths and Adults http://www.helenkeller.org	Provides technical assistance, including training, information, and support, to families and agencies serving children, youth, and young adults who are deaf–blind.
Deafblind Children Home Page http://www.geocities.com/Heartland/Meadows/5939	A resource for parents of children who are deaf–blind.
The National Technical Assistance Consortium for Children and Young Adults Who Are Deaf–Blind (NTAC) http://www.tr.wou.edu/ntac	NTAC provides technical assistance to families and agencies serving children and young adults who are deaf–blind.
Science Curriculum for Deaf–Blind Howe Press at Perkins School for the Blind http://www.perkins.org/accessiblescience/ http://www.perkins.org/accessiblescience/	A four-level curriculum guide for students, ages 2 to 9, who are deaf–blind with cognitive abilities.

ASSISTIVE TECHNOLOGY DEVICES FOR SENSORY IMPAIRMENTS

Assistive Technology Devices for Students with Visual Impairments

Students with visual impairments benefit by using technology to access information. To use technology successfully and independently, students like Miranda and Josh need AT devices. The use of AT devices, whether light tech or high tech, enable students with visual impairments to access immense amounts of information that are needed for success in the general education curriculum and daily life. However, each student with visual impairment is different. For this reason, each AT device is usually individualized for a particular student's needs, and Miranda and Josh provide good examples. Josh needed the font enlarged to 16 points on his computer screen. Miranda needed a much larger 24-point font. Some students with visual impairments do not need a larger font but do need the font to be displayed in a different color. It is important for the multidisciplinary team to provide explicit information in the student's IEP so that teachers and other service providers know exactly what devices the student needs. This section provides an overview of devices that are available for students with visual impairment.

ACCESS TO PRINT AND MULTIMEDIA MATERIALS   Teachers of students with visual impairment play a key role in making appropriate AT devices available so the student can access information displayed on a computer screen. Kapperman and Sticken (2003a) suggested that providing access to screen information revolves around (a) magnifying images and visual information on the screen, (b) providing screen readers, and (c) making information available in braille.

MAGNIFICATION OF COMPUTER IMAGES AND VISUAL INFORMATION   With accommodations, such as enhancement of the operating system of the computer, many students with low vision can read the computer screen and access information. For example, the word processor that we used to write this chapter has accessibility options that require little time and effort to employ. The display, keyboard, sound, and mouse can be adapted for the student with visual impairment. Our operating system can adjust text size and font size and has a magnifier. It also offers an option for entering information for the user with a visual impairment. Josh would benefit from this kind of adaptation because his low vision requires only a 16-point font.

This is an example of a 16-point font.

Some persons with visual impairment need specialized software to enhance visual images. Screen-enlargement software can be used to increase the size of the onscreen images. Students like Miranda can be taught the strategies necessary to invoke special commands to enlarge the images to predetermined sizes. In addition, portions of the text can be magnified while the remaining text is left at the unmagnified size. This software is designed for use on computers with specific dimensions and can be designed for the individual student's needs. See Table 8-4 to find shareware and commercial products available for this purpose.

Explore the accessibility options on your personal computer.

Using Table 8-4, identify a resource that a classroom teacher could use to provide closed captioning on classroom media materials.

TABLE 8-4	Assistive Technology Resources for Visual Impairment
American Printing House for the Blind, Inc. (APH) http://www.aph.org	A nonprofit organization promoting the independence of persons who are visually impaired by providing specialized materials, products, and services needed for education and daily living. APH provides technical support for its electronic products.
Braille Translation Software Duxbury Braille Translator MegaDots http://www.duxburysystems.com	Braille translation and word-processing program for computers; includes the Nemeth Code translation program.
Descriptive Video Services Media Access Group at WGBH http://main.wgbh.org/wgbh/pages/mag/description.html	The service provides descriptive narration of key visual elements, which is then inserted within the natural pauses in dialogue to help a person with a visual impairment better understand the story.
Note-Taking Device TransType https://www.msu.edu/~mjh/atc-bvi.htm	TransType is two products in one tiny package: a synthesizer and an advanced note taker.
Braille Sense Plus http://www.enablemart.com	Functional note taker and braille display
Franklin Company http://www.franklin.com	Dictionaries with enlarged displays and speech output.
Independent Living Aids http://www.independentliving.com	Low-vision products for independent living. Includes auxiliary AT devices such as magnifiers, talking watches, talking clocks, and other daily-living tools.
Personal Digital Assistants (PDA) PAC Mate http://www.freedomscientific.com	The PAC Mate is a handheld computer that provides on-the-go access to information and computing. Freedom Scientific manufactures assistive technology products for those who are blind and vision-impaired and products for the special education and learning disability markets.
Delphi http://www.aagi.com	Provides navigation and orientation information to the computer user who is visually impaired.
Screen Enlargement Hardware and Software ZoomText Xtra http://www.aisquared.com	Hardware and software that enlarge the display of a monitor. ZoomText Xtra is a screen magnifier or integrated magnifier/reader.
Screen Enlargement MagniSight Explorer B/W CCTV http://www.lssproducts.com	Source for closed circuit television.
Screen Enlargement The Screen Magnifiers Homepage http://www.magnifiers.org	Provides free information about software and hardware to improve access to computers, information, and the Internet for people with vision problems.

(Continued)

TABLE 8-4   *(Continued)*

Speech Output Systems JAWS 10 for Windows http://www.freedomscientific .com/products/fs/jaws-product-page.asp	JAWS is an enhanced, multilingual software speech synthesizer. Includes nine languages. JAWS also outputs to refreshable braille displays, providing braille support.
Speech Output Systems Texthelp http://www.texthelp.com	Texthelp Systems Ltd. has developed accessibility software, dyslexia software, and text-to-speech software.
Tactile Products Repro-Tronics http://www.repro-tronics.com	Repro-Tronics is the designer and manufacturer of the Tactile Image Enhancer, Flexi-Paper tactile imaging paper, and Thermo Pen II. These products are designed to assist blind and visually impaired individuals in the creation and understanding of tactile graphic images. Explore this website and gain an understanding of how each of these unique products can assist in deciphering and designing tactile images.
Optical Devices for Science Carolina Biological Supply Company http://www.carolina.com	Useful tools in biology lab work, allowing enlarged images of small objects through the lens of a microscope to be viewed on a computer monitor, television, or projection screen.
Optical Devices for Science Frey Scientific Science Products http://www.freyscientific.com/index.jsp	Useful tools in biology lab work, allowing enlarged images of small objects through the lens of a microscope to be viewed on a computer monitor, television, or projection screen.

SCREEN READERS   Many students with visual impairment need to have information on the computer read aloud. Reasons may include that the student (a) has no usable vision, (b) cannot read, or (c) needs to supplement print reading with screen-reading software. Whatever the reason, students can use **speech output devices** to gain information from print materials. Speech output devices, such as a computer with a speaker, communicate information to the student in a form that meets the student's individual needs.

Two components are necessary to provide screen-reading capability. First, the computer must have the appropriate hardware to support the software that reads and produces the sounds. Most computers have a voice synthesizer built into the machine; for those that do not, a synthesizer must be connected to the computer. Although models are improving, the voice synthesizer has a robot-like voice quality. Many software programs allow the user to choose a male or female voice, and even different languages. Second, the system must have software that converts the images to speech. Most software is user-friendly, but the student must receive instruction in how to use the software. Text can be uploaded from scanned materials or read from the Internet. Guidelines provided in the Americans with Disabilities Act (1990) and the Telecommunications Act of 1996 have encouraged many organizations, government agencies, commercial software companies, and websites to provide information that can be read with a screen reader. A word of caution: The student must know how to use the computer operating system *and* the application software. Training in computer skills is a prerequisite for using these devices.

BRAILLE FORMAT   Braille is a communication system of touch that allows persons who are blind to read, review, and study the written word. It consists of raised dots in a six-cell configuration, and each configuration represents a letter in the alphabet. In addition to the alphabet and punctuation, braille also includes 186 contractions and short forms of words. Braille is read using the index fingers and moving the hand or hands from left to right along each line (American Council for the Blind, 2005. Two methods are available for transforming print material from the computer into braille: an electronic refreshable braille display and a braille printer.

An electronic refreshable braille display is a hardware device combined with software that converts print into braille. The user scans the printed screen and the information is converted to braille. The information is then displayed on the hardware device in braille. The student reads the braille by moving his or her fingers across the display. Portable refreshable braille devices are available. These devices provide braille for devices such as notebooks, cell phones, and personal digital assistants (PDAs). Table 8-4 has more information about these devices.

The second type of technology for converting printed information from the computer to braille is braille translation software, which is used with a braille printer. Students can enter the information to be converted to braille by (a) typing the material into a word processor; (b) using a scanner and optical character recognition software to input the material; and (c) retrieving the information from another source, such as scanned materials, the Internet, or a CD (Kapperman & Sticken, 2003a). In all three methods, the information is translated into braille and sent to the braille printer. Kapperman and Sticken suggested that the production of braille using translation software and braille printers provides an efficient method of producing high-quality braille that is easy for both novice braille users and sighted persons to use effectively.

INTERNET ACCESS   One of the long-standing problems for students with visual impairments is the lack of accessibility and instant availability of visual information. The Internet provides access to vast amounts of information and allows for almost instant communication with others all over the world. Enabling students with visual impairment to access the Internet provides a rich source of information, communication, and social opportunities. Websites that are accessible and examples of how to design webpages for accessibility can be found in Table 8-1.

To access the Internet, the student with a visual impairment needs the same equipment as his or her peers. However, the student also needs the types of AT described previously in this chapter so that she or he can access the Internet. In addition, the student with a visual impairment also needs explicit or direct instruction in how to use AT and how to access information found on the Internet. Specifically, the student needs instruction in how to access, send, and receive email; use databases; navigate websites, and enter and participate in chat rooms.

Computer access through the use of AT devices comprises only a portion of the AT devices that are available for students with visual impairments. Other devices that allow the student to be a successful learner are discussed in the following section.

SUPPLEMENTAL OR SUPPORTING ASSISTIVE TECHNOLOGY DEVICES FOR VISUAL IMPAIRMENT Students with visual impairments have access to a plethora of supplemental devices that support their access to the general education curriculum. High-tech AT devices found on the AT continuum include portable electronic note takers, electronic dictionaries with enlarged screens and voice output, talking calculators, personal digital assistants for braille users, portable book-reading devices, electronic travel aids, wireless reading devices, and compasses with tactile and braille displays and speech output. Light-tech devices on the AT continuum include tactile markings, timekeeping devices, and tactile paper. Table 8-4 provides resources for obtaining these materials.

What information can the classroom teacher contribute to the IEP team meeting that might prevent AT abandonment?

AT devices for students with visual impairments enhance instruction and provide the student with access to participation within the general education curriculum. The multidisciplinary team must be deliberate and specific in determining what AT would be the most helpful in accomplishing these goals. When products are chosen for any reason other than what is best for the student, they may suffer the fate of AT abandonment. The multidisciplinary team provides the foundation for successful student use of AT devices by collaborating to learn about and address each student's individual needs.

Assistive Technology Devices for Students with Hearing Impairments

As in teaching students with any impairment, teachers of students with hearing impairments must understand the individual needs of the student. For the student with a slight or mild hearing loss, very few accommodations may be needed. However, if a student like Josh has a moderate to profound loss, accommodations may be needed to help the student gain access to and benefit from classroom instruction. The teacher of the hearing impaired collaborates with other members of the multidisciplinary team regarding the instructional strategies and AT devices that the student may use successfully for learning.

To assist the student who has sensory needs, environmental accommodations may be necessary. These types of accommodations might include (a) seating placement of the student, (b) modifications to the classroom, and (c) accommodations and modifications for instruction and instructional materials (Heller et al., 1996). As we discussed in detail in Chapter 1, accommodations allow access while modifications alter the expectations of the student in content or level.

AT devices can be enhanced by accommodations and modifications, or they provide the adaptation, modification, or accommodation. For example, preferential seating allows the student with a hearing impairment to pair his AT device that amplifies or provides sounds with speech reading. If the student has an interpreter, the classroom must be arranged so that the student can see the teacher and interpreter at the same time. Modifications to the classroom may include improvement in the acoustics of the room, thus providing the student with less interference from background sounds and enabling the AT device to work more efficiently. Also, when a student uses an interpreter, the room must have sufficient light so the student can see the interpreter, which is especially important when a video or slides are shown with the lights turned off. Finally, the classroom teacher can use AT devices to make accommodations to instructional materials, such as allowing the use of note-taking devices so a peer can take notes for a student with a hearing impairment.

ASSISTIVE TECHNOLOGY FOR AMPLIFYING OR PROVIDING SOUND   For students who benefit from sound amplification, the hearing aid will most often be prescribed. According to the American Speech-Language-Hearing Association (2004a), children as young as 4 weeks of age can be fitted with amplification such as hearing aids and assistive technology.

There are many types of hearing aids. Josh wore in-the-ear models with green ear molds. The color is an opportunity for the hearing specialist to allow the student some choice in design and ownership of the hearing aid. Special hearing aids are also built to handle very specific types of hearing losses. For example, a bone-conduction hearing aid uses a headband and a bone vibrator for individuals who have no ear canal or outer ear. Hearing aids for use by individuals who have no hearing in one ear route sounds coming to one ear over to the other ear. Still other hearing aids can be worn behind the ear, worn on the body, or incorporated within eyeglasses (American Speech-Language-Hearing Association, 2004b).

Students like Josh wear hearing aids in both ears (binaural aids). A binaural aid is different from a bilateral aid because it is more technologically advanced. Unlike the bilateral aid, it allows for the two aids to work together to provide a much more natural mode of hearing. However, many children need a hearing aid for only one ear (monaural aid). The purpose of the hearing aid is to pick up sounds, magnify them, and then deliver the sounds to the middle ear. It is important for those who work with the student with a hearing impairment to know that sound is amplified but not always made clearer (Heward, 2009). However, hearing aids should be fitted on a child as early as possible so he or she will learn to use the device for awareness and communication. As part of the IEP, the student and all those who work with him or her should be trained in how to take care of the hearing aid and troubleshoot hearing aid problems. Tips for taking care of hearing aids can be found in Table 8-5.

From the resources found in Table 8-5, list tips for taking care of a hearing aid.

Hearing aids are effective only if the student can actually hear and understand spoken language. A student in a noisy classroom receives little or no benefit from the hearing aid. For this reason, group assistive listening devices increase the use of important sounds for learning while decreasing the less meaningful noises of the classroom. In most instances, the teacher wears a microphone for the transmitter and the student has a receiver that may be like a hearing aid or actually part of a hearing aid. These devices may include an FM system, an infrared system, an electromagnetic induction loop, or a sound field system. In all cases, the teacher should be trained in how to use the system chosen for the student's individual needs.

TABLE 8-5 Assistive Technology Resources for Hearing Impairment	
Amplifiers http://www.harriscomm.com	LightLink Infrared Neckloop Receiver.
Butte Publications http://www.buttepublications.com	A publisher of educational materials for students who have hearing impairments.
Captioned Media Program (CMP) http://www.cfv.org	CMP provides a free loan program of more than 4,000 open captioned media in the form of videos, CD-ROMs, and DVDs. Materials may be borrowed by and for anyone who has a hearing impairment.
Media Access Group at WGBH http://main.wgbh.org/wgbh/pages/mag/services/captioning/	Media Access Group, the Caption Center, provides captioning for films, home videos, music videos, DVDs, teleconferences, and CD-ROMs.

An FM system uses radio waves. It has a transmitter, a receiver, and a monitor. The infrared system uses infrared lights. It has a transmitter–emitter panel that is similar to the infrared diode on a remote-control device and emits a signal in a 360-degree conelike radius, much like the light of a flashlight. The electromagnetic induction loop uses an electromagnetic field of energy with a transmitter and receiver to receive sound from a T-coil that is implanted in a hearing aid or from a desktop receiver. The sound field uses an FM microphone to transmit the teacher's voice to speakers placed around the room that amplify speech 10 to 12 decibels; this particular device improves the signal-to-noise ratio (SNR). An SNR of at least +15 is necessary to achieve maximum benefit from an amplification device. Table 8-5 describes sources for more information about these devices.

A teacher may have in his or her class a student with a hearing loss who has had a **cochlear implant**. This is an electronic device designed to provide enhanced sound detection and the potential for greater speech understanding to children with severe or profound hearing loss who do not benefit from hearing aids (Niparko, 2001). The cochlear implant does not amplify sounds but bypasses the damaged portion of the ear and directly stimulates the auditory nerve. Parents; teachers; other service providers; and, when appropriate, the student must know how to care for the external components of the cochlear implant. These components include a microphone (to pick up the sound and transmit it to the speech processor), a speech processor (to select and code useful sounds), and a transmitter with a magnet (to send the code to the receiver). The transmitter is worn on top of the skin behind the ear. A cord connects the transmitter to the speech processor. The speech processor is worn in a pocket or clipped to a belt. Users may also choose systems in ear-level styles that look like behind-the-ear hearing aids.

Go to the Companion Website to see pictures of a cochlear implant.

ASSISTIVE TECHNOLOGY THAT REPLACES SOUND   A technology that is becoming more prominent and offers the student with a hearing impairment access to real-time presentations, such as a class lecture, is speech-to-text transcription or translation. This technology enables the student access to the general education curriculum while allowing the teacher to meet the communication demands of these students. Speech-to-text translation enables a trained captionist to type the teacher's instruction and student comments into a laptop computer using a shorthand code. The text is instantly reproduced on a screen or a student's personal laptop computer monitor. It is not a verbatim translation but keeps as close as possible to the original. For more information about how this technology can be implemented in a school setting, visit the National Technical Institute for the Deaf (NTID) website (see Table 8-5).

Most persons with hearing are aware of television captioning found on regular television programming. This is similar to watching a movie with subtitles. Students who would benefit from captioning must have a closed caption television set with a built-in closed caption decoder chip. This makes invisible captions visible on the screen. The captions contain both narration and sound effects in print. Analogue television sets made after 1993 were equipped with a feature so that the captioning can be placed anywhere on the screen. Digital television is equipped with captioning capability. However, once the United States made the change in 2009 from analogue television to digital television, problems with live captioning emerged. This is because most of the captioning is analogue and will not appear on the digital screen.

In the general education classroom, students are exposed to information through the use of media such as videos, CD-ROMs, and DVDs. Students with hearing impairments may benefit from having these captioned. The Captioned Media Program (CMP) provides access to communication and media through the use of captioned educational media and supportive materials. CMP also acts as a captioning information and training center. Teachers may borrow materials for students who need captioning. More information about CMP may be found in Table 8-5.

The Americans with Disabilities Act, described in Chapter 1, mandated that all states provide persons with hearing impairments access to telecommunication. For the student with a hearing impairment, this law provides independence and access to information, in addition to safety. Text telephones (TTs), originally called TTY (Teletype) or TDD (Telecomunications Device for the Deaf) systems, enable the person with a hearing impairment to communicate with persons with hearing on a conventional phone. The student must have a TTY and relay numbers to participate in telephone conversations. The user contacts the telecommunication relay service (TRS) and types in his or her message. The TRS relays this message to the person who is receiving the call. The person responds in voice, and the TRS types in the reply to the sender. In essence, the message goes from written form to voice via the TRS operator. For social and safety reasons, instruction in how to use the TRS should be included as part of a student's IEP.

Using your local phone directory, find the instructions and TRS for making a telephone call to a person who is deaf.

ASSISTIVE TECHNOLOGY FOR DAILY LIVING FOR HEARING IMPAIRMENT The student with severe to profound hearing impairment may need AT devices for help with daily living needs. These devices promote independence and self-determination. They reduce student dependency on others. For example, bells in the school that ring but also flash give the student warning of class changes and emergency signals. A vibrating alarm clock that can be placed under the pillow gives the student responsibility for starting her or his day. Doorbells can be designed to make a light flash when someone is at the door. Other such devices can be found in Table 8-5. The multidisciplinary team should collaborate to find AT devices that promote independence within the student's daily living environment.

Assistive Technology Devices for Students with Deaf–Blindness

Although many curriculum areas benefit students with deaf–blindness through the use of AT devices, other areas cannot be accessed without the ability to communicate. Improved communication can give the student independence, allow more participation in school, help develop friendships, and increase acceptance from family and peers (Engleman, Griffin, Griffin, & Maddox, 1999). AT devices that allow students to communicate with their caregivers, teachers, and peers may fall at different places on the AT continuum (see Chapter 1). Communication systems include any combination of objects, pictures, drawings, and symbols. The teacher can easily understand these systems because they are labeled in print or have voice output. Students who are deaf–blind may combine the use of a communication device with manual communication so that they may communicate with persons who do not sign (Heller et al., 1996). (See Chapter 7 for additional information about AT devices for communication.)

As mentioned previously, the age of onset and the degree of sensory loss determines what AT devices are appropriate for the student with deaf–blindness. Many of the AT devices useful for students with visual impairment and hearing impairment can be individualized for use by the student with deaf–blindness. As always, the multidisciplinary team's role is critical in determining the appropriateness of the device and the training that the student and caregivers must have to be able to use it.

ASSISTIVE TECHNOLOGY FOR STUDENT LEARNING

Students with sensory impairments who have no additional disabilities are held to the same academic standards as their peers without disabilities. To enable these students to access and succeed in the general education curriculum, they need the assistance of specially trained and qualified persons to design and deliver instruction. A collaborative effort is essential for the multidisciplinary team so that students who are visually impaired, hearing impaired, or deaf–blind have appropriate support and specially designed instruction for learning. This section highlights some ways that AT affects access to the general education curriculum and promotes student learning.

Age of Onset: Implications for Assistive Technology and Student Learning

In this chapter, the age of onset of a sensory impairment has been emphasized repeatedly as being critical in providing services to students with sensory impairments. Knowing if the student has a congenital or an adventitious sensory loss affects how the student will gain access to instruction. Age of onset raises

Because of her disability, Beth is eligible for related services. What related service might help her adjust to her visual impairment?

other issues, such as the procurement of AT devices and training and instruction for its use. The following examples illustrate that point:

> Beth received a head injury that resulted in vision loss when she was 13 years old. Before the accident she was a healthy, outgoing teen. Since the accident, she has experienced periods of depression and is receiving medical treatment and group therapy. However, when her multidisciplinary team met with her to discuss the use of a CCTV in the classroom to help her with reading, she refused to learn how to use the device. At that point, she was also refusing to use large-print materials at school but was spending several hours each night reading large-print materials to prepare for class. She is exhausted from these efforts. Her parents are still adjusting to the emotional issues of the accident and vision loss. They do not want her to "look" different at school.

> Ponte is an 8-year-old boy who is congenitally and prelingually deaf. He uses sign language to communicate. At age 5, he had an unsuccessful cochlear implant. At age 7, he asked his parents to allow him to have another implant because he wanted to talk. This implant was successful, and Ponte now uses his voice paired with manual signs. Ponte is improving his conversational language by engaging in real-time chats on the Internet with friends in cyberspace.

How might the classroom teacher find safe cyberfriends for Ponte?

> LaKeezia is an 11-year-old who is deaf–blind. She was born without eyes and with one ear missing. Although she has no visual memory to use in her learning, she is a braille reader and uses software calendar programs to help her stay organized. Her computer has refreshable braille, and she enjoys communicating with her friends and family using email with a screen reader. She is a cane user but hopes one day to have a guide dog. Her teachers use explicit and direct instruction to teach her to use new AT devices.

These three examples illustrate the issues that teachers and caregivers face in providing instruction and care to students with sensory impairments. Multidisciplinary team members must take many factors into account as they identify the student's learning styles and the teaching styles that will be used for learning. Determining the appropriate AT devices is a critical responsibility of the team. (Team roles and responsibilities are discussed in detail in Chapter 3.)

Assistive Technology for Learning for Students with Visual Impairments

Knowing whether a student with a visual impairment is a braille reader or a print reader is very important for the teacher. For students to become literate in braille, they need regular and systematic instruction from a trained specialist. The TVI is the person who should deliver this instruction. The multidisciplinary team must ensure that enough time is allotted for instruction in braille (Koenig & Holbrook, 2003). This should be part of the IEP. Many AT devices can assist the braille reader. For example, a student who needs to take notes from a lecture has several options, depending on the number of notes he or she has to take. The use of a tape recorder, a slate and stylus, a braille writer, an electronic note taker, or a desktop or laptop computer may serve the purpose of note taking for a braille reader (Ross & Robinson, 2003).

Historically, people with visual impairment are poorly represented in the mathematical, scientific, and technical fields in schools and in employment (Kapperman & Sticken, 2003b). *The Nemeth Code of Braille Mathematics and Science Notation* allows students with visual impairment to access mathematics. Students should always be presented with the most accurate braille. It is critical that the TVI work closely with the teachers of mathematics and science to provide the most accurate translation of printed mathematics terms, codes, and symbols into the braille code of mathematics. Table 8-1 provides information about computer-based tutorials for sighted teachers to learn the Nemeth Code.

Tactile models, maps, and other graphics for content areas such as health education, social studies, math, and science should be provided for the student with visual impairment who is a braille reader. Maps and graphs can be reproduced for the braille reader by utilizing a tactile graphic kit. Braille labels can be attached to the graphics by using a braille label maker or printing them using a braille translator program.

Tactile models for the human anatomy are available for students with a visual impairment. If typically developing students have the opportunity to view models for learning the human anatomy, the student who is blind should have the opportunity to explore it through the use of tactile models. This may need to be done outside the general education classroom so that the student will not be embarrassed and will have the opportunity to ask questions (Farrenkopf & McGregor, 2003). See Table 8-4 for sources for tactile graphics.

Science and social studies present an ongoing challenge for the teacher who teaches a student with a visual impairment, primarily because of the large number of illustrations, diagrams, graphs, timelines, and other visual information that is crucial in understanding concepts. Students who use their vision for learning may need AT devices, such as CCTV, to enlarge the materials. Others who rely on other senses for learning may benefit from three-dimensional models, tactile graphics, and adapted tools.

Science activities can be adapted for use by students with visual impairments and physical disabilities. Table 8-4 contains science resources. These materials and activities may also be used for students without disabilities. The *Science Activities for the Visually Impaired/Science Enrichment for Learners with Physical Handicaps* (SAVI/SELPH) materials can be ordered from the Lawrence Hall of Science (see Table 8-4). The materials include nine teaching units, and the modules may be purchased separately or as a group. If the student with a visual impairment is included in a science class where it is not feasible to use the program, the tools can be ordered separately to allow participation within the inclusive environment.

Assistive Technology for Learning for Students with Hearing Impairments

One of the most important considerations for learning for students with hearing impairments is how the student communicates. Just as students with a hearing impairment represent a heterogeneous group, the individual communication needs vary greatly. Easterbrook & Baker (2001) suggested that, in the inclusive school environment, many multidisciplinary teams fail to address the issue of communication in a comprehensive manner. Yet the communication needs of the student determine how successful the student will be in learning. The multidisciplinary team should ask and explore areas that provide the most information about the communication needs of the student. These areas should include (a) the student's preferred learning style, (b) where and how the student will receive instruction, (c) access to language models, and (d) the provision of AT services and the use of AT devices (Easterbrook & Baker

As the team members address communication needs, they must take an indepth look at how any AT service or device will aid the student with hearing impairments. The team must evaluate the use of current and future AT considerations by asking questions such as the following:

1. How does the AT device contribute and promote student learning?
2. How does the AT device enable the student to respond in meaningful ways to learning?
3. What AT devices will the parents or caregivers support?
4. What kind of training might students, parents, and teachers need to use the AT device?
5. How and when will the student's use of the AT device for learning be evaluated?

For students like Josh, who is learning in a school environment that has limited expertise in educating students with hearing impairments, questions like these may allow the IEP team to address AT learning needs related to communication in depth (Easterbrook & Baker, 2001).

Assistive Technology for Learning for Students with Deaf–Blindness

Students who are deaf–blind usually do not benefit from either a program for students who are blind or a program for students who are deaf. Much of the curriculum for students with deaf–blindness is designed to help the student develop communication skills and social skills. The curriculum should also include instruction in basic skills. This makes the educational program for students with deaf–blindness more like programs for students who have severe disabilities. Depending on the degree of blindness and deafness, the student may use some visual and auditory modalities for learning. However, the student will need direct instruction from the teacher to make use of these during instruction. Effective instruction for students with deaf–blindness must include tactile teaching strategies so that the sense of touch is incorporated in learning.

Depending on the age of onset, students with deaf–blindness may or may not have spoken language. Many students benefit from the use of augmentative and alternative communication (ACC). Sign language systems, communication boards, and electronic communication aids are effective for enabling students with deaf–blindness to access the general education curriculum. The student's IEP team should consider ways for the student to use AT and thus actively participate in learning activities with their peers without disabilities. (More about ACC can be found in Chapter 7.)

Assistive Technology and Art Activities for Students with Sensory Impairments

Students like Josh and Miranda are engaged students in inclusive classrooms. Art activities play an important role in the development of children in the general education classroom. Art is an important learning process for children. It allows them freedom to explore a variety of important developmental processes such as movement, sensation, and perception. Research indicates that students who participated in arts-integrated curricula gained more academically than those who did not have the opportunity to do so (Ingram & Riedel, 2003; Stronge, 2002). Even though some teachers may not think so, many students with sensory impairments can participate in art activities. Using AT, students who once may have been excluded from visual art activities now may enjoy the multiple benefits of experiencing nonstructured, nonjudgmental, and developmental aspects of art making. Josh and Miranda should have access to, as well as the opportunity to participate in, any art activities that their peers enjoy.

Miranda might use her CCTV to participate in a drawing lesson. A paint palette might be secured to her workstation to enable her to find the colors she needs for a painting project. It is the responsibility of the IEP team to address not only AT for academics but also how AT might facilitate participation in art activities.

Table 8-6 lists multiple sources for assistive technology for art activities. Assistive Technology Spotlight 8-1 highlights two national organizations that promote art activities for students with disabilities: the Helen Keller International Art Show for students with sensory impairments and the VSA Arts organization for persons with disabilities.

TABLE 8-6   Assistive Technology and Art Resources

Ability Hub http://www.abilityhub.com	AT simplifies the lives of artists with disabilities, but AT is not necessarily simple. This Web site offers an easy and organized way to find adaptive equipment, answers to questions about AT you might already have, and a host of resources for alternative solutions to using computers.
AbleNet, Inc. Art for Me, Too! http://www.ablenetinc.com	Every child loves to create art! Here's a great resource book to help support all students in art activities using assistive technology.
Alimed http://www.alimed.com	This site points predominantly to medical and generalized orthopedic and rehabilitative supplies, but many of these adaptive tools could be useful to an artist with a disability.
Extensions for Independence http://mouthstick.net/index.htm#Products	This Web site, designed by Arthur Heyer, who paints with a mouth stick, offers many adaptive tools for artists and all kinds of work situations. Mouth-stick paintbrush holders, motorized easels, turntable desks, and even used wheelchairs are all featured here. The site also has a community atmosphere to it, with links to related Web sites and personal articles.
Mobility Store http://www.mobilitystore.com	This Web site offers adaptive tools for every aspect of life, and many can be applied to art.

PARTIAL PARTICIPATION AND ASSISTIVE TECHNOLOGY   In the general education environment, it is inevitable that a student with a sensory impairment may not be able to participate fully in some learning activities. The more severe or extensive the sensory loss or losses (as in a dual sensory loss), the more the opportunities for full participation diminish. However, by employing the principle of partial participation, the teacher can provide increased opportunities for these students to participate in meaningful ways. The principle of partial participation, first described by Baumgart et al. (1982), implies that every student has a chance to participate in classroom learning activities to any extent possible. Students can engage in some parts of an activity with supports such as AT. For example, LaKeezia, mentioned previously, is deaf–blind. She uses a computer with refreshable braille to communicate. While LaKeezia may not be able to give an oral report in her social studies class, she may be able to use her computer with voice output to demonstrate what she knows about the topic.

When the classroom teacher plans for instruction, he or she should determine ways that the student with deaf–blindness can partially participate. This should be an integral and ongoing part of planning for daily instruction.

ASSISTIVE TECHNOLOGY SPOTLIGHT 8-1

Art and Students with Sensory Impairments

Art is an important component of a student's growth and development. AT allows students access and opportunity to participate in art activities like those sponsored by the following organizations.

The Helen Keller Art Show

The Helen Keller Art Show is a juried, statewide, and international exhibit of artwork by children and youth with sensory impairments. The philosophy of the exhibit is that all participating students are considered winners. Teachers are encouraged to incorporate visual arts into the individual educational plan of each student. The exhibit is shown throughout Alabama with selected international pieces traveling throughout the United States and displayed in various government buildings in Washington, DC. More information, including submission forms, may be found at the Helen Keller Art Show website: http://www.vsrc.uab.edu/deafblind/hk.html

VSA Arts

VSA Arts is an international nonprofit organization founded in 1974 by Ambassador Jean Kennedy Smith. VSA Arts strives to create a society where people with disabilities can learn through, participate in, and enjoy the arts. The VSA Arts website includes information on performing and visual arts. Go to http://www.vsarts.org

AT should be a large consideration in helping the teacher plan meaningful and age-appropriate activities that allow access and opportunities for learning for students with sensory impairments.

How can LaKeezia use AT to research a social studies project?

Chapter Review

- Visual impairment is considered a low-incidence disability. Congenital loss of vision occurs before or at birth. Adventitious loss of vision is usually the result of an accident or disease.
- The legal definition of blindness is based on loss of visual acuity and field of vision.
- Students with a hearing impairment are considered to have a low-incidence disability. Progressive hearing loss refers to a loss caused by a disease the mother passes to the child early in the prenatal stage of development. Prelingual deafness may result in children not developing speech and language.
- Hearing impairment is caused by a conductive hearing loss or a sensorineural hearing loss. A student may have either a unilateral or bilateral hearing loss. Students who are deaf–blind, sometimes referred to as having a dual-sensory impairment, usually have severe communication, developmental, and significant learning needs. Sometimes more specialized services are needed for these children.
- Students who are deaf–blind require specialized instructional strategies. These students must be considered for AT devices to promote access to the general education curriculum.
- Technology provides a wealth of aids for the student with a visual impairment: increased font size, different color font, enhancement of a computer operating system, specialized software to enhance a visual image, screen readers that produce sounds, transformation of print material into braille, braille translation software, and access to the Internet.
- Other AT devices that support a student with visual impairment include electronic note takers, electronic dictionaries, talking calculators, personal digital assistants for braille readers, portable book-reading devices, electronic travel aids, and compasses with tactile and braille displays and speech output.
- AT devices for students with hearing impairment can provide modifications and accommodations for the classroom. AT can be light tech, for example, changing the location of the student's seating and the modifications made for use with instructional materials.
- Some students with hearing impairment need sound amplification. Some need hearing aids. The selection of a hearing aid must be based on the individual needs of the student. Hearing aids are effective only if the student can actually hear and understand spoken language. An FM system that operates by radio waves and has a transmitter, receiver, and monitor can transmit a teacher's voice to speakers placed around a classroom. This can amplify speech 10 to 12 decibels. Some students have received cochlear implants in the last few years. Cochlear implants are electronic devices that provide enhanced sound detection and potential for much improved speech comprehension to children

with severe or profound hearing losses. A tactile aid is designed to provide information about sounds by having the student "feel the sound." Tactile aids are used to teach speech and improve receptive communication.

- Speech-to-text transcription or translation is becoming more popular for students who have a hearing impairment. This type of technology allows the trained captionist to type the teacher's instructions and student comments into a laptop computer using a shorthand code. The text is instantly reproduced on a screen or a student's personal laptop computer monitor.

- Students with hearing impairment can also use the television captioning found on regular television programming. The television set must have a built-in closed caption decoder chip for this to work. Students with hearing impairments can be exposed to the same type of information as their typically developing peers through videos, CD-ROMs, and DVDs.

- The environment must be changed to accommodate the student with hearing impairment both at home and in the classroom. Bells with flashers, alarm clocks that vibrate, and doorbells that make a light flash are useful accommodations.

- Students who are deaf–blind need improved communication to give them a sense of independence with all individuals and to provide access to the general education curriculum. These AT communication devices can be in the form of pictures, symbols, objects, or drawings. They can be tactile, electronic, or nonelectronic.

- Knowing the age of onset of the sensory impairment of a student is critical for planning services. The type of sensory impairment, which could be congenital or adventitious, affects how the student gains access to the general education curriculum.

- Students with a visual impairment may need a braille or print reader. Some children need systematic instruction from a trained specialist. A tape recorder, slate and stylus, braille writer, electronic note taker, or desktop or laptop computer can assist students with a visual impairment in the classroom. Tactile models, maps, and other graphics for content areas can provide assistance for the student with a visual impairment who is a braille reader. The use of CCTV to enlarge materials helps students in the areas of science and social studies.

- For students with a hearing impairment, AT must be fully addressed as it relates to communication. The multidisciplinary team should consider the student's preferred learning style, where and how the student receives instruction, access to language models and AT services, and the use of AT devices.

References

American Council for the Blind (2005). *Braille: History and use of braille*. Retrieved May 8, 2006, from http://www.acb.org/resources/braille.html

American Speech-Language-Hearing Association. (2004a). *Children and hearing aids*. Retrieved July 9, 2004, from http://www.asha.org/public/hearing/treatment/child_aids.htm

American Speech-Language-Hearing Association. (2004b). *Hearing aids*. Retrieved July 9, 2004, from http://www.asha.org/public/hearing/treatment/hearing_aids

Baumgart, D., Brown, L., Pumpian, I., Nisbet, J., Ford, A., Sweet, M., et al. (1982). Principle of partial participation and individualized adaptations in educational programs for severely handicapped students. *Journal of the Association for Persons with Severe Handicaps, 7*, 17–27.

Easterbrook, S. R., & Baker, S. K. (2001). Considering the communication needs of students who are deaf or hard of hearing. *Teaching Exceptional Children 33*(3), 70–76.

Engleman, M. D., Griffin, H. C., Griffin, L. W., & Maddox, J. I. (1999). A teacher's guide to communicating with students with deaf–blindness. *Teaching Exceptional Children, 31*(5), 64–70.

Farrenkopf, C., & McGregor, D. (2003). Physical education and health. In M. C. Holbrook & A. J. Koenig (Eds.), *Foundations of education: Vol. 2. Instructional strategies for teaching children and youths with visual impairments.* New York: American Foundation for the Blind.

Heller, K. W., Alberto, P. A., Forney, P. E., & Schwartzman, M. N. (1996). *Understanding physical, sensory, and health impairments: Characteristics and educational implications.* Pacific Grove, CA: Brooks/Cole.

Heward, W. L. (2009). *Exceptional children: An introduction to special education* (9th ed.). Upper Saddle River, NJ: Merrill/Pearson Education.

Huebner, K. M. (2003). Visual impairment. In M. C. Holbrook & A. J. Koenig (Eds.). *Foundations of education: Vol. 1. History and theory of teaching children and youths with visual impairments.* New York: American Foundation for the Blind.

Ingram, D., & Riedel, E. (2003). *Arts for academic achievement: What does arts integration do for students?* Minneapolis, MN: University of Minnesota, Center for Applied Research and Educational Improvement.

Kapperman, G., & Sticken, J. (2003a). Assistive technology. In M. C. Holbrook & A. J. Koenig (Eds.), *Foundations of education: Vol. 2. Instructional strategies for teaching children and youths with visual impairments.* New York: American Foundation for the Blind.

Kapperman, G., & Sticken, J. (2003b). A case for increased training in the Nemeth Code of Braille mathematics for teachers of students who are visually impaired. *Journal of Visual Impairment, 97*(2), 110–113.

Koenig, A. J., & Holbrook, M. C. (2003). Professional practice. In M. C. Holbrook & A. J. Koenig (Eds.), *Foundations of education: Vol. 2. Instructional strategies for teaching children and youths with visual impairments.* New York: American Foundation for the Blind.

Niparko, J. K. (2001). *Kids and cochlear implants: Getting connected.* Retrieved June 29, 2004, from http://www.agbell.org

Ross, D. B., & Robinson, M. C. (2003). Social studies and science. In M. C. Holbrook & A. J. Koenig (Eds.), *Foundations of education: Vol. 1. Instructional strategies for teaching children and youths with visual impairments.* New York: American Foundation for the Blind.

Stronge, J. H. (2002). *Qualities of effective teachers.* Alexandria, VA: Association for Supervision and Curriculum Development.

Topor, I. L., Holbrook, M. C., & Koenig, A. J. (2003). Creating and nurturing effective educational teams. In M. C. Holbrook & A. J. Koenig (Eds.), *Foundations of education: Vol. 2. Instructional strategies for teaching children and youths with visual impairments.* New York: American Foundation for the Blind.

U.S. Department of Education. (2009). *Twenty-eighth annual report to Congress on the implementation of the Individuals with Disabilities Improvement Act.* Washington, DC: Author.

9

Assistive Technology for Transition to the Adult World

CHAPTER VIEW

CHAPTER FOCUS

1. Why should assistive technology be included in transition planning?
2. What is the role of assistive technology in postsecondary education?
3. How does the student with a disability use assistive technology in the workplace?
4. Describe how assistive technology can enhance interpersonal relationships.
5. How can assistive technology enable students to become independent adults in residential environments?
6. How is assistive technology included in the curriculum so students make successful transitions to adult environments?
7. How can secondary teachers prepare students for the transition to the adult world?

Assistive Technology Snapshot

MEET MARY MCCLAIN

Mary McClain is 18 years old and is currently in the 11th grade at Warner High School. She lives at home with her mother, Patricia McClain, a nurse at a local hospital, and her father, Henry McClain, a mechanic at a local automobile service station. She has two younger siblings, Ruben, age 15, and Emily, age 10.

Mary has been receiving special education services in a resource room for students with mild disabilities since she was in the second grade. She was initially determined eligible for services based on a specific learning disability in reading. When Mary was 16 years old, she was involved in an automobile accident that left her with right **hemiplegia**, or paralysis on the right side of her body. Her gross motor skills, including walking, and fine motor skills in the area of writing were affected. In addition, she experiences some lingering articulation problems related to her speech.

Mary's individualized education program (IEP) team began the process of planning for her transition from school to the adult world when she was 14. At that time, Mary expressed an interest in pursuing a profession in the medical field, such as nursing. Since the accident, with the help of her family and school counselor, Mary has determined that nursing may not be an option, but she still expresses an interest in the medical field. The IEP team met to evaluate Mary's current IEP and transition plan. The team members included Mary, her parents, her special education teacher, her current high school English teacher, her math teacher, the school counselor, the transition specialist, her occupational and physical therapists, the local education agency representative, the assistive technology (AT) specialist, and the vocational rehabilitation counselor.

Prior to the meeting, Mary had been reevaluated. At the meeting, the assessment data were examined and considered in the planning of her transition. The team learned that Mary had passed three of the four parts of the state-required graduation examination. She would have three more opportunities to take the reading portion of the examination before graduation the next year. Her English teacher spoke optimistically about Mary passing the examination due to her motivation and the remedial services she would receive.

With the assistance of the AT specialist, Mary had prepared a short electronic portfolio presentation for other team members. The presentation showcased her accomplishments and interests without emphasizing her disabilities. She indicated that she was interested in attending the local postsecondary technical college to explore a two-year degree in the medical support field. She would like to learn more about programs offered by the college so she would be prepared to make choices about her career. Her parents expressed an interest in Mary living at home while she is in college, but they were willing to begin a discussion of independent living so she would be prepared when she left the college setting to pursue an independent life and career. Mary and her parents would like Mary to obtain a part-time summer job and perhaps work during her senior year. Mary indicated that she would like to participate in extracurricular activities but is having problems making friends and finding out what activities she would like. She stated that she likes music but is unable to participate in the school choir because of her speech problems.

Mary wanted to know more about special services she might receive in the college setting. In her high school content-area classes, Mary receives accommodations for her reading disability and also uses AT for written language. She was concerned about how all of that would work in a college setting. In her current high school setting, Mary's special education teacher makes all the contacts with Mary's teachers for accommodations and services. Mary stated that the prospect of having to do this is scary and that she is uncertain she can do it.

At the conclusion of the meeting, the team, with significant input from Mary, revised Mary's comprehensive transition plan. It included elements of self-advocacy, self-determination, career exploration, and visits to the local college and other agencies that would help support her in the postsecondary environment. In addition, the team suggested that Mary become involved in a service-learning project that might help her with decisions about a career in the medical field. With the assistance of the special education teacher and vocational rehabilitation counselor, Mary will identify a service-learning project and begin looking for a part-time job, perhaps something related to the medical field. Mary's mom believes she can help Mary get a part-time job at the hospital where she works. The team also included the goal for Mary to improve her computer skills for communication and information gathering. The AT specialist will work with Mary to determine what AT she will need for these skills.

ASSISTIVE TECHNOLOGY AND TRANSITION

Mary will soon be leaving the secondary school environment. Transition planning for students with disabilities is designed to prepare them to live and participate actively and successfully in their homes, communities, and workplaces. Without preparation, many students with disabilities experience poor postschool outcomes, such as unemployment, underemployment, low participation in postsecondary education, and general dissatisfaction with their adult lives (Conderman & Katsiyannis, 2002; Will, 1986). Transition services for students with disabilities focus on all domains of successful adult functioning. The three domains defined by Halpern (1985) have long served as a successful model for planning and integrating transition services for students with disabilities. These domains include promoting quality of life in (a) the residential environment, (b) employment, and (c) social and interpersonal networks. The needs of the student and the demands of the environment determine whether services that are needed by the student are generic in nature, time-limited, or ongoing special services.

Webquest
9.1

To read about transition and assistive technology, go to http://ici.umn .edu/products/ impact/192/ over16.html

Transition Defined

Students like Mary need intensive planning and specific instruction in how to use AT to support transition to and successful living in the adult world. Transition services are a coordinated set of activities for a child with a disability that:

A. is designed to be within a results-oriented process, that is focused on improving the academic and functional achievement of the child with a disability to facilitate the child's movement from school to post-school activities, including post-secondary education, vocational education, integrated employment (including supported employment), continuing and adult education, adult services, independent living, or community participation;

    B. is based on the individual student's needs, taking into account the child's strengths, preferences, and interests;

    C. includes instruction, related services, community experiences, the development of employment and other post-school adult living objectives, and, when appropriate, acquisition of daily living skills and functional vocational evaluation. (Individuals with Disabilities Education Improvement Act, 2004, Sec. 300[34])

Webquest 9.2

To see an example of how to plan for transition and assistive technology, go to http:// transitioncoalition .org/transition/ tcfiles/files/docs/ attransitionpacket12 24259340.pdf/ attransitionpacket .pdf

The Individuals with Disabilities Education Improvement Act (IDEIA) requires that IEPs include information on how the student's transition from school to the adult world will be supported. This IEP must be in effect when the child is 16 years old. However, transition efforts and the role of AT in supporting transition should begin much earlier. (See Table 9-1 for the AT transition planning timeline.) Early planning allows the student and the other IEP team members to address all the issues and concerns related to AT and transition to the adult environment.

Barriers to Transition

Failure to plan for AT use in the adult environment creates barriers and issues that prevent the much needed use of AT in the successful transition to adulthood. These barriers and issues include (a) lack of early transition planning in

TABLE 9-1 Assistive Technology Transition Planning Timeline

Student Age	Action Needed
Before age 14	• The student's IEP should include goals for the use of AT in the school, home, and community.
By age 14	• Include in the transition process the role that AT will play in transition and exit options.
	• Begin self-advocacy training for AT services and devices.
No later than age 16	• Identify ways that AT can provide access and support in career exploration, job sampling, and some job training.
	• Begin to identify how AT will be used in job training and placement.
	• Explore funding sources for AT needed by the student in employment, postsecondary education, residential living, and/or leisure activities.
Ages 16–18	• Contact adult services programs; assess the student's needs and demands of the adult environments to determine how AT can be used for access and support.
	• Begin AT training in the proper use of AT devices to maximize success in postschool environments.
Ages 18–21*	• Continue to review transition plans and update AT devices to meet the demands of the adult environment.
	• Develop a long-term financial support plan that includes the renewal, refurbishment, or updating of AT.

*Some students may remain in school until age 21.

Which individual will guide the student in learning to use the AT device during the transition phase of his or her school career?

Has an assessment been conducted in the selected workplace to determine the appropriate AT device?

the secondary program, (b) lack of adequate training for the student and other professionals, (c) lack of follow-up once the student has AT equipment, (d) AT abandonment, (e) the inability to find funding sources, and (f) resolving eligibility issues for accommodations in the workplace and postsecondary settings (Houchins, 2001; Mull & Sitlington, 2003).

According to the IDEIA, the student must have a transition plan in place by age 16. Best practice and common sense demand that the transition process begin much earlier. For Mary and others like her, AT is vital to academic and career success. Thus, the IEP should include opportunities to teach how AT is used in environments other than the school environment. A comprehensive and well-written plan ensures that the student and the parents/caregivers are aware of opportunities in employment, postsecondary, residential, social, and interpersonal areas. Timelines and procedures help make the transition a smooth one. AT can play a large part in ensuring that the student has access to full participation in these environments.

**Webquest
9.3**

To see an example of a guide for assistive technology and transition, go to http://www.ednet.ns.ca/pdfdocs/studentsvcs/assistive_technology.pdf

ASSISTIVE TECHNOLOGY AND TRANSITION TO POSTSECONDARY EDUCATION

For many high school students, the future includes college. Postsecondary education improves the chances for meaningful employment, increased vocational options, and greater lifetime earnings (Heward, 2003). Many young adults with disabilities are ill prepared to meet the significant demands of accessing postsecondary education. These challenges include academics, self-advocacy, social networks, and daily functional skills (Babbitt & White, 2002). Assessing a student's readiness is one way of assisting the student in making an effective transition. Assessment tools enable the IEP team to gain a perspective on the student's readiness skills and assist in addressing needs. Babbitt and White developed such a tool in the form of a questionnaire that promotes awareness of the use of AT for access to learning in the postsecondary setting. This information can provide the direction for instruction related to transition.

Preparing for the Postsecondary Environment

The National Center for the Study of Postsecondary Education Supports (2002a) suggested several areas that should be addressed to prepare students with disabilities for the postsecondary environment while the student is in secondary education. First, the student must have opportunities during secondary education to understand themselves and their disability in relation to needed services and supports. AT services and devices are among such supports and services for many students with disabilities. Attention should focus on advocating for these services and devices in the postsecondary setting.

Second, secondary programs must develop models of assistance that are individualized to meet the needs of the student with a disability in the postsecondary setting (National Center for the Study of Postsecondary Education Supports, 2000a). These models should be personally responsive, flexible, and integrated with the overall real-life support needs of the student. The student should be aware that some AT will be time-limited and some will be ongoing services across the time the student is in the postsecondary setting. An example of a time-limited AT service would be AT for an English composition course (for example, word-prediction software) but not for a wellness course. An ongoing service across all courses might be the use of a personal digital assistant for organization. A generic service would be the use of a computer lab for Internet access or word processing. AT is highly individualized and the preceding are examples of postsecondary environments in which the student will use AT. The transition process is outcome-oriented, so it is important to relate it to functional goals for the student.

Perhaps one of the most difficult challenges for the parent and student in transition is that the student and the IEP team must coordinate and manage post-secondary education supports and services provided by an outside agency (National Center for the Study of Postsecondary Education Supports, 2000b). It is important to note that, during the high school years, the student's rights are pro-tected and regulated under IDEIA. However, after graduation and entrance into the postsecondary adult world, the student's rights are protected and regulated under other legal mandates (see Chapter 1). During the transition process, it is the responsibility of the student's IEP team to determine which agencies can pro-vide the appropriate resources, funding, and accommodations that the student will need. The AT needs of the student should be a topic of discussion and prior-ity with any agencies. The roles and responsibilities in obtaining, training, and evaluating the AT should be determined long before the student enters the post-secondary setting (Johnson, Stodden, Emanuel, Luecking, & Mack, 2002).

One area of concern that is most often represented at the IEP meeting for tran-sition services is vocational rehabilitation (VR). Mandated by federal law and con-sidered a related service, VR has the primary goal of integrated competitive employment for persons with disabilities. The services provided by VR can include postsecondary education supports for students with disabilities in higher educa-tion. IEP team members (and yes, you may be such a team member) must consider how they can assist the student in coordinating and managing supports and services and recognizing the importance of technology for access and success. It is helpful to note that many agencies provide services in a format very different from services delivered under IDEIA. The team members should educate themselves about these differences so that provision of services can truly be a collaborative effort.

The IEP team has the responsibility of ensuring that the resources, accommo-dations, modifications, services, and supports required in the postsecondary education programs transfer from the secondary education setting to the postsec-ondary education environment and then eventually to employment (National Center for the Study of Postsecondary Education Supports, 2000a). Sitlington (2003) suggested that training in the secondary setting is essential to ensuring the proper use of AT in the postsecondary environment. Training opportunities maximize educational gains and decrease the high level of abandonment. A word of caution: Professionals should carefully consider the impact of removing a stu-dent from eligibility at the secondary level. Removal of eligibility at the secondary level may make the student ineligible to receive reasonable accommodations that include AT devices and services at the postsecondary institution (Sitlington, 2003).

SELF-ADVOCACY   Students should be trained in self-advocacy skills. The student must begin to advocate for his or her needs in the postsecondary setting, and it is important for the student to learn how to self-advocate. At this point in the student's college career, parents have no standing, and the institution is required only to react to the student's specific requests for needs (Field, Sarver, & Shaw, 2003). The student also must self-identify and provide documentation of the need for accommodations for a disability. College requires more self-advocacy than high school. When students make requests of the postsecondary institution for AT, they should be aware that AT may be expensive. If the institution is funding the AT, it will require significant documentation that the student actually will benefit from its use. Preparation should begin at the secondary level so that students use the AT devices they need to be successful. (Activities to promote self-advocacy can be found later in this chapter, in the section titled Assistive Technology for Student Learning.)

ASSISTIVE TECHNOLOGY AND TRANSITION TO EMPLOYMENT

Preliminary data from the *National Longitudinal Transition Study—2* indicated that transition programs for students ages 15 to 19 are making a positive difference in the areas of (a) secondary education completion, (b) living arrangements and social involvement, (c) education after graduation, (d) employment rates and job characteristics, and (e) overall engagement in the community (Wagner, Newman, Cameto, & Levine, 2005). Differences include the following: (a) The school completion rate for students with disabilities increased by 17% between 1985 and 2003, (b) the rate of postsecondary enrollment doubled in the same period of time, and (c) the number of students who left school and worked for pay increased from 55% in 1987 to 70% in 2003 (Wagner, Newman, Cameto, & Levine). Looking at these statistics, one can understand the importance of a good, strong transition plan that meets the individual needs of students with disabilities.

As students with disabilities begin the process of making decisions about adult life, employment is an important part of the discussion. The ability to be successfully employed offers a person a sense of pride and satisfaction with life, as well as the opportunity to be independent. Not only do we gain financially from work, but the workplace offers additional incentives. For example, many social relationships are formed and nurtured in the workplace. Transition for the student with a disability should include components of employment—whether during the secondary years, while enrolled in a postsecondary program, or after secondary or postsecondary education. Family-centered planning enables family members to develop and use strategies so that all are true partners in the transition process.

When planning for transition in the area of employment, students and family members must be made aware of the real-life skills that are important for 21st-century employment. The Secretary's Commission on Achieving Necessary Skills (SCANS) (2005) was established to advise the secretary of labor on the skills necessary for employment; the commission identified five competency skill areas that employers feel are necessary. These five competency skill areas are in addition to the basic skills, thinking skills, and personal qualities identified for individuals to be successful on any job. The five competency areas are listed in Figure 9-1.

Resources	Interpersonal	Information	Systems	Technology
Time	Participates as a member of a team	Acquires and evaluates information	Understands systems	Selects technology
Money	Serves clients/customers	Organizes and maintains information	Monitors and corrects performance	Applies technology to the task
Material and facilities	Exercises leadership	Interprets and communicates information	Improves and designs systems	Maintains and troubleshoots equipment
Human resources	Teaches others			
	Negotiates	Uses computers to process information		
	Works with diversity			

FIGURE 9-1 SCANS Competencies

Decisions related to transition made by the IEP team must take into account the individual needs of the family and the student, the existing strengths of the family, and the student's preferences and interests. The SCANS competencies must be part of the student's curriculum if they are to become real-life skills. For Mary, for example, the IEP team should gather as much information as possible about her and her interests, with consideration being given to the SCANS competencies. This and other assessment data enable the team to make decisions that plan transition for integrated employment.

Establishing networks of relationships for employment purposes is one way to help secure job experience for secondary students. Family relationships and networks can be great resources for providing employment experience and opportunities. Using family-centered strategies empowers the family to participate actively in the transition process. IEP team members can use other natural supports such as community resource agencies to help the student find work experience.

As the team helps the student explore possible career paths, the student and family should be made aware of all the employment options. After decisions are made about what employment option the student will pursue, the team looks at what supports and services the student will need to prepare for, secure, and keep employment. For many students with disabilities who depend on AT for success in the academic world of secondary education, AT may be a major consideration in the workplace. Certainly it is an important issue for the IEP team to address.

Consider the AT continuum. Have all technology options, including light- to high-tech options, been considered?

Guidelines for Transition to Employment

When consideration is given to AT for transition to employment, several issues should be addressed by the IEP team. Figure 9-2 provides a short list of AT guidelines for transition. Attention to guidelines such as these prevents wasted time during transition for students who require the use of an AT device for success.

Is the AT device user-friendly for the student in the workplace environment, as well as in other environments?

- Which individual will guide the student in learning to utilize the AT device during the transition phase of his or her school career?
- Has an assessment been conducted in the selected workplace to determine the appropriate AT device?
- Consider the AT Continuum. Have all technology options been considered, including light- to high-tech options?
- Is the AT device user-friendly to the student and the workplace environment, as well as to other environments?
- Can the student utilize the technology on a trial basis within the workplace to determine its effectiveness?
- What person(s) will maintain the AT device?
- What funding options are available to lease or to purchase the AT?

FIGURE 9-2   Assistive Technology Guidelines for Transition

Many professionals have a tendency to disregard the employment needs of students with severe disabilities. When these students leave school, Section 504 of the Rehabilitation Act of 1973 provides continuing protection of their rights to gainful employment (see Chapter 1). Supported employment is an area that can be considered in the transition process. Supported employment is a means by which individuals with severe disabilities can be provided with intensive services and supports and extended time to perform their work responsibilities. Intensive services could include a job coach who works directly with students to teach them specific tasks. Intensive supports could include an adapted computer keyboard (keyboard on the monitor or a keyboard used with only one hand), a computer monitor (a large monitor for a visually impaired person), or an adapted workstation (such as a raised desk or table). Individuals with severe disabilities have unique learning styles that may require AT devices and supports as mentioned to access and to succeed in the workplace.

Secondary educators who work with students with severe disabilities must provide effective and thorough employment-training programs (Smith & Stuart, 2002). Students with severe disabilities require supports such as AT to ensure success in employment settings. As stated previously, the engagement of the student with a disability in the workplace increases the person's independence. Consequently, the student with severe disabilities is not primarily dependent for long-term benefits on **Supplemental Security Income (SSI)**, a federal income supplement funded by general tax revenues. It is designed for persons with disabilities and provides money to meet the basic needs for food, clothing, and shelter.

As noted, the secondary student must develop and improve skills of self-determination and self-advocacy for the postsecondary education environment. These skills will be needed to access the workplace accommodations he or she will need. Under the Americans with Disabilities Act (ADA) (see Chapter 1), it is the right of the individual to choose when or even whether to disclose his or her disability or any information related to the disability. It is important for the individual to recognize when it is appropriate to self-identify and ask for reasonable accommodations.

Reasonable accommodations vary according to the needs of the individual. They may range from simple to complex, light tech to high tech, inexpensive to expensive. AT may be a reasonable accommodation to request so that the person can be successful in his or her job (Wonacott, 2003). Exploring the student's prospective career and assessing what AT might be needed in the particular workplace is one way to empower the student so that he or she will disclose that AT is needed in the workplace. Opportunities to use the AT in a workplace setting are also essential in facilitating the successful use of AT in future work environments.

Can the student use the technology on a trial basis within the workplace to determine its effectiveness?

Students with disabilities engaging in transition activities should learn how to use the Internet to search for employment and for communication. Many students will need AT devices to access the Internet. The federal government has many websites that provide employment information for persons with disabilities (see Table 9-2). Families and school personnel will find these websites valuable sources of information.

What person(s) will maintain the AT device?

ADULT AGENCIES   As families and school personnel engage in the transition process for employment, they will find many opportunities to collaborate with adult service agencies. Again, VR will be an important contact in reaching the goal of integrated competitive employment for persons with disabilities (Wonacott, 2003). Use of AT has long been a priority of VR. Since the passage of the Technology-Related Assistance for Individuals with Disabilities Act (1988), all 50 states receive grants to develop and coordinate AT services for the ultimate purpose of career development culminating in employment (Butler, Crudden, Sansing, & LeJeune, 2002). (Table 9-2 displays resources for finding AT services for adults.) VR can be a source for lending AT for trials and for seeking funds for purchasing AT outright. The IEP team should become familiar with resources within the community. The identification of resources and supports within a community are an essential part of the transition plan for students with disabilities.

What funding options are available for leasing or purchasing the AT?

ASSISTIVE TECHNOLOGY AND INTERPERSONAL NETWORKS

Quality of life for successful adults includes social competence, as well as making and maintaining healthy interpersonal relationships. Having adequate social skills allows individuals to respond and adapt to the expectations of society. These skills begin developing at birth and continue throughout the life span. Students with disabilities often have difficulties with the skills that lead to social competence and positive relationships (Vaughn, Bos, & Schumm, 2003). At the secondary level, the IEP team should plan instruction and experiences that allow the student to develop occupational social skills. Statistics have indicated that deficits in occupational social skills are responsible for almost 90% of job loss (Elksnin & Elksnin, 2001). When the IEP team meets to plan for transition, this area of social and interpersonal networks must be addressed and assessed, and the team should include the student's social, interpersonal problem solving, and leisure skills.

TABLE 9-2 Resources for Transition	
Vocational & Educational Services for Individuals with Disabilities http://www.workforcenewyork.org/ulster/vesidjob.htm	Assists individuals with disabilities to find a place in the workforce.
Office of Special Education Programs http://www.ed.gov/about/offices/list/osers/osep/index.html?src=mr	Provides an overview of laws and services related to special education programs.
Vocational Evaluation & Career Assessment Professionals http://www.vecap.org	Promotes the professions and services of vocational evaluation and work adjustment.
Job Accommodation Network http://janweb.icdi.wvu.edu	Consulting service designed to increase employability for people with disabilities.
Center for Assistive Technology http://cat.buffalo.edu	Conducts research to increase knowledge about AT devices for persons with a functional impairment.
National Institute on Postsecondary Education, Libraries and Lifelong Learning (PBLLI) http://www.ed.gov/offices/OER/PLLI	Supports research to help improve libraries, postsecondary education, literacy, and lifelong learning.
Alliance for Technology Access http://www.ataccess.org	Network of community-based resource centers, developers, vendors, and services for children and adults with disabilities.
National Transition Alliance for Youth with Disabilities http://www.dssc.org/nta	Academy of Educational Development established 1994 to design programs that meet the unique information, technical assistance, training, and research needs of professionals and programs that serve to improve the lives of infants, toddlers, children, youth, and adults with disabilities and their families.
Social Security http://www.socialsecurity.gov	The government website resource for Social Security.
Supplemental Security Income http://www.ssa.gov	A federal income supplement program for people with disabilities.
Internet Resources for Students in Transition http://cat.buffalo.edu/transition	This resource facilitates access to the Internet and to information related to planning transition. This site is specifically designed to enable students using computers with assistive technology to access search engines and online resources, including online dictionaries, books, and computer tutorials.
National Center on Secondary Education and Transition (NCSET) http://www.ncset.org	NCSET coordinates national resources, offers technical assistance, and disseminates information related to secondary education and transition for youth with disabilities in order to create opportunities for them to achieve successful futures.

Social Skills

The social skills required to keep a job are occupational social skills. For many students with disabilities, AT can assist in meeting the individual needs of the student in this area. For example, one skill a person may need to get a job is to telephone a potential employer to arrange a job interview. Students with hearing impairments must know how to use telecommunication devices to make telephone calls. This and other situations fall into the category of having adequate communication skills.

Communication is vital in developing relationships, improving social skills, and participating in leisure activities. Although communication is described in depth in Chapter 7, it is important to note its importance in this area. Students who cannot communicate effectively have problems with social skills and ultimately in forming and maintaining appropriate relationships. Students with communication difficulties should be taught to use AT to communicate not only with teachers and caregivers but also with their peers.

Interpersonal Problem Solving

Interpersonal skills are important in human interactions and activities and are at the heart of the labor market. Interpersonal skills enable a person to work, assume responsibility, collaborate with fellow workers, and solve problems in a cohesive manner. For students with disabilities, this area requires more time to develop and refine. It is important that such students begin to develop these skills early in the transition process and to learn and practice interpersonal problem-solving skills. This can be accomplished through course work, projects, simulations, and on-the-job training. The basic strategies for developing interpersonal problem-solving skills can be taught within the classroom and then generalized to real-life situations. During the transition process, teachers can provide students with opportunities related to interpersonal problem solving that will enhance their opportunities to be successful during their postsecondary years.

Leisure and Recreation

Another area that is often overlooked in academic settings is that of leisure and recreation. Quality of life is improved for individuals who have opportunities for meaningful leisure and recreational activities. Recreational activities provide a venue for social interaction and are intended to help students learn how to use leisure and recreation time in meaningful and constructive ways. These services may include assessment of leisure function, identification of therapeutic recreation services, exploration of recreation programs in schools and community, and development of leisure activities. Leisure activities, under related services, may also include artistic and cultural programs that the student may require if such programs allow the student to benefit from special education (Mattson, 2001).

AT can play an important role in leisure and recreation for students with disabilities. This depends on the needs of individual students, and the IEP team should look at ways that AT can provide access to recreation and leisure. The team should also determine how AT allows the student to become proficient in these skills.

In the case of Mary, the IEP team may consider what AT Mary will need to participate in one of the school music programs. Is there some way that AT will allow her access to the programs so that she can explore her interest in music? Working with Mary and other school personnel, such as the music teacher, the AT specialist can help determine how AT might allow Mary to do this.

ASSISTIVE TECHNOLOGY AND DAILY LIVING

Some students with disabilities need AT not only in the school and work environment but also on a daily basis. AT in all areas can improve the quality of life for the student. AT within the residential environment can be included in the student's transition plan if one of the goals is to live independently.

Such AT devices range on the AT continuum from light tech to high tech. Eating utensils with handles that are built up for an easy grip can result in the student being able to eat independently. This can be accomplished through wrapping the handle of the utensil with a piece of foam rubber and taping it in place. Velcro can be used to stabilize a dish, book, or writing tablet so it won't slip across a surface. A section of a drinking cup can be cut out to help the student sip from the cup.

For individuals with a visual impairment, tactile markings on various objects, such as measuring cups, thermostats, appliances, telephones, and clocks, can decrease some of the challenges faced in everyday living. Those with a hearing impairment might need an alarm clock that vibrates, a bulb that flashes when the doorbell or telephone rings, and closed captioned television. For those with more severe cognitive disabilities, visual representations of objects could be taped on various items throughout the environment to help with identification. Individuals can learn to point to specific pictures when they need or want something. Visual representation with pictures can be used across all environments and can be easily adapted for the specific environment. Many students in transition make use of visual representations of objects through pictures and communicate very well in this manner. This can be carried over into daily living in the transition plan.

Other light-tech AT that can be modified to increase independence in one's daily life includes large-print newspapers, computer software that magnifies objects and reading material, Dycem to stabilize various objects, a magnifying glass or mirror, lap trays, armrests, pillows for support, shower seats, bed rails, sliding board for transferring an individual, lever handles for opening and closing a door, lowered sinks and tables, and a phone holder that makes it easy to pick up the receiver. Mobility aids for individuals within the home could include wider doors for ease in manipulating a wheelchair and ramps to replace stairs. Many objects within the home can be adapted to meet the needs of the individual. During transition planning, daily living should be a consideration for the student; parents should work with other members of the IEP team to ensure that, if AT is needed within the home for the student, the equipment, accommodations, and modifications are purchased or made.

ASSISTIVE TECHNOLOGY FOR STUDENT LEARNING

Transition occurs throughout one's life span. It begins in the preschool years and continues throughout the student's school years. All students with disabilities are eligible for transition services at all levels. The only requirement is that they must meet the criteria as mandated in IDEIA. Regardless of the student's disability, AT must be considered as part of the IEP. AT is an important part of transition services for many students and should begin early in the student's education.

As we look at learning activities that promote successful transition, consider two questions: (a) What activities are needed to help the student make a successful transition? and (b) What AT devices and services will assist the student in accessing these activities? Transition was defined previously in this chapter, as were services that will aid the student in the transition process from high school to postsecondary school and future life activities. Transition activities can be considered vocational, postsecondary school employment, postsecondary education, living independently, and becoming an active member of the community. If AT is needed for the student to be successful in each of these areas, it must be addressed in the IEP. As part of the student's IEP, the goals and benchmarks that relate to the goals of the student are developed. As in the case of Mary, the goals are reviewed on an annual basis and are subject to further review if deemed appropriate by the IEP team. Because Mary is utilizing AT to improve her communication skills, it is important that the team monitor Mary's progress in this area by reviewing her IEP more frequently than on an annual basis. Mary is taking an active part in this process to be sure the goals match her interest in lifelong activities.

Assistive Technology and Transition in the Elementary School

Many transition activities in the elementary school years can begin to introduce students to various types of opportunities that are available to them and how AT can fit into the workplace. Transition in the elementary school years can be incorporated into the subject-area content. For example, in the health area, the teacher might introduce a unit on nutrition. This instruction could evolve into the various vocations related to nutrition that are available to students. A student with a visual impairment might develop an understanding of various software programs that are used within a hospital setting so a dietitian can better perform his or her job. Other activities that can be included in the curriculum are field trips to various area industries, career fairs, individuals who serve as mentors to students, and discussions of careers related to certain parts of the curriculum.

Certain parts of the elementary curriculum can include career exploration activities, for example, simulation activities within the classroom, guest speakers who can connect information with actual vocations, and visits to job sites for a day. To prepare students for certain vocations, teachers can begin introducing related courses or opportunities that are available as part of the secondary curriculum, thus encouraging students and parents to begin thinking very early about transition to postsecondary school activities.

Another area that teachers might begin looking at during the elementary years includes the various learning styles of students and how these might coincide with different vocations later in students' lives. Learning-style inventories determine the preferred mode of learning. These learning styles can be kinesthetic (hands on), visual, auditory, or a combination. The learning styles can be incorporated into various types of group activities that allow students to begin learning the process of collaboration and how everyone's contributions are important to the task, as well as learning to work with individuals from very diverse backgrounds. If a student is utilizing an AT device during elementary school, peers can gain an understanding of how the AT device works to enhance student participation in an activity. This type of school activity can be the beginning of a lifelong process for many students in understanding how all students can contribute to society.

Assistive Technology and Transition in the Middle School and Secondary School

As the student progresses to middle and secondary school, it is important that transition activities become a major part of the curriculum. Students should begin to understand where their interests lie and should begin thinking about lifelong goals. They should also begin to establish as much as possible an independent lifestyle for themselves. Self-determination and self-advocacy are important skills for students to become more independent and must be part of the middle and secondary schools curricula.

SELF-DETERMINATION   Self-determination involves students in helping to make critical decisions affecting their futures. If students are to become independent, they must have a big say in the direction they wish to take, rather than IEP team members or related service providers making decisions for them. Collaboration among team members is important, but the student should be the team member with the final say about all aspects of the transition plan. Self-determination must be incorporated into the IEP for the student to begin evaluating options for postsecondary activities.

Mary presented her accomplishments and interests to her IEP team members through a portfolio presentation, which in itself told them much about the knowledge she had of herself and her determination to be successful. For self-determination activities to be successful, services must be accessible, coordinated, and assessed, and students must be aware of their needs, must be advocates for themselves, and must set and work toward goals (Morgan, Ellerd, Gerity, & Blair, 2000).

Students should have enough information from documentation, assessments, interest inventories, parents, teachers, and AT specialists to determine if AT support is needed for success during the transition phase of their school career. Information must be readily available for all IEP team members so that the best decisions can be made to ensure the student's success.

SELF-ADVOCACY   Self-advocacy must also be an integral part of the student's transition plan. Teachers should begin providing students with opportunities to become their own advocate as early as the elementary years. Students must have knowledge of the laws that provide them with certain rights. As students begin to transition from middle school to high school and become advocates for themselves, teachers should make certain that an understanding of the IDEIA, Section 504 of the 1973 Rehabilitation Act, and the ADA are included in their curricula. Students who need AT should also have knowledge of the law that provides them with this option and an understanding of how to advocate and fund the AT needed for success in postsecondary, community, and work environments.

At the middle and secondary school levels, students should begin to take the initiative to have a major say in the development of their IEP. This may include a student (a) leading his or her own IEP meeting, (b) deciding on the courses in which to enroll, (c) meeting with the high school counselor to explore various postschool opportunities, and (d) informing each of his or her teachers about specific IEP-mandated modifications and accommodations that are required to meet certain course requirements. Students should begin participating in these ways during the middle school years, and some as early as the upper elementary school years. Students who use AT within the regular education classroom should be sure the regular education teacher has knowledge of the device. If a student needs an alternate keyboard or adapted mouse for computer use, the teacher should have a working knowledge of how the device works. If not, perhaps the student can train the teacher for its use in specific instances.

The manner in which a student learns to advocate for him- or herself within the school setting can be carried over into the postschool years, in either the vocational or higher education setting. This can be part of helping the student know and understand what AT is available to her or him and will help the student to be successful on the job or in school. Students must know and understand how to fill out a job or college entrance application, use appropriate interview skills, and make an employer or college professor aware of both the environmental and academic modifications needed to be a successful student.

O*NET is an interactive and accessible occupational database sponsored by the U.S. Department of Labor (see Table 9-3). Information about employment, occupations, and job skills can be found on it website. O*NET and similar websites provide sources of information that can be incorporated into the curriculum to help students make informed decisions about their futures. The use of such websites will also help determine which type of AT and other accommodations might be needed in specific job situations.

The school setting can serve as a pilot site for AT. As mentioned previously, a student can be provided many simulation activities within the general education curriculum that use AT and can be of value in making informed decisions. When students practice using AT in simulation-type settings, they can transfer these experiences to real-life settings to see if the AT is appropriate for a potential postschool activity. This type of activity should be a major part of the curriculum, beginning during middle school and continuing through high school. This type of simulation can result in less discouragement for the student in later years, as well as in the opportunity to explore other options if one does not prove to be successful.

After the IEP team has determined what vocation or area the student wants to pursue, it is important that the team consider the need for AT. Mary's IEP team decided it was important for her to improve her computer skills for communication and information gathering so she could transition successfully

TABLE 9-3 Tools for Transition	
Assistive Technology and Rehabilitation Equipment ABLEDATA http://www.abledata.com	ABLEDATA provides objective information about assistive technology products and rehabilitation equipment available from domestic and international sources. Although ABLEDATA does not sell any products, it can help you locate the companies that do.
Rehabilitation Engineering & Assistive Technology Society of North America (RESNA) http://www.resna.org	RESNA is an interdisciplinary association of people with a common interest in technology and disability. The purpose is to improve the potential of people with disabilities to achieve their goals through the use of technology.
The Alliance for Technology Access (ATA) http://www.ataccess.org	ATA is a network of community-based resource centers, developers, vendors, and associates dedicated to providing information and support services to children and adults with disabilities and to increasing their use of standard, assistive, and information technologies.
Information Resources DisabilityInformation http://www.disabilityinfo.gov	This website covers a variety of topics related to employment for people with disabilities: advice for individuals with disabilities seeking work; help for employers looking for hard-working and dedicated employees; information on employment rights, laws, and regulations; resources for employment programs; and job accommodations for people with disabilities.
National Rehabilitation Information Center (NARIC) http://naric.com	According to the homepage, NARIC is the gateway to an abundance of disability- and rehabilitation-oriented information organized in a variety of formats designed to make it easy for users to find and use.
Employment Services Job Accommodation Network (JAN) http://www.jan.wvu.edu	JAN is a free consulting service designed to increase the employability of people with disabilities by (a) providing individualized worksite accommodations solutions, (b) providing technical assistance regarding the ADA and other disability-related legislation, and (c) educating callers about self-employment options.
Occupational Information Network (O*NET) http://online.onetcenter.org	This website has an accessible database and search engine for finding occupations and skill information.
Just One Break, Inc. (JOB) http://www.justonebreak.com	The mission of JOB is to find competitive employment for people with disabilities through partnerships with companies in all industries.

(Continued)

TABLE 9-3 *(Continued)*

Note-taking Neo by AlphaSmart http://www.alphasmart.com	Neo is easy to use, lightweight, and affordable—designed to provide a wide range of computing capability on its own and to integrate effortlessly with desktop and laptop computers. Neo offers a full-size keyboard and extraordinary battery life but adds a 50% larger display and twice as much memory than prior models.
Organization Draft: Builder—Writing and graphic organizer software http://www.donjohnston.com	Draft: Builder breaks down the writing process into three distinct skills: planning and concept mapping, note taking and resource citing, and composing a first draft. Each view supports the student by providing considerate scaffolds appropriate for each task. In addition, a split-screen view remains constant, reflecting all of the work students have done and thus helping them to transfer information and build on ideas as they work through writing's recursive process.
Organization Inspirations http://www.inspirations.com	Organize class material using pictures, shapes, and colors. Can assist students as they create presentations for employment and postsecondary environments.
Recording for the Blind & Dyslexic http://www.rfbd.org	Recording for the Blind & Dyslexic, a nonprofit volunteer organization, is the nation's educational library serving people who cannot effectively read standard print because of visual impairment, dyslexia, or other physical disability.
Braille and Talking Books Library http://www.perkins.org	A service of Perkins School for the Blind. Users will find an online products catalog, large-print services, audio-described video services, and a reference library. *Newline* is, a free telephone-based service for listening to newspapers.
Rehabilitation Services Administration (RSA) http://www.ed.gov/about/offices/list/osers/rsa	RSA oversees formula and discretionary grant programs that help individuals with physical or mental disabilities to obtain employment and to live more independently through the provision of supports such as counseling, medical and psychological services, job training, and other individualized services. RSA's major Title I formula grant program provides funds to state vocational rehabilitation agencies to provide employment-related services for individuals with disabilities, giving priority to individuals who are significantly disabled.
Workforce Investment Act of 1998 http://www.afscme.org/pol-leg/wiahome.htm	One-stop career centers for workforce preparation and employment.

ASSISTIVE TECHNOLOGY SPOTLIGHT 9-1

Using Assistive Technology to Meet Transition Goals

Teaching the SCANS Competencies

SCANS Competency: The student will use a computer to process information.

Transition Goal: Jade will employ computers to acquire, organize, analyze, and communicate information.

Meet Jade: Jade is a 14-year-old student who is blind. She is a braille reader. Her desktop computer is equipped with a refreshable braille keyboard, a screen reader, and braille and print printers. Using this AT, Jade's computer teacher, in collaboration with her teacher of students with visual impairments (TVI), is teaching Jade to use a computer spreadsheet to develop a budget. In addition, her history teacher is teaching her to use online computer databases to research reports.

It's Your Turn: Using the example of Mary from the chapter-opening Assistive Technology Snapshot and information and websites found throughout this text, create examples of how AT can be used to meet this SCAN competency and transition goal selected by Mary's IEP team.

SCANS Competency: The student participates as a member of a team.

Transition Goal: Mary will work cooperatively with others and contribute to group ideas, suggestions, and effort.

It's Your Turn:

Your Examples: _____

_____

_____

Source: Information adapted from Kopple, C., Kane, M., Matheson, A. M., Packer, A., & White, T. (1993). SCANS in the schools. In the U.S. Department of Labor, Teaching the SCANS Competencies (p. 10). Retrieved August 11, 2005, from http://wdr.doleta.gov/SCANS/teaching/teaching.pdf

into the postsecondary environment. The plan to use the computer to enhance Mary's communication and information-gathering skills requires the use of AT for both skill areas. The AT must be provided by the school system for Mary to meet the annual goals of her IEP.

Chapter Review

• Transition services focus on all domains of successful adult functioning. Halpern (1985) defined three domains for planning and integrating transition services for students with disabilities: (a) residential environment, (b) employment, and (c) social and interpersonal networks.

- AT that will support transition should be part of the planning process in IEP development. Failure to plan for AT during transition planning can result in barriers and issues for the student in becoming a successful adult.
- Issues related to AT that create problems during the transition process include (a) lack of early transition planning in the secondary program, (b) lack of adequate training for the student and other professionals, (c) lack of follow-up once the student has the AT equipment, (d) AT abandonment, (e) inability to find funding sources, and (f) resolving eligibility issues for accommodations in the workplace and postsecondary settings.
- Challenges that young adults meet in accessing postsecondary education settings include academics, self-advocacy, social networks, and daily living skills. Assessing the student's readiness is one way of assisting the student in making an effective transition from high school to a postsecondary setting. Appropriate AT services and supports are available to students in the postsecondary setting. The development of models to meet the needs of students with a disability in a postsecondary setting is essential if the student is to be successful. The models must be personally responsive, flexible, and integrated with the overall real-life support needs of the student. Some AT services will be time-limited and some will be ongoing.
- Students who enter postsecondary education institutions are served under different laws than those that apply during their high school years. Students who enter postsecondary education settings are no longer served under the Individuals with Disabilities Education Improvement Act of 2004.
- An agency that assists with transition services for students with disabilities is Vocational Rehabilitation (VR). The primary goal of VR is integrated competitive employment and may also include postsecondary education supports. Training in the secondary setting is essential to ensure the proper use of AT in the postsecondary environment.
- Students must begin to advocate for themselves during the secondary education years. In the postsecondary education setting, students must self-advocate; their parents have no standing. The student must also self-advocate with the disability and provide documentation of the need for accommodations. If the student needs AT at the postsecondary level, he or she must provide significant documentation that he or she actually needs and will benefit from the use of AT. This is particularly true if the institution is paying for the device or service.
- Transition planning should include awareness activities for the student regarding the real-life skills that are important for 21st-century employment. SCANS, a group that advises the U.S. Department of Labor on skills necessary for employment, identified five competency skill areas that employers feel are necessary. These include resources, interpersonal skills, information, systems, and technology. Combined with assessment data, the SCANS competencies enable the IEP team to make decisions related to transition into employment.
- Considerations for AT during transitions should be addressed by the IEP team. Nine guidelines for transition include the following: Which individual

will guide the student in learning to use the AT device during transition? Has the assessment been conducted in the workplace to determine the appropriate AT device? Have all technology options, from light tech to high tech, been considered? Would light-tech AT devices meet the need for the student as well as high-tech devices would? Is the device user-friendly for the student in the workplace and all environments? Can the device be used on a trial basis? Who will maintain the AT device? What funding options are available? Has the workplace environment been assessed for functional mobility?

- AT must be a reasonable accommodation in the workplace so the employee with a disability can be successful. Exploration, assessment, and opportunity to use AT during the transition process are essential for successful use of AT in the work environment.
- AT can assist students with disabilities in the occupational social skills area. Students with varying abilities may need simple AT devices such as a telecommunications device to make telephone calls. Individuals who lack communication skills have problems with social skills and ultimately in forming and maintaining appropriate relationships.
- Recreational activities provide a venue for social interaction. Services related to accessing leisure and recreation activities include assessment of leisure functions, identification of therapeutic recreation services, exploration of recreation programs in schools and communities, and development of leisure activities. These may include artistic and cultural activities.
- Some students with disabilities may need AT for daily living skills. AT in the residential environment can also be included in the transition plan. Individual needs vary. Appropriate AT can range from the use of Velcro to stabilize a dish to tactile markings on everyday objects.
- Transition begins in the preschool years and continues throughout the student's education and into adulthood. The use of AT should begin early if it is needed. Transition can be thought of in two ways: (a) What is transition? (b) What are the activities related to transition that are important for the student?
- Transition in the elementary years may include incorporating various vocations within a subject content area.
- In the middle and secondary school years, transition activities become an integral part of the student's curriculum. During these years, students should begin thinking about their interests and lifelong goals.
- Self-advocacy involves the students in helping to make decisions regarding their futures. This encourages and fosters a level of independence. Self-advocacy must also be part of the transition plan. Teachers should begin providing students with opportunities to become their own advocates during the middle school and secondary school years. During all these phases of the student's education, it is important to determine if AT is needed for the student to be successful, to access the general education curriculum, and to be considered for specific job and/or postsecondary opportunities.

References

Babbitt, B. C., & White, C. M. (2002). "R U Ready?": Helping students assess their readiness for postsecondary education. *Teaching Exceptional Children, 35*(2), 62–66.

Butler, S. E., Crudden, A., Sansing, W. K., & LeJeune, B. J. (2002). Employment barriers: Access to assistive technology and research needs. *Journal of Visual Impairment & Blindness, 96*, 668.

Conderman, G., & Katsiyannis, G. (2002). Instructional issues and practices in secondary special education. *Remedial and Special Education, 23*, 169–179.

Elksnin, N., & Elksnin, L. K. (2001). Adolescents with disabilities: The need for occupational social skills training. *Exceptionality, 9*, 91–105.

Field, S., Sarver, M. D., & Shaw, S. F. (2003). Self-determination. *Remedial and Special Education, 24*, 339–350.

Halpern, A. S. (1985). Transition: A look at the foundations. *Exceptional Children, 51*, 479–486.

Heward, W. L. (2003). *Exceptional children: An introduction to special education* (7th ed.). Upper Saddle River, NJ: Merrill/Prentice Hall.

Houchins, D. (2001). Assistive technology barriers and facilitators during secondary and post-secondary transitions. *Career Development for Exceptional Individuals, 24*, 73–88.

Individuals with Disabilities Education Improvement Act. Pub. L. No. 108-446, 300 STAT.43.

Johnson, D. R., Stodden, R. A., Emanuel, E. J., Luecking, R., & Mack, M. (2002). Current challenges facing secondary education and transition services: What research tells us. *Exceptional Children, 68*, 519–531.

Mattson, B. (2001). *Related services.* (Report no. NICHCY-ND16). Washington, DC: National Information Center for Children and Youth with Disabilities, Academy of Educational Development. (ERIC Document Service ED459567)

Morgan, R. L., Ellerd, D. A., Gerity, B. P., & Blair, R. J. (2000). That's the job I want! *Teaching Exceptional Children, 32*, 44–49.

Mull, C. A., & Sitlington, P. L. (2003). The role of technology in the transition to postsecondary education of students with learning disabilities. *Journal of Special Education, 37*(1), 26–33.

National Center for the Study of Postsecondary Education Supports. (2000a). *Technical report: Postsecondary education and employment for students with disabilities: Focus group discussion on supports and barriers to lifelong learning.* Honolulu: University of Hawaii at Manoa.

National Center for the Study of Postsecondary Education Supports. (2000b). *Technical report: National survey of educational support provision to students with disabilities in postsecondary education settings.* Honolulu: University of Hawaii at Manoa.

Secretary's Commission on Achieving Necessary Skills, U.S. Department of Labor. (2005). *Teaching the SCANS Competencies.* Retrieved August 11, 2005, from http://wdr.doleta.gov/SCANS/teaching/teaching.pdf

Sitlington, P. L. (2003). Postsecondary education: The other transition. *Exceptionality, 11*(2), 103–114.

Smith, S. W., & Stuart, C. H. (2002). Transition planning for students with severe disabilities: Policy implications for the classroom. *Intervention in School & Clinic, 37*, 234–238.

Vaughn, S., Bos, C. S., & Schumm, J. S. (2003). *Teaching exceptional, diverse, and at-risk students in the general education classroom* (3rd ed.). Boston: Allyn & Bacon.

Wagner, M., Newman, L, Cameto, R., & Levine, P. (2005). *Changes over time in the early postschool outcomes of youth with disabilities: A report of findings from the National Longitudinal Transition Study (NTLS) and the National Longitudinal Transition Study—2 (NTLS2).* Menlo Park, CA: SRI. Retrieved August 11, 2005, from http://www.nlts2.org/pdfs/str6_completereport.pdf

Will, M. C. (1986). Educating children with learning problems: A shared responsibility. *Exceptional Children, 52*, 411–415.

Wonacott, M. E. (2003). *Employment for people with disabilities* (Report No. EDO-CE-03-247). New York: New York University, Institute for Education and Social Policy. (ERIC Document Reproduction Service No. ED478950)

10

Assistive Technology for Distance Learning

CHAPTER VIEW

- Assistive Technology Snapshot
- Distance Education
- Distance Teaching
- Assistive Technology for Student Learning
- Assistive Technology Spotlight 10-1
- Chapter Review

CHAPTER FOCUS

1. What is distance learning?
2. What types of distance learning may students with disabilities access for education?
3. What kinds of assistive technology might a student with a disability need to access distance learning?
4. How can distance learning be used to promote home–school communication?
5. What information does the course designer of distance learning need to make the distance-learning experience accessible for students with disabilities?
6. How might distance learning be used for social as well as educational networking?

Assistive Technology Snapshot
MEET JEREMY JOHANSEN

Jeremy Johansen is a 10th-grade student at Carver High School. Jeremy lives with his single father and older brother, Aaron. Jeremy's father, James Johansen, is a major in the United States Air Force. Because of Major Johansen's job, the family has moved many times. Jeremy is now in his second high school. Aaron is a senior at the same high school. When Jeremy was in the ninth grade, he took a dare and was riding a borrowed motorcycle without a helmet. Jeremy had a wreck and was diagnosed with traumatic brain injury, or an acquired brain injury, caused when his head struck the road. According to Jeremy's medical and educational records, he has experienced numerous complications and severe personality changes, sometimes becoming violent for no apparent reason. These complications, alongside some physical and health issues, have caused Jeremy to miss many days of school. As a consequence of his numerous absences from school, Jeremy struggles to be a successful learner and to stay engaged with his peers. When Jeremy is absent due to long episodes, the district provides a teacher who goes to his home or to the hospital.

Jeremy's special education teacher, Mr. Hanjab, has called an individualized education program (IEP) meeting to discuss the plan for providing services to Jeremy while he is undergoing treatment for his brain injuries as well as counseling for his extreme mood shifts. In addition to the regular members of Jeremy's IEP team, Mr. Hanjab has invited the assistive technology (AT) specialist and the distance education specialists to the meeting to suggest distance-learning technology. He hopes such technology will keep Jeremy in real-time contact with his classes and will help him access course work via his computer when he is feeling up to participating.

DISTANCE EDUCATION

Distance education is a viable learning alternative to traditional classrooms for all students. However, a student with disabilities who cannot meet the standard rigor of attending classes may need an alternative way to receive his or her education other than attending classes. Jeremy's IEP team must consider what types of AT will allow him the opportunity to continue his studies in possible alternative settings. These settings may include nontraditional educational settings such as the home, hospital, or nursing home, and educational goals in these settings may best be met via distance education.

As Jeremy's IEP team members make decisions about how distance education can help him be a successful learner, they also must understand the different components of providing this service for Jeremy. Moore and Kearsley (1996) define **distance education** as planned learning that typically occurs in a geographical location different from the source of the instruction. Distance education requires a well-defined and well-planned system of technology-based instructional delivery that includes a variety of effective pedagogical features that are feasible through the use of technology. Other important elements of distance education are (a) design for effective modes of communication between the facilitator and learner, (b) administrative and organizational considerations, and (c) issues of accessibility to both settings and instruction for students with disabilities.

Webquest

10.1

To see about types of online learning opportunities, go to http://distancelearn .about.com/

Components of Distance Education

Two components of distance education must be understood as the team plans services for Jeremy. The first is that of **distance teaching,** which consists of the pedagogical elements that the facilitator or instructor uses to deliver instruction to a place where he or she is not physically present. This element is viewed from the perspective of the facilitator (Belanger & Jordan, 2000). The other component, **distance learning,** is viewed from the perspective of the learner and is closely related to distance teaching. However, the successful distance learner must have full access to the technology that allows him or her to interact with the instructor and benefit from instruction. AT, as well as instructional accommodations, may be required so that students with disabilities gain access to the general education curriculum through distance education.

Distance education may be delivered in a variety of ways for students. The team may want to consider both real-time distance education and asynchronous distance education.

Jeremy's father wanted him to stay engaged with his peers and to continue learning. Real-time distance education for Jeremy might be the opportunity for him to participate from his home or from the hospital in class activities as they occur. He would be able to interact with his peers and with his facilitator and ask and answer questions. His participation would have the advantages of actual engagement with his class and authentic learning opportunities as his classmates are engaging. For example, every day from 12:30 p.m. until 2:15 p.m., Jeremy could go online using a webcam and participate in his science and social studies classes. Through emails or the class website, his facilitator could prepare him for instruction by sending him a class outline and notes. Jeremy could access the school website for the homework hotline. His facilitator could also plan learning activities that required Jeremy to participate with his peers.

Due to the serious nature of Jeremy's illness and the additional medical procedures he may require, at times Jeremy may not feel well enough to participate in class. In such cases, Jeremy might benefit from asynchronous distance education, which allows students like Jeremy to learn at their own pace and in their own time. Online learning modules can be designed to meet the school district's course of study standards for the particular grade level. Many times, a homebound teacher, who provides the instruction to the student in the student's home environment, may have a schedule that allows visits only at certain times of the day, but these may not be the optimal learning times for the student. Online courses allow Jeremy to access instruction at the times that are best for him. Students like Jeremy need instruction from a facilitator in how to use the modules. Jeremy's father and older brother may also need training so that they can assist Jeremy.

What other terms are used for the term *homebound teacher*?

Other asynchronous learning opportunities can enhance learning for the student who is geographically distant from the learning environment. School and classroom webpages, email, e-newsletters, and homework hotlines are resources that should be considered to support the student with a disability and to keep him or her engaged in learning. When these learning opportunities are available, the team must consider how the student will access them and if AT is needed for access.

Other students with and without disabilities may have the opportunity to participate in asynchronous distance learning for reasons other than illness. Such an example would be the student in the secondary setting who takes advantage of courses that are not available at his or her school but are available online or by teleconferencing in real time. Many secondary students participate this way in course work such as foreign languages, higher-level mathematics, and college preparatory classes.

Real-time distance education and asynchronous distance education, combined with the services of a homebound teacher who makes visits to the home or hospital, allow a student with a disability the best opportunity to be a successful learner. As mentioned throughout this book, the IEP team must consider whether the student will need AT to access the learning opportunity and, if AT is required, how the AT can best meet the student's individual educational needs.

DISTANCE TEACHING

Real-Time Teaching

As a team makes decisions about how a student may use distance education to access the general education curriculum, certain issues must be considered. In Jeremy's case, the team wants to provide an opportunity for him to have productive and successful interactions with his facilitator and peers. The team must consider what equipment will be needed; the training necessary for the facilitator, peers, family and student; and the types of AT that would allow the student access to this type of learning.

What kinds of AT devices will Jeremy need to participate in real-time teaching?

TELECONFERENCING   When most people think of distance learning in real time, teleconferencing comes to mind. For students with disabilities who are participating in course work originating in another site, such as a college or university, teleconferencing may be the primary mode of learning. The IEP team must consider what accommodations the student may need to participate. AT may also be needed. For example, a student with a hearing impairment may need a closed caption monitor to benefit from instruction. (Closed caption media is discussed in Chapter 7.)

For Jeremy, it would be unnecessary to provide the learning opportunity through teleconferencing. Although the school may have the equipment (satellite or webcam) to do so, it would be improbable that the school would provide a similar setup at the student's home or in a hospital setting. Let's explore what kind of equipment Jeremy needs to have access to his classroom and for his peers and facilitators to have access to him.

EQUIPMENT   There is a relatively efficient way of providing this learning experience. Both the school and the student at home or in a hospital would need a personal computer, Internet access, a webcam or network camera, software, and microphones. Some computers come with built-in webcam and microphones that are ready to use with an Internet connection. Most add-on webcams or network cameras come with the necessary software and built-in microphone. Depending on the type of webcam and its features, the price is often affordable

Review a lesson plan. As a teacher, how would you make plans for a student like Jeremy?

for such an endeavor. The team should consider a laptop with wireless capability for Jeremy so he can move from one environment (home) to another (hospital) as necessary and use the computer while he is in bed.

TRAINING ISSUES After the equipment has been purchased and assembled, the next step is to provide training to the facilitator in how to use the equipment for providing instruction. She or he must know what the student at home actually will be able to view. Will the student need to see maps, boards, or other visual aids? If these cannot be clearly seen by the student, the facilitator must provide these instructional materials in another format, such as handouts or CDs. Another consideration may include the facilitator's training in making modifications and/or accommodations to the instruction so it will better fit the needs of the student. Also, how is the facilitator to include the student in class participation and how will the student be assessed to determine what he or she has learned? As the facilitator prepares each lesson, clearly he or she must consider the student connected to the classroom via the computer. Accommodations and even some modifications for learning will have to be made.

In addition to training for the facilitator, the students in the classroom must have information about their interactions with the student via the computer. Rules and routines should be explained carefully to the students so they will know how to interact appropriately with the student at home or in the hospital. The education of the students in the classroom must not be impeded by the interjection of the distance education element. Nor should the education of the student who is learning in alternative settings be impeded by the students in the regular classroom.

The student away from the school also needs training. The classroom facilitator must work collaboratively with the AT specialists, the distance education specialists and the homebound teacher to ensure that the student at home understands the rules and routines of the classroom and how to use the equipment. The homebound teacher also needs to provide training to the student's family, including a plan of action if something does not work properly. One example is the Internet going down temporarily.

ACCESSIBILITY The IEP team must also consider issues of accessibility for the student with a disability. What kinds of AT might the student need to access the instruction? The team must identify what AT might allow the student with a disability to use a computer for real-time distance education. The use of the computer requires the use of input and output devices. For example, the student with limited fine motor skills may need an alternative input device. Many examples of AT devices are found in other chapters in this book. Table 10-1 lists resources for distance education. Failure to consider AT for access lessens the opportunity for the student to be a successful learner.

Webquest
10.2

To learn about Blackboard, an online teaching tool, go to http://www.blackboard.com/

Asynchronous Teaching

ONLINE COURSE DELIVERY For many years, educators, especially those in higher education, have debated whether online courses match the more traditional on-campus teaching. The concept of distance learning is not new to colleges

TABLE 10-1 Resources for Distance Education	
Universal Design http://www.cast.org/udl	Resources, research, and examples to assist in the design of learning materials and activities for all learners.
Information Technology Technical Assistance and Training Center (ITTATC) http://www.ittatc.org	Through training and assistance, ITTATC strives to increase the availability of accessible technology in the United States. In particular, ITTATC focuses on improving the accessibility and usability of information and telecommunications technology, such as computers, websites, and telephones, and office technology such as copiers and fax machines.

of education. Correspondence schools opened in the late 1800s and were recognized as a viable means to obtain a degree. With the advent of radio and television in the 1950s and 1960s, universities were able to reach even more students.

The University of Phoenix (http://www.universityofphoenix.com) is an accredited institution that offers both undergraduate and graduate degrees through Web-based instruction. The university uses technology as a means to expand accessibility to learning resources that enhance both collaboration and communication to improve learning. In 2005, the university with the highest enrollment was the University of Phoenix Online Campus, with 117,309 students (NCES, 2008). Further, 5.5% of the U.S. population in 2003 and 14.9% of college students used the Internet for online instruction (NCES).

WebCT provides institutions of higher education with the capacity to engage students while increasing student enrollment. WebCT's vision is to provide educational innovations that will connect people and technology (WebCT, 2006). WebCT can provide instruction through distance education. This vision is important for two reasons. First, it implies that instruction no longer needs to be constrained by a single building or setting. Instruction can be delivered to the student instead of the student having to attend classes. Second, it implies that instruction is no longer limited by geographical boundaries, only by Web access. This creates the opportunity for offering online instruction not just to campuswide communities but also to other audiences. For example, it could open many doors for Jeremy to receive instruction while he is away from his classmates, or if he chooses to accompany his father to one of his duty stations. Online instruction would allow Jeremy the opportunity to complete his education with his classmates in an almost seamless manner. Jeremy could complete his education from the same school system with his classmates regardless of geographic location.

DISTANCE LEARNING AND HIGHER EDUCATION   According to the National Center for Education Statistics (2000–2001), 90% of public 2-year institutions and 89% of public 4-year institutions offered distance education courses. Among all 2- and 4-year institutions in 2000–2001, 19% had degree or certification programs that were designed to be completed totally online. Of the 2- and 4-year institutions that had offered distance education courses in the academic year 2000–2001, a total of 45% reported they had received requests to provide accommodations in the distance education courses for students with disabilities.

Much more than peripheral technology, distance learning plays an integral role in helping institutions all over the world to advance their mission-critical goals. In North America, nearly every institution of higher education conducts some form of distance learning. Australia has adopted distance-learning technology on a broad scale to bridge the distances separating its population centers. The United Kingdom, Europe, and Japan use distance-learning technology to deliver instruction, and interest continues to grow in other parts of the world (WebCT, 2003).

Online instruction is an alternative for people who may have to travel long distances for instruction and for individuals with disabilities who cannot fit onsite or on-campus instruction into their schedules. Students have responded well to the flexibility of scheduling and ease of use (Beard & Harper, 2002; Beard, Harper, & Riley, 2004). However, the primary reasons to incorporate Web-based instruction into programs are the following: (a) The technologies enable universities to reach a broad base of students previously considered unreachable, (b) new technologies allow universities to demonstrate new teaching strategies and techniques to students, and (c) these technologies allow universities another way to integrate technology into the teacher education programs and to model new strategies for students (Mehlinger & Powers, 2002).

DISTANCE LEARNING AND SECONDARY EDUCATION   Distance education in the secondary school setting goes beyond the traditional classroom with walls to deliver instruction to a classroom without walls. Distance learning allows elementary schools and secondary schools to expand course offerings and to create flexibility in scheduling and instructional delivery (Doherty, 2002; Kennedy-Manzo, 2002; Trotter, 2002; Wildavsky, 2001). According to the National Center for Education Statistics (NCES) (2002), during the 12-month, 2002–2003 school year, more than one third of public school districts (36%) had students enrolled in distance education courses. These courses included foreign language studies; content areas such as math, science, language arts, and social studies; and advanced placement or college-level courses. NCES also reported that the types of technologies used as primary modes of instructional delivery for any distance education courses included Internet courses using real-time computer-based instruction, Internet courses using asynchronous computer-based instruction, two-way interactive video, and one-way prerecorded video. Reasons for using distance learning included being able to offer courses not otherwise available at the school, meeting the needs of specific groups of students, and offering advanced placement or college-level courses. In addition, school districts cited that reducing scheduling conflicts for students was an important rationale for utilizing distance education (National Center for Education Statistics, 2002).

Think about your own experiences with distance learning. How would your experiences have been different if you had a visual impairment or a physical disability?

A related issue centers on whether students can learn as much via online course delivery as they can via onsite teaching. For students with disabilities, or other students who may need distance learning, the online delivery method can be very effective. With AT devices specific to the needs of the student, online delivery can be a very effective means for a student who may need to be away from the actual school setting for a time.

As the student's IEP team considers online course delivery, the team should ask a series of questions to determine how the student can be a successful online

1. What types of AT devices or software are needed for the student to be successful?
2. Who will be responsible for ensuring that the AT device and any software are working for the student?
3. Who will be responsible for updating the online materials?
4. Who will be responsible for monitoring the student's progress throughout the course or subject matter to be covered?

FIGURE 10-1   IEP Team Considerations for Online Course Delivery

learner (see Figure 10-1). These questions must be addressed during the student's IEP meeting and during assessment. The issues must be made clear to the student prior to starting any online delivery.

> Think about Jeremy in the Assistive Technology Snapshot at the beginning of the chapter and refer to Figure 10-1. How might the team answer the questions?

When consideration is given to online course delivery, the developer can keep certain details in mind so the student will feel like part of the class group. For students to be as involved as possible with actual group activities, the developer should promote discussion that is very interactive. The discussion forum with classmates can be useful for the student to interact with classmates at certain times and in specific subject areas. For students with disabilities to excel, they must have the proper AT devices and services, as determined by the IEP team.

Within the classroom, students can also benefit from asynchronous discussions because they can post thoughts and ideas related to the discussion through a discussion board, instant messaging, or other means. Such discussions can last as long as the facilitator feels it is necessary to cover the subject content. While students with disabilities are utilizing online course delivery, facilitators also have the opportunity to create virtual visits related to the topic being covered. Students can take virtual tours of historic places, such as the White House or the birthplace of Martin Luther King, Jr.; museums; and outdoor places that relate to the topic. This type of learning can offer all students the opportunity to enrich their knowledge. Interaction and support can be offered through online delivery with electronic slide presentations, assessment feedback, and email, in which the instructor provides feedback to the student about his or her work. Online delivery offers options such as chat rooms, discussion boards, and other group activities that can foster inclusion of a student with disabilities during the time he or she is away from the main classroom (Kassop, 2003).

Academic Development

USING THE INTERNET   Students with disabilities often have difficulty with research projects in inclusive settings. The Internet is currently one advanced technological mode used to support distance education for course presentation (Owston, 1997; Rossman, 1992). While such courses are used in higher education, the Internet is also useful in K–12 settings as a means of instruction and source of information. Chamberlin (2001) suggested that, by taking advantage of the pedagogical strengths of onsite and online teaching, instructors can offer students the greatest chance to discover their strengths and weaknesses as learners and to find the best opportunity for achieving success. For some students, the Internet can help achieve this goal.

Students who participate in distance education that is Internet-based spend less time in the classroom and can complete course work at their convenience within settings of their own choice. For students like Jeremy, this approach would work during the time he is away from the actual classroom. It would grant him the opportunity to participate with his peers in classroom assignments and activities. Online communication often eliminates students' inhibitions regarding communication. It can remove both psychological and social barriers to student–facilitator interactions (Chamberlin, 2001).

WEBQUEST   One tool related to distance learning that is used by many students and can be useful for students with disabilities is Webquest, a very structured, scaffolded research tool that involves the utilization of some Internet sites. This research tool can assist all students in their research. Webquest must be carefully organized and structured for it to be successful. Students with cognitive disabilities often find this process easier due to the structure of the design. A basic outline for students to follow in utilizing Webquest could include the topic, a brief introduction, expectations, an outline of the process, and the evaluation. These areas can be subdivided into smaller sections, with activities in each section that build on each other. A good feature of Webquest is that facilitators can use it either for online course delivery or for cooperative learning groups within the classroom, thus enhancing more inclusion of students with disabilities. For example, Jeremy could participate in a Webquest assignment while away from the classroom.

VIRTUAL REALITY   Students with disabilities can experience virtual reality as a means for a positive learning experience. All students experience virtual reality through computer games and simulations. A positive aspect of virtual reality is that all students can benefit from participating in an environment that may not be offered during a typical school day. AT can be part of virtual reality for students with disabilities. A sensor can provide movement on a computer game such as tennis, soccer, or ping-pong. Students can engage in many academic subject areas that provide real-life situations, such as museum tours, safaris, and visits to foreign countries and other educational sites. Virtual reality programs are also being developed to assist students with appropriate behavioral skills. Students can practice social skills or use the programs as outlets for creativity or self-expression (McComas, Pivik, & Laflamme, 1998). Ongoing research is needed to determine how students with disabilities may use AT to access these experiences and how virtual reality can be customized to meet the various needs of the students (McComas, Pivik, & Laflamme, 1998). IEP teams must determine what AT is needed for virtual experiences to be meaningful learning events for students with disabilities.

Web Development and Accessibility

The Internet became a great source of information beginning in the 1990s. Individuals from all walks of life now use it. The Internet provides the most up-to-the-minute information on everything from news developments to books, to ordering from online companies. Today's interactive forms of pictures, cartoons, and audio programming make the Internet a useful teaching tool for the classroom facilitator. The Internet can be a wonderful tool for accessing information for individuals with disabilities, in addition to using the AT devices and software that offer the best opportunities for information retrieval in an inclusive setting.

Section 508 of the 1998 Rehabilitation Act Amendments covers access to federally funded programs and services. The law requires access to electronic and information technology provided by the federal government. Federal agencies must make technology accessible to employees and the public with disabilities and while not posing an undue burden on the agency providing the access (Amendment to Section 508 of the Rehabilitation Act of 1988, (1998). The Access Board, the governing body charged with assisting U.S. federal agencies to achieve Web access, announced the guidelines that can help the agencies comply with Section 508. The board, in an effort to coincide with the law, mandated that federal agencies make electronic information available to all federal employees and all individuals in the public, including those with disabilities, unless "an undue burden would be imposed on the agency" (Access Board, 2001). While the guidelines were imposed to guide federal agencies, they can also be applied to the classroom facilitator to ensure that all students have Web access.

Facilitators who create websites related to their classrooms, academic content areas, or schools will find the descriptions useful in the development. Descriptions, such as those listed in Figure 10-2, ensure that the Web is developed to be accessible for all individuals (Access Board, 2001).

The concept of universal design for learning (UDL) (see Chapter 1) has enhanced the design of many products by making them usable by a wider range and greater number of individuals. What has become a necessity for some individuals has resulted in many conveniences for a large segment of the population. Many companies are developing more conventional methods of technology and combining them with AT devices to be used by everyone. Touchscreens, once used only by individuals with disabilities, are now used by nearly everyone to pay bills, check in at airports, withdraw money from automatic teller machines (ATMs), and so on.

Some AT devices used to enhance inclusion of a student with a disability in the general education curriculum or in a distance education setting are today the same as conventional technologies. Three such areas include input, processing, and output. When a student with a disability uses conventional technologies properly, she or he can have total access to the Internet. These devices have been discussed in previous chapters as they pertain to specific disabilities.

With the appropriate alternative keyboards, students with disabilities can access much information on the World Wide Web, which can further ensure their success in the general education curriculum. When consideration is given to such, a facilitator must consider the appropriate type of switch for the student. Various Websites can be accessed with a Web browser, a modem, and an Internet service provider (ISP). For the browser to be useful to a student with a disability in an inclusive setting, the method of input and output must be addressed appropriately. This can be done as part of the student's IEP. Various software programs use a talking word processor and can provide the student with auditory feedback. Some programs can benefit students with both visual and cognitive disorders. Word processors provide the student with the option of viewing text without a large screen. A few examples of input, processing, and output AT devices are listed in Figure 10-3.

Guideline	Description
Text tags	Words are added to represent the nontext element.
Multimedia presentation	Equivalent alternatives are synchronized with the presentations.
Color	Webpages are designed so that information conveyed in color is available without color.
Readability	Documents are organized to be readable without the use of an associated style sheet.
Server-side image maps	Redundant text links are provided for each active region of a server-side image map. When the webpage uses a server-side image map to present the user with a selection of options, browsers cannot indicate the URL; therefore, the redundant text link helps to provide access to the page for anyone not able to see or accurately click on the map.
Client-side image maps	Allows the author to assign text to each image map "hot spot." This type of map identifies the regions of a map with different URLs, which can be read by a screen reader.
Data tables	Row and column headers are identified for data tables, and markup is used to associate data cells and header cells in the data tables.
Frames	Text in the body of each frame helps to identify the frame.
Flicker rate	Webpages are designed to avoid screen flicker with a frequency greater than 2 Hz and lower than 55 Hz. Some individuals with photosensitive epilepsy can have a seizure triggered by displays that flicker, flash, or blink if the flash has a high intensity and is within a certain frequency range.
Text-only alternative	Text-only pages contain the same information and functionality as the primary pages of the website. The text-only pages are updated whenever the primary pages are updated.
Scripts	The same information in the script is identified with functional text that can be read with AT.
Applets and plug-ins	When the webpage requires an applet, plug-in, or other application, the page provides the appropriate link.
Electronic forms	When a form is to be completed online, the form allows individuals using AT to access the information, field elements, and functionality required for completion and submission of the form, including directions and cues.
Navigational links	A method is provided to facilitate the easy tracking of page content that provides AT users with the option of skipping repetitive navigation links.
Time delays	The user is alerted and given sufficient time to indicate that he or she requires more time.

FIGURE 10-2 Web Accessibility Descriptions

WEB AUTHOR'S TOOLKIT For students with disabilities to access the Web and be successful, we as a society must acknowledge and remedy the barriers that exist on a number of websites. To ensure accessibility for everyone, individuals can use several tools when authoring a website. These tools can scan webpages and identify potential accessibility problems. Validating and correcting such barriers should be standard practice. Web accessibility tools are useful for evaluating, correcting, and repairing webpages. Resources for these tools are found in Table 10-2.

Input Devices	Processing Devices	Output Devices
Alternative keyboards	Browser	Talking word processors
Access utilities	Word prediction	Speech synthesizers
Switches	Menu management	Screen readers
Voice recognition		Braille translators
Joysticks	AT input	Manipulates objects on the screen
Trackballs	AT input	An alternative pointing device used by rotating the ball with the palm of the hand; manipulates objects on the screen

FIGURE 10-3   Examples of Assistive Technology Input, Processing, and Output Devices

In addition to Web accessibility tools like those found in Table 10-2, online companies, such as Adobe Systems Incorporated (2005), help make electronic information more accessible to people with disabilities. In partnership with leading technology companies, Adobe Systems Incorporated can help computer users do the following:

- Access content using assistive technologies, such as screen readers or screen magnifiers.
- Create accessible content using Adobe authoring tools.
- Use Adobe Acrobat software to create accessible Adobe PDF files.
- Use Adobe tools to generate accessible forms.

Web designers and developers can be confident that products and services like those available from Adobe Systems Incorporated assist in complying with accessibility mandates, such as Section 508 of the U.S. Rehabilitation Act (Adobe Systems Incorporated).

TABLE 10-2   Web Accessibility Tools

Web Access Tools http://trace.wisc.edu/world/web	Information on Web access tools and accessible website guidelines.
Evaluation Tool http://validator.w3.org	This is the W3C Markup Validation Service, a free service that checks Web documents in formats such as HTML and XHTML for conformance to W3C recommendations and other standards.
Web Accessibility Verifier http://aprompt.snow.utoronto.ca	Web authors can use A-Prompt to make their webpages accessible to people with disabilities. The A-Prompt software tool examines webpages for barriers to accessibility, performs automatic repairs when possible, and assists authors in making manual repairs when necessary.

ASSISTIVE TECHNOLOGY FOR STUDENT LEARNING

Newsletters

Many schools have developed a periodic newsletter to keep parents and the community informed about what is happening within the schools. Newsletters can be published in either electronic or printed forms. One advantage of an electronic format is that it can be updated quickly by the school administrator or a facilitator so parents receive information as quickly, even on a daily basis. Individuals with disabilities (both in and out of school) may require AT devices to access the electronic format. Via a school newsletter, Jeremy could keep up with information and activities that are going on within his school while he is away from the classroom. In the design of such an electronic newsletter, or a website, the developer must be sure it is accessible for all. The accessible Web author's Toolkit can ensure that the website is accessible. If the printed form is used, it may be necessary to translate it into braille for those individuals with a visual impairment.

Homework Hotlines

Many school systems now incorporate a homework hotline to assist students with assignments outside class. Licensed professional educators in content-specific areas staff the homework hotlines and assist students as they call. A text telephone allows students who are deaf or nonverbal to communicate using the telephone. The student types in questions on a keyboard and looks at a visual display for a response (Lewis & Doorlag, 2003). See Chapter 7 for more information.

Homework hotlines can also be set up to use AT for connecting with email, as appropriate for the student. With a homework hotline, Jeremy could receive additional assistance with homework when he cannot attend class. Local educational agencies that incorporate a homework hotline should address accessibility issues so that all students can use the service.

Email

Email is an effective and efficient method of communication. Most students in today's classrooms have access to a computer and email. Email has taken the place of many print materials. Facilitators and students communicate via email almost every day. For students with disabilities, email can be accessed with the use of AT devices. As mentioned in multiple chapters, AT software programs are available to help students with a disability use email efficiently. Alternative keyboards, computer monitors, and software are designed for certain disabilities and can also enhance the student's use of email. Email can also provide students who may not be in the actual classroom with an opportunity to communicate with facilitators and students. Jeremy can use email to communicate with his fellow classmates on a daily basis, and email will provide Jeremy with up-to-the-minute communication and social opportunities.

Locate the accessibility features or options on your personal computer. What changes can you make in the use of the keyboard?

SOCIAL NETWORKING

Many Internet sources are available for students to meet and make friends outside the public school facility. Many of these services offer online dating and promises that you will meet your ideal mate, but there are also services that allow you to meet with your schoolmates and friends or to make new friends. Services such as Facebook (www.facebook.com) and MySpace (www .myspace.com) are social networks where students can meet other people from around the world and develop virtual friendships. Email address books and instant messaging partners can be added so the user doesn't need to individually add existing friends to the account. These services are a little complicated to navigate and they keep asking for a cell phone number with texting capability, but with time, they will be a good way to maintain social contacts.

ASSISTIVE TECHNOLOGY SPOTLIGHT 10-1

Are Your Students Ready for Distance Learning?

Distance learning requires much in the way of self-discipline, and not everyone is suitable for a distance-learning class. The following guidelines can help determine if a student is a candidate for a distance-learning class. The questions may need to be adapted to the student's age and learning level. If the student answered "No" or "Not sure" to any of the questions, these may be areas the student needs to develop before taking an online course.

1. I have the necessary equipment and/or material for taking the distance education class that I am interested in at this moment.
   Yes   No   Not sure
2. If my computer breaks down at some point during the course, I will get it fixed immediately and will use another system in the meantime.
   Yes   No   Not sure
3. Flexibility in scheduling my classes and studying is important to me.
   Yes   No   Not sure
4. I am willing to learn through the use of new technologies.
   Yes   No   Not sure
5. I have anywhere from mid- to high-level computer skills.
   Yes   No   Not sure
6. As a reader, I usually understand the text without help.
   Yes   No   Not sure
7. I am self-disciplined, self-motivated, and capable of working independently.
   Yes   No   Not sure
8. I am open to seeking assistance from other students or my instructor.
   Yes   No   Not sure
9. I am willing to contact my instructor by email, phone, or other methods if I have problems with anything in my distance education class.
   Yes   No   Not sure
10. I feel that distance education can provide me with the level of education equivalent to courses delivered via a traditional method (on campus).
    Yes   No   Not sure
11. When an instructor hands out directions for assignments, I usually prefer figuring out the instructions on my own.
    Yes   No   Not sure
12. When I consider my personal life, the amount of time I have to work on an online course is more than enough.
    Yes   No   Not sure
13. If I have to go to campus to take exams or complete labwork, I can rearrange my schedule and make time to go.
    Yes   No   Not sure

14. I am comfortable with word processing.
     Yes   No   Not sure
15. I have an email account and use it regularly.
     Yes   No   Not sure
16. I send and receive email attachments regularly.
     Yes   No   Not sure

Chapter Review

- Distance education is defined as planned learning that occurs in a geographical location different from the source of instruction. Distance education consists of distance teaching and distance learning. Distance teaching involves the pedagogical elements that a facilitator or instructor uses to deliver instruction elsewhere. Distance learning requires that a student have full access to the technology that allows interaction with the instructor and allows the student to benefit from instruction. AT may be required for a student with a disability to use distance education.

- Distance education can be delivered as real-time or synchronous distance learning or as asynchronous distance learning. Synchronous teaching involves opportunities for the student to have productive and successful interactions with facilitators and peers and can include teleconferencing with a computer, Internet access, a webcam or network camera, software, and microphones. Accessibility issues must be addressed. Training for both the facilitator and student in the use of certain equipment must take place for the teleconferencing to be beneficial. AT must be a consideration for a student with a disability using a computer for real-time distance education.

- Asynchronous teaching can include online course delivery, academic development, the Internet, and Webquest. Web development and accessibility are important for all individuals using the Internet. The Internet can provide up-to-the-minute information and can be accessed through many types of AT devices and software. Section 508 of the 1998 Rehabilitation Act Amendments requires access to electronic and information technology provided by the federal government. Federal agencies must make sure that technology is accessible to employees and to individuals with disabilities. While guidelines were imposed on federal agencies, these guidelines can be useful for educators who want to create websites for their classrooms.

- Universal design for learning (UDL) has enhanced the design of many products by making them usable to a wider range and greater number of individuals. Many companies are combining more conventional methods of technology with AT devices so that the products may be used by everyone.

- Various tools are available for authoring a website and making it accessible to everyone. Such tools can scan webpages and identify potential problems.

- Three major areas that many schools use in the area of technology are e-newsletters, a homework hotline, and email. Newsletters in electronic format can be updated quickly, and the information can be sent and received easily and quickly. Individuals with a disability may require AT devices to access the electronic format. A homework hotline can be used with certain AT by all students.

A student with a hearing impairment may need a telecommunications device. Homework hotlines may be connected to email and appropriate AT devices. Email can be accessed efficiently and easily. Alternative keyboards, computer monitors, and software are designed for certain disabilities and can also enhance the student's use of email.

- Students can use the Internet to keep up with friends and classmates. Social networking services such as Facebook and MySpace are excellent ways for students to keep up with old friends as well as make new ones.

References

Access Board. (2001). *Web-based Intranet and Internet information and applications guidelines.* Retrieved May 8, 2006, from http://www.accessboard.gov/sec508/guide/1194.22.htm

Adobe Systems Incorporated. (2005). *What is Adobe PDF? More secure, reliable, electronic document distribution and exchange.* Retrieved August 16, 2005, from http://www.adobe.com/products/acrobat/adobepdf.html

Amendment to Section 508 of the Rehabilitation Act of 1998 (1998). Retrieved March 10, 2005, from http://www.section508.gov/index.cfm?FuseAction=Content&ID=14

Beard, L., & Harper, C. (2002). Student perceptions of online versus on campus instruction. *Education, 122*(4), 658–663.

Beard, L., Harper, C., & Riley, G. (2004). Online versus on campus instruction: Student attitudes and perceptions. *Tech Trends, 48*(6), 29–31.

Belanger, F., & Jordan, D. H. (2000). *Evaluation and implementation of distance learning: Technologies, tools, and techniques.* Hershey, PA: IDEA Group.

Chamberlin, W. S. (2001). Face to face vs. cyberspace: Finding the middle ground. *Syllabus, 15*, 11.

Doherty, K. M. (2002). *Students speak out.* Retrieved May 8, 2006, from http://counts.edweek.org/sreports/tc02/article.cfm?slug=35florida.h21

Kassop, M. (2003). *Ten ways online education matches, or surpasses, face-to-face learning.* Retrieved May 8, 2006, from http://technologysource.org/article/ten_ways_online_education_matches_or_surpasses_facetoface_learning

Kennedy-Manzo, K. (2002). *Sizing up online content.* Retrieved May 8, 2006, from http://www.teachermag.net/sreports/tc02/article.cfm?slug=35curric.h21

Lewis, R. B., & Doorlag, D. H. (2003). *Teaching special students in general education classrooms.* Upper Saddle River, NJ: Merrill/Pearson Education.

McComas, J., Pivik, J., & Laflamme, M. (1998). *Current uses of virtual reality for children with disabilities.* Retrieved May 9, 2006, from http://citeseer.ist.psu.edu/mccomas98current.html

Mehlinger, H., & Powers, S. (2002). *Technology and teacher education: A guide for educators and policymakers.* New York: Houghton Mifflin.

Moore, M., & Kearsley, G. (1996). *Distance education: A systems view.* Belmont, CA: Wadsworth.

National Center for Education Statistics. (2000–2001). *Postsecondary education quick information system.* Retrieved March 16, 2009, from http://nces.ed.gov/surveys/peqis/publications/2003017

National Center for Education Statistics. (2002). *Distance education courses for public elementary and secondary school students.* Retrieved August 22, 2005, from http://nces.ed.gov/surveys/frss/publications/2005010

National Center for Education Statistics. (2007). Digest of education statistics. Retrieved January 27, 2010 from http://nces.ed.gov/pubs2008/2008022.pdf

Owston, R. (1997). The World Wide Web: A technology to enhance teaching and learning. *Educational Researcher, 26*(2), 27–33.

Rossman, P. (1992). *The emerging worldwide electronic university: Information age global higher education.* Westport, CT: Greenwood Press.

Trotter, A. (2002). E-learning goes to school. *Education Week.* Retrieved May 9, 2006, from http://teachermagazine.com/sreports/tc02/article.cfm?slug=35elearn.h21

WebCT. (2003). *Learning without limits: Flexible e-learning solutions for institutions across the educational spectrum.* Retrieved April 4, 2005, from http://www.webct.com/service/ViewContent.contentID=17980017

WebCT. (2006). *The WebCT vision.* Retrieved May 8, 2006, from http://www.webct.com/vision

Wildavsky, B. (2001). *Want more from high school?* Retrieved May 9, 2001, from http://www.keepmedia.com/pubs/USNewsWorldReport/2001/10/15/220261?ba=a&bi=4&bp=24

AUTHOR INDEX

SUBJECT INDEX

Note: Page numbers followed by f or t refer to Tables or Figures